Fresh From the

the Bible for a cha

2018

FRESH from the WORD

the Bible for a change

Foreword by Lucy Winkett

Edited by Nathan Eddy

IBRA
International Bible Reading Association

MONARCH
BOOKS

Oxford, UK & Grand Rapids, Michigan, USA

Text copyright © 2017 International Bible Reading Association
This edition copyright © 2017 Lion Hudson

Published by Monarch Books (an imprint of Lion Hudson IP Ltd)
Wilkinson House, Jordan Hill Road, Oxford OX2 8DR, England
Email: monarch@lionhudson.com www.lionhudson.com/monarch
and by the International Bible Reading Association
5–6 Imperial Court, 12 Sovereign Road, Birmingham, B30 3FH
Tel: 0121 458 3313; Fax: 0121 285 1816
www.ibraglobal.org
Charity number 1086990

ISBN 978 0 85721 798 1
e-ISBN 978 0 85721 868 1
ISSN 2050-6791

First edition 2017

A catalogue record for this book is available from the British Library

Printed and bound in the UK, July 2017, LH29

Fresh From the Word aims to build understanding and respect for different Christian perspectives through the provision of a range of biblical interpretations. Views expressed by contributors should not, therefore, be taken to reflect the views or policies of the Editor or the International Bible Reading Association.

The International Bible Reading Association's scheme of readings is listed monthly on the IBRA website at www.ibraglobal.org and the full scheme for 2018 may be downloaded in English, Spanish and French.

Contents

Foreword – Reading the Bible with your feet ... and heart and head

Reading the Bible isn't always straightforward. For many Christians, alongside all the amazing and inspiring stories, there are bits we don't like, wish weren't there and find it difficult to defend. And although we say we know what's in there, quite often when we read it we are surprised. The American writer Mark Twain said that it wasn't the bits of the Bible he didn't understand that caused him most trouble, it was the bits he did understand. The people we meet in the pages of scripture are as varied as we are: doing their best, praying their hardest, making countless mistakes along the way.

It has never been more important, in this generation which is often suspicious about organised religion and wary of sacred texts, to get to know our Bible afresh. And we can do that by reading it with our heart, with our head and with our feet. What do I mean?

When we read the Bible with our heart, we let it touch us; we let the gospel get under our skin. We weep with Martha over the death of her brother Lazarus, we despair with Job and his family at the series of unearned catastrophes he endures, we laugh at Jonah's petulance and we smile at Sarah's scepticism, and we are struck silent by the healing power of Jesus. This emotional engagement with the Bible is really important. We let it touch us and we are more fully alive.

When we read the Bible with our head, we become interested in the original Greek language and the many layered meanings of Hebrew; we want to know what other scholars have said before us and how their interpretations can help ours. This can be really invigorating and stimulating. When we read the Bible with our head, we obey the commandment to love the Lord our God with our mind as well as everything else.

And finally when we read the Bible with our feet, we acknowledge that this scripture is good news for our lives as they are lived now. Not the life we think we should have, or the life we wanted or didn't get to choose. The life we are actually living day to day. Because these are the kind of lives that are vivid in scripture and these are the lives that, with us, are transformed by its power.

Reading the Bible with your mind, your heart and your feet – transformational power, every day.

Lucy Winkett

How to use *Fresh From the Word*

How do you approach the idea of regular Bible reading? It may help to see daily Bible reading as spiritual exploration. Here is a suggestion of a pattern to follow that may help you develop the discipline but free up your mind and heart to respond.

• Before you read, take a few moments – the time it takes to say the Lord's Prayer – to imagine God looking at you with love. Feel yourself enfolded in that gaze. Come to scripture with your feet firmly planted.

• Read the passage slowly before you turn to the notes. Be curious. The Bible was written over a period of nearly 1000 years, over 2000 years ago. There is always something to learn. Read and reread.

• If you have access to a study Bible, pay attention to any echoes of the passage you are reading in other parts of the biblical book. A word might be used in different ways by different biblical authors. Where in the story of the book are you reading? What will happen next?

• 'Read' yourself as you read the story. Be attentive to your reactions – even trivial ones. What is drawing you into the story? What is repelling you? Observe yourself 'sidelong' as you read as if you were watching a wild animal in the forest; be still, observant and expectant.

• What in the scripture or in the notes is drawing you forward in hope? What is closing you down? Notice where the Spirit of Life is present, and where negative spirits are, too. Follow where life is leading. God always leads into life, even if the way feels risky.

• Lift up the world and aspects of your life to God. What would you like to share with God? What is God seeking to share with you?

• Thank God for being present and offer your energy in the day ahead, or in the day coming after a night's rest.

Introduction from the Editor

The last few years have seen tumultuous changes in centres of power around the world. Mass movements of people in North and South Sudan, Syria and across the Middle East were fixed in the headlines, and over 25 African nations held national elections in the last two years. Recent popular political movements swept outsiders into power and changed the political landscape in the UK, Europe, and the US. The world seems be asking new, hard questions of its leaders – and it seems that at times our leaders don't know how to respond. It's appropriate, then, that this year at IBRA we turn to the theme of leadership in our Bible reading. What does the Bible imagine good leadership to be? What are the qualities of a good leader? These are the very timely questions we put to scripture, to God, and to you, this year.

As people of faith, we believe we can be part of the flourishing of our communities. At IBRA, we believe this can happen through reading and pondering the Bible; that God in the Spirit will work through our reading practice to help us be the leaders the world needs. The founding principle of IBRA is to make a habit of reading the Bible and discussing our thoughts with others. Will you take up this challenge this year with us – to read the Bible daily, and to let God make you all that you can be in your community?

As in previous years, our hallmark is to feature creative and faithful writers from around the world. This year we have writing from South Africa, India, Argentina, Brazil, Nigeria, Samoa, the US, the Caribbean, Sweden and elsewhere, as well as from a spread of regions within the UK. In addition to the theme of leadership, 2018 features the weeks: A place to stay, Going viral (communication in the Bible), Held in God's hand, and continuous readings through Hosea, Proverbs, Colossians, Mark and the Psalms.

Our sales rose last year, and our future as an association is looking bright. I pray this book will help take IBRA further along the path this year that God has set out for us. And I pray that God will work deeply, joyfully and surprisingly in your life through your Bible reading.

N.the trp

Acknowledgements and abbreviations

The use of the letters a or b in a text reference, such as Luke 9:37–43a, indicates that the day's text starts or finishes midway through a verse, usually at a break such as the end of a sentence. Not all Bible versions will indicate such divisions. We are grateful to the copyright holders for permission to use scriptural quotations from the following Bible versions:

NIVUK Scripture quotations marked NIVUK taken from the Holy Bible, New International Version Anglicised. Copyright © 1979, 1984, 2011 Biblica, formerly International Bible Society. Used by permission of Hodder & Stoughton Ltd, an Hachette UK company. All rights reserved. "NIV" is a registered trademark of Biblica. UK trademark number 1448790.

NRSVA Scripture quotations marked NRSVA taken from the New Revised Standard Version Bible: Anglicised Edition, copyright © 1989, 1995 the Division of Christian Education of the National Council of the Churches of Christ in the United States of America. Used by permission. All rights reserved.

Quotations from poetry by David Merritt on pages 79–84 are used with the kind permission of the author.

Here I am

Notes by **Clare Nonhebel**

 Clare Nonhebel is the author of 13 fiction and non-fiction books, magazine features and a blog. Her most recent novel, *The Healing Place*, is set in the context of the popular self-help industry. Visiting death row inmates resulted in a book, *Survivor on Death Row*, which she co-wrote with execution survivor Romell Broom. She has been involved in prison ministry and groups for survivors of childhood sexual abuse and currently volunteers on a gardening project for mental health. Clare has used the NIVUK for these notes.

Monday 1 January
Wake-up call

Read 1 Samuel 3:1–10

Then Eli realised that the Lord was calling the boy. So Eli told Samuel, 'Go and lie down and if he calls you, say, "Speak, Lord, for your servant is listening."'

(verses 8–9)

Hearing God for the first time is always a wake-up call.

Samuel has no experience of God speaking; Eli has. So why doesn't God speak to Eli? The message turns out to be for Eli anyway – one that he will find hard to hear. Is that why it needs to come through another listener?

Christians have different responses to the voice of God. Some believe God only speaks through scripture, or in silent promptings, or through visible signs. Some believe he only speaks to special holy people. Others say, 'If God has a message for me, he will tell me directly – not through another person, especially a less experienced Christian – or a non-Christian!'

Eli knows that God speaks to whomever he chooses, however and whenever he chooses. He also knows the response: 'Here I am, Lord. Speak – I'm listening.'

If we say, 'I wish God would speak to me!' is there one thing we don't want to hear? In this year ahead, let's pray that we don't block our ears to anything God might want to say to us, in any way, through any other person or directly.

† Lord, if you want to speak to me, open my heart to hear. Give me a spirit of obedience, to act on whatever you say. Amen

Monday 8 January
Baptised

Read Mark 1:9–13

And a voice came from heaven, 'You are my Son, the Beloved; with you I am well pleased.'

(verse 11)

When you see the son, you see the father. When a son helps his father run the family business, he acts in his father's name, his workers treat him with the same respect that they give to his father. In the parable of the vineyard (Mark 12:1–12) the workers that the owner sends to end the takeover of the vineyard are badly treated, but he expects the rebellious workers to respect his son (verse 6). In today's reading, the voice from heaven affirms that when you see Jesus, you see his Father. In his words and actions, Jesus represents God the Father – he is part of the divine family, a beloved son who has his father's full approval and backing. It is not clear whether everybody present at the baptism of Jesus heard the voice from heaven and saw a dove (verse 10), or whether the words were said only to Jesus and he later shared the experience with his disciples. But by recording this incident, Mark makes clear right from the start of his Gospel that Jesus is not simply another human prophet. He is the son who helps his father run the family business, and that business is the kingdom of God. When Jesus bursts onto the scene, the kingdom also arrives; regime change has happened.

† 'Your kingdom come.' Help me to live now as a citizen of your kingdom, and to look forward to its final coming. Amen

For further thought

• As you read through Mark's Gospel this year, note down the words and actions of Jesus that show what the kingdom of God is like.

Tuesday 9 January
What kind of kingdom?

Read Psalm 2

> 'Ask of me, and I will make the nations your heritage,
> and the ends of the earth your possession.
> You shall break them with a rod of iron,
> and dash them in pieces like a potter's vessel.'

(verses 8–9)

After centuries of occupation by invading foreign powers, most recently the Greeks and the Romans, the Jews saw God's final intervention as victory over their enemies, the physical destruction of invading armies and tyrannical rulers, the restoration of an independent Jewish kingdom and the Jews being put in the top spot, celebrated by a great feast. Today's reading of Psalm 2 highlights the difference between hopes at the time and the reality of Jesus. Jesus does not come to physically fight actual kings and rulers or restore a political kingdom, though even at his final moments on earth, his disciples still ask, 'Lord, is this the time when you will restore the kingdom to Israel?' (Acts 1:6).

Rather, Jesus demonstrates what God's kingdom is like. When John, his forerunner, is imprisoned and wonders if his life's work has been useless, Jesus replies, 'Go and tell John what you have seen and heard: the blind receive their sight, the lame walk, the lepers are cleansed, the deaf hear, the dead are raised, the poor have good news brought to them. And blessed is anyone who takes no offence at me' (Luke 7:22–23). The gospel accounts enable us too to see and hear how Jesus embodies the kingdom of God – and to recognise the kingdom at work in our own lives.

† Lord, help me to recognise your kingdom at work in the world and in my own life. Amen

For further thought

• In what ways does the picture of God's Son and his work described in Psalm 2 differ from the reality of Jesus described in Mark's Gospel?

Wednesday 10 January
Fishing for people

Read Mark 1:14–20

*And Jesus said to them, 'Follow me and I will make you fish for people.'
And immediately they left their nets and followed him.*

(verses 17–18)

After a time of preparation spent in the wilderness (Mark 1:12–13), Jesus now embarks on his own public ministry, proclaiming the good news of the arrival of the kingdom of God. One of his first tasks is to bring together a group of followers to train up as his helpers. The first people he asks to join him aren't the most obvious choice. They are busy professional fishermen, working on the Sea of Galilee. How can they drop everything and become followers of a wandering preacher they have never seen before? Simon and Andrew were out on the lake throwing out their nets ready to haul in a catch, so Jesus must have shouted to them from the shore. They probably couldn't even see very clearly who he was. Yet Mark tells us that they didn't hesitate: '… immediately they left their nets.'

At least James and John were tied up by the shore, sitting in their boat with their father, mending their nets. So they could see the man walking past, who stopped by their boat and out of the blue told them to join him. They too did not hesitate, but left their father, who must have wondered what his sons were doing, climbing out of the boat and walking off along the shore with a total stranger. And what did he mean when he said he would turn them into fishermen for people? Something about Jesus led these four men to make a split-second decision that changed their lives forever.

† Lord, make me attentive to you, so that I can always hear your call and follow you. Amen

For further thought

• What do you think is meant by being a 'fisher of people'? How might you go about it in your own life?

Thursday 11 January
They were all amazed

Read Mark 1:21–28

They were all amazed, and they kept on asking one another, 'What is this? A new teaching – with authority! He commands even the unclean spirits, and they obey him.'

(verse 27)

Jesus has already acquired a reputation as a teacher, so when he goes to the synagogue at Capernaum on the Sabbath, he is asked to preach. But he is no ordinary teacher. Mark portrays Jesus as someone who is completely sure of who he is and what he has come to do. He frequently uses the phrase 'and immediately' to describe Jesus moving from one situation to another; he knows what he has to do, he knows what is involved in living the kingdom of God, he speaks for God in a way that his hearers had never heard before, with authority.

And the regime change that Jesus signifies is able to put things right. The kingdom of God is a realm of wholeness and healing, of compassion and forgiveness, of mercy and justice. The onlookers are amazed when Jesus delivers the man in the synagogue from the evil spirit that torments him, but Jesus is no publicity-seeking wonder worker. Delivering the oppressed is simply the power of God working in his kingdom. The suffering man does not ask Jesus to heal him, to rid him of the spirit that possesses him; he seems frightened of Jesus more than anything, because what is happening here is a clash of spiritual powers. The spirit that possesses the man is faced by a much greater power, that of the kingdom of God in the person of 'the Holy One of God'. Jesus speaks to the unclean spirit with the assurance of who he is and what he represents – with authority.

† Lord, I choose to be a citizen of your kingdom, to know that you can guide and heal me and share your love and joy with me. Amen

For further thought
• When and how does God speak to you with authority?

Friday 12 January
Proclaiming the message

Read Mark 1:29–39

He answered, 'Let us go on to the neighbouring towns, so that I may proclaim the message there also; for that is what I came out to do.' And he went throughout Galilee, proclaiming the message in their synagogues and casting out demons.

(verses 38–39)

Right from the start, Mark shows Jesus plunging into a busy, crowded ministry. He responds to the needs of all who come to him, from Simon's mother-in-law in bed with fever to those who crowd around the door begging for healing. It is an exhausting scenario, so it is not surprising that Jesus also needed to get away, rising early in the morning and walking through the sleeping town to a place where he could be quiet and alone. A place where he could spend time with his Father. But the crowds of needy people came knocking at the door even at first light and Simon and the other disciples went searching for Jesus. Jesus could have spent days healing the sick just in Capernaum, and as word of his work spread, people would have come from further afield.

But Jesus needs to move on. His mission is not to heal every sick person in Israel, but to let people know that the kingdom of God has arrived, that his actions and words show what this kingdom is like. Physical and mental healing is not all that the kingdom is about. It is also about teaching, and challenging wrong ideas about God. Mark's use of 'and immediately' also gives a sense of urgency to Jesus' ministry – given the situation in Israel, a challenging preacher will not be allowed to roam around freely for very long. So Jesus needs to confront as many people as possible with the kingdom of God.

† Lord, help me to live in such a way that through me others may glimpse what the kingdom of God is like. Amen

For further thought

• Jesus could have spent days healing the sick in Capernaum. Why do you think he needed to move on to other places?

Saturday 13 January
Healing

Read Mark 1:40–45

But he went out and began to proclaim it freely, and to spread the word, so that Jesus could no longer go into a town openly, but stayed out in the country; and people came to him from every quarter.

(verse 45)

Jesus began his teaching ministry in the local synagogues (Mark 1:39). But his healing ministry required a low profile – above all, the people who crowded round him asking for healing had to be prevented from disrupting the life of the town he was visiting. But this was not easy to achieve. He might ask someone like the healed leper to keep quiet about what had happened, but everyone would know that the leper had been healed and the man himself wanted to tell everyone about it. So even more people came to Jesus asking for healing, blocking the narrow streets and crying out for his help. The only answer was to move to the outskirts of the town and let the people come to him there.

The exchange between Jesus and this leper (whose disease may not have been leprosy as we know it, but some other skin complaint) is short but significant. The leper isn't sure that Jesus will choose to heal him; he no longer trusts people to be good to him, most of them wouldn't even touch him in case they caught his disease. The compassion that Jesus feels may be for what his disease has done to this man: isolated him from the community, destroyed his trust in people, made him unsure that even a godly preacher who has healed so many will want to heal him. Jesus touching the man was healing in itself; the removal of the skin disease gave him a new life and a new trust in people.

† As Jesus chose to heal the leper, so I know, Father, that you always choose to do what will make me whole and give me new life.

For further thought

• Do you find it difficult to believe that God always chooses to do good to you? How has God been at work in your life?

Thursday 18 January
Restorer of the Sabbath

Read Mark 3:1–12

And he said to the man who had the withered hand, 'Come forward' … He looked around at them with anger; he was grieved at their hardness of heart and said to the man, 'Stretch out your hand.' He stretched it out, and his hand was restored.

(verses 3, 5)

In yesterday's reading, Jesus was judged because his disciples did the unfathomable and reaped corn on the holy day. It seems that Jesus used his authority, declared that the 'Son of man was Lord even of the Sabbath' and deliberately broke the law again. Indeed, a wider gap developed between the Pharisees' religious understanding and Jesus' interpretation.

This story serves as a caution for those in the Church today who love systematic ideologies more than they love God and fellow brothers and sisters in Christ. It is possible that traditions are maintained at the expense of spirituality, impassioned faith and vital congregations.

Jesus believed that doing good transcended rule-keeping. Restoration of a withered hand surpassed rules, and an embarrassing situation gave way to newness of life. Darkness was lifted and possibilities were endless. Here lies the assurance of God's healing spirit again and again, reminding us that nothing is beyond Jesus' ability to take what seems dried up and lifeless and bring abundant restoration.

† Restoring God, step into the midst of my dryness and water me afresh, so my life and the life of the world will flourish. Amen

For further thought

• What traditions in your church community need challenging?

Friday 19 January
Authority to appoint apostles

Read Mark 3:13–20

And he appointed twelve, whom he also named apostles, to be with him, and to be sent out to proclaim the message, and to have authority to cast out demons.

(verses 14–15)

To be called by name expresses several meanings: chosen, known, special, set apart; all of which are visible in the reading for today. This selection process was a vastly important moment as 12 men were chosen amongst the many who followed Jesus. Most importantly, they were not selected for some cushy role, but one that was hard, thankless and sacrificial. Jesus, who knew the demands of the role, reserved the right to choose, and to authorise their duties: to preach and exorcise spirits.

The many reality shows on the television today – *The X Factor*, *The Apprentice*, *The Great British Bake Off* and others – all involve a selection process. Contestants are given the opportunity to fulfill lifelong dreams, and there is no denying the significance of being chosen. However, there is a difference between being selected for a reality show and for apostleship. The role of an apostle does not lead to glory and a celebrity lifestyle, but the opposite: persecution, criticism and alienation.

In spite of hardships, there is no denying the privilege of being called by name, set apart and chosen to fulfill God's purpose in your life. Will you risk following Jesus? To respond in the affirmative, you are declaring that your life is in God's hands and your desire is for his will to become your will.

† Commissioning God, I give myself to be used for your glory and praise! Amen

For further thought
- Discipleship and sacrifice are inextricably linked together, inviting surrender to the authority of Jesus.

19

Saturday 20 January
Authority to adopt

Read Mark 3:31–35

And looking at those who sat around him, he said, 'Here are my mother and my brothers! Whoever does the will of God is my brother and sister and mother.'

(verses 34–35)

It appeared at face value that Jesus was breaking another decree, the honouring of one's parents. It appeared as if he dealt with his family in total disregard, as outsiders. It appeared as if he was claiming strangers as family at the expense of his own family relationship. Yet on closer inspection Jesus is not denying his familial connection, but extending the boundaries of family; not just those who were related by blood, but those who were willing to listen and follow his teachings belonged to his family. Jesus was exercising his authority and fulfilling his mission by embracing those outside his family unit as adopted sons and daughters of God.

I have friends who adopted their two sons a few years ago and speak of their decision as one which created a family and shared love with the unrelated, thus making them relatives. To belong and to be accepted and valued are essential for the well-being of every human being, which is reflected in Jesus' spiritual lesson to his family and disciples about the kingdom of God. Jesus went beyond human limitations to show how God's kingdom is about relationship full stop, thus reminding us that genuine relationship is not just a matter of flesh and blood.

Are we inclined to embrace only those like us? Jesus taught that not only blood relatives but obedient disciples are part of his new family. Therefore, those who were and are prepared 'to take up [their] cross and follow him' were and still are his 'brothers, sisters and mother'.

† Father of all, through your Son Jesus we have become adopted children. May we embrace the privilege of belonging to a new family. Amen

For further thought

• Doing the will of God gives us new identity, new worth and a sense of deep belonging.

Readings in Mark (1)
3 The word and the storm

Notes by **Simei Monteiro**

Simei Monteiro is a Brazilian poet and composer. She worked as Worship Consultant at the World Council of Churches in Geneva, Switzerland. She is interested in worship and the arts, and her book, *The Song of Life* (ASTE/IEPG 1991), explores the relationship between hymnody and theology. As a retired missionary from the United Methodist Church, USA, she lives in Curitiba, Brazil, with her husband Revd Jairo Monteiro. They have two daughters and three grandchildren. Simei has used the NRSVA for these notes.

Sunday 21 January
The fruitful life

Read Mark 4:1–20

And he said to them, 'To you has been given the secret of the kingdom of God, but for those outside, everything comes in parables' ... And he said to them, 'Do you not understand this parable? Then how will you understand all the parables?'

(verses 11, 13)

Parables are meant to be simple to understand; intended to enable hearing and move people to reflection and action. In Jesus' time, and even now, parables confront us, provoke thought and demand a response in action.

When I was a little girl I loved stories of mystery and secrets. It was always exciting to discover the secret or the key that disclosed a hidden plot. In this parable, there is a mysterious relationship between seed and soil and it is up to us to discover the 'secret of the kingdom of God': the secret for a fruitful life.

Surely we want to hear, understand and respond to the word just as the good soil reacts to the vital movements of the seed. However, notice that in almost all the described situations the seed is in danger. How can we save the seed? How can we avoid it being spoiled?

But sometimes there is enough strength in the seed to survive even in a dry soil. Let us nurture the soil of our lives this week with courage and determination so the word can bear enough fruits in us for the sake of life.

† Divine Sower, transform our hearts into good and fertile soil so the seeds of your kingdom can bear fruits of justice and peace! Amen

Monday 22 January
Hidden secrets coming to light

Read Mark 4:21–34

He said to them, 'Is a lamp brought in to be put under the bushel basket, or under the bed, and not on the lampstand? For there is nothing hidden, except to be disclosed; nor is anything secret, except to come to light.'

(verses 21–22)

In this parable, Jesus speaks about hidden things we need to disclose under the power of the light. The lamp is a metaphor for disclosure, revelation of darkness in us, hidden thoughts in our minds, lost things in our lives.

We use light to illuminate the space around us, even small corners. Sometimes we are able to see things and places more clearly and take away things we want to get rid of.

Why fear being exposed to light or being shown as we really are? If the light of God reveals our deficiencies and enlightens us we can even become transparent. Even more, when touched by God's powerful light we can be transfigured into a new person.

The best news is that this is a liberating process! Growing in the grace of God we can be free of guilt and shame. God wants us to be a white-hot light, a beacon in this world, a sign of God's love to our neighbours. Being a transparent person means that nothing can be hidden in us, even if we are still struggling to overcome our imperfections.

The light of God can inundate our inner being and make us a light which reflects God's image. 'And all of us, with unveiled faces, seeing the glory of the Lord as though reflected in a mirror, are being transformed into the same image from one degree of glory to another,' writes Paul in 2 Corinthians 3:18, 'for this comes from the Lord, the Spirit.'

† O Light of the World! Search and clean my heart and mind so your light can freely shine in me. I want to reflect a real image of your grace! Amen

For further thought

• Which hidden things do you think need to be brought to light in our world today?

Tuesday 23 January
When fear brings hope

Read Mark 4:35–41

*He woke up and rebuked the wind, and said to the sea, 'Peace! Be still!'
Then the wind ceased, and there was a dead calm. He said to them, 'Why
are you afraid? Have you still no faith?'*

(verses 39–40)

Storms in life are natural but always unexpected. They appear
without warning and in seconds our life can change. In the middle
of the storm, when we feel scared, helpless and alone, we are
tempted to forget that God is there for us. We still have faith but
fear and doubt keep us paralysed, panicked and even unable to
look for help. In some circumstances, we can be completely taken
over by the storm, give up our hope and perish. How to deal with
the unpredictable? Normally in our despair, we would say, 'I am not
prepared for this; I do not know what to do!'

As a child, living by the sea, I always was afraid when a thunderstorm
approached. I rushed to close the windows to avoid seeing the
waves beating against the pier across our street. Then I searched
for my mother in the house. I remember her face; just her smile
was enough to bring peace and calm to my heart. I knew she was
there for me.

However, when there is no immediate solution to the storms in our
lives, we can still be moved by faith and leap into the dark. Even
crawling in the dark, faith will move us towards salvation!

Faith in action is the answer when we feel powerless. Faith will
certainly draw us closer to our helper, our Saviour Jesus! In all
times, all ages in the past, present and future, he will remain our
Saviour.

† O Jesus, my Pilot, help me to deal with fears; let me always be sure you are by
my side when facing things I cannot control or when I feel abandoned and alone.
Amen

For further thought
• What habits help you deal with fear and stress?

Wednesday 24 January
The storm is passing over, Hallelujah!

Read Psalm 107:23–32

> ... they cried to the Lord in their trouble,
> and he brought them out from their distress;
> he made the storm be still,
> and the waves of the sea were hushed.

(verses 28–29)

What can we do in the middle of the storm? Is there an alternative to despair?

The night after one of my operations was very difficult. I was alone at the hospital and because I was in so much pain I couldn't sleep; time was not passing and the night seemed endless. Longing for the dawn, I feared that all the hospital staff had disappeared and I cried out for help several times. Then, I heard a whisper in my heart: 'All shall be well' and I was filled with stillness. Later, recovering at home, I wrote a song, *Vigília* (Vigil), based on Psalm 130.

> In anguish and sorrow,
> from depths of depression
> I cry out to you.
> The dark night is endless,
> my heart longs awaiting
> the dawn of the day!
> You come to my rescue;
> a whisper, that tells me
> that 'all shall be well'!

In the middle of a storm, we can discover the dimensions of grace. To be still is difficult, but the waves are not bigger than God's power. Soon you can smile and say, 'Thanks be to God, it is over!'

† God, our Pilot! Give us the courage to face storms in our lives. Whisper words of comfort. Amen

For further thought

• Rewrite verses of Psalm 107 in your own words, using a situation that relates to your life.

Thursday 25 January
The secret of integrity

Read Mark 5:1–20

He lived among the tombs; and no one could restrain him any more, even with a chain … They came to Jesus and saw the demoniac sitting there, clothed and in his right mind, the very man who had had the legion; and they were afraid.

(verses 3, 15)

Human beings are not as strong as they seem to be. Sometimes the wholeness of a personality can be broken and the unity of body, mind and spirit of an individual is dissociated and disintegrated. When Jesus asked the possessed man, 'What is your name?' he replied, 'My name is Legion; for we are many.'

If we lose our integrity we can become a legion; our mental images, all our psychological life will become fragmented and our identity exists no more. The presence of a legion in the midst of a community can destroy and disrupt its life.

Only God can reunite all these fragments and restore our human communion. God calls us by our very name and claims divine ownership: 'I have called you by name, you are mine' (Isaiah 43:1). We belong to God and we want to be part of God's family. The man begged to stay with Jesus but he told him to go and tell what happened to him to the entire village.

Nowadays, in Brazil, we are facing a kind of political schizophrenia with more than 35 registered political parties and new ones asking for recognition, each one pursuing its own interests and agenda. In this situation, it is really hard to find someone that can represent us.

We are praying for a social and political unity that could allow us to really go forward in the right direction of social integration. We believe that the assurance of 'belonging' is stronger than all the negative forces in us and in the life of our country.

† Let us pray for countries divided by ethnic identity, class or religion so that God's love can transform not only the hearts of people but also their entire life.

For further thought
• 'Every kingdom divided against itself is laid waste, and no city or house divided against itself will stand' (Matthew 12:25).

Friday 26 January
Dare to believe

Read Mark 5:21–43

... *'If I but touch his clothes, I will be made well.' Immediately her haemorrhage stopped; and she felt in her body that she was healed ... He said to her, 'Daughter, your faith has made you well; go in peace, and be healed of your disease.'*

(verses 28–29, 34)

Jesus the Master is being pressed by a multitude; a woman approaches him. She is looking desperately for healing. If only her father or brother or another relative was there to intercede on her behalf, she might be thinking! She was a woman and Jesus a rabbi; she had a haemorrhage and was thus considered impure. Anything she dared to do would be considered a violation of the community laws.

In most biblical accounts we see Jesus acting as Master: teaching, healing, exhorting. Nevertheless, this episode shows us a woman being the master of her actions. She knows what she needs and what she was longing for. She does not cry out or beg Jesus for healing; she had been suffering so many years and she thought it was enough. She took her opportunity and dared to believe in something unlikely. She had nothing to lose, she was freed from her perceived disgrace and she was on the way to grace.

Logically, we believe that faith is a condition for moving forward. This woman simply dared to touch Jesus. She was not sure what would happen but she thought, 'If I but touch'. If she asked for help, perhaps she would not have gotten permission to be closer to Jesus and, if discovered, probably she would have suffered the consequences of her transgression.

Perhaps this is a disturbing thought: can we dare to take the way of faith even when we are not sure about the results or the risks? For this woman, her faith made her well!

† God, our Healer, give us courage and boldness even when there is no hope, even when we feel abandoned and oppressed. Amen

For further thought

• Have you ever felt abandoned? How did you keep your faith in God and in humanity?

Saturday 27 January
The secret of discipleship

Read Mark 6:1–13

He called the twelve and began to send them out two by two, and gave them authority over the unclean spirits. He ordered them to take nothing for their journey except a staff; no bread, no bag, no money in their belts …

(verses 7–8)

Jesus' advice to the disciples is strange and mysterious. How do we understand such a call for discipleship that spells weakness and poverty? Would it not be more appropriate to imagine the disciples of the King of kings as a wealthy and powerful group whose members go everywhere distributing God's blessings?

Nevertheless, being a servant of Jesus does not mean being a famous preacher. It means having no greed, no plans except to accomplish God's will when and where it is needed.

This call is also to accept Jesus' call to a simple life and, more than this, to a low-consumption way of living: less power, less money and fewer belongings. Perhaps not to be a powerful person but a person empowered by God's love. Then we will be surprised to realise how much lighter we are and how ready to love and serve our neighbours.

Despite the inversion of values in our society, the poor and simple people are able to recognise immediately a servant of Jesus Christ.

Many years ago, a new missionary came to the Amazon region in Brazil 'to preach the gospel to the indigenous people'. He started saying: 'I want you to know Jesus, how he humbly lived among us and healed sick people …' Then he was surprised when the chief of the community came to him and said: 'O yes! Of course, we know Jesus! He has passed by here …' and he told him about an anonymous doctor missionary who came, lived and even died among them.

† God, help us to choose a simple life, to listen to your call on the streets, and to travel the journey you planned for us, and may the Holy Spirit surprise us on the way! Amen

For further thought
- Do you truly appreciate the little things in life; that life's wonders and joys are God's blessings to be shared with others?

History of IBRA and the International Fund

The International Bible Reading Association (IBRA) was founded by the Sunday School Union (SSU) committee under Charles Waters in 1882. At the time Waters was the manager of a bank in King's Cross. A devout young man and Sunday school teacher, Waters had arrived in London in 1859 to further his career, and there encountered the brilliant and inspirational teaching of Charles Spurgeon. He threw himself heart and soul into working with Spurgeon and the Sunday School Union. In 1882, the SSU wrote to all members in Britain and overseas inviting them to join the newly formed International Bible Reading Association, circulating lists of daily Bible readings, supported by brief commentary notes.

The response was amazing. Readers appreciated that each day they were provided with a portion of scripture that was thoughtfully brief, selected with the utmost care to link to the week's topic. There was a living, personal touch which was seemingly the secret of its success.

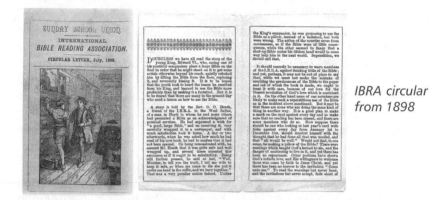

IBRA circular
from 1898

By 1910 the readership had exceeded a million people and was touching the lives of soldiers fighting wars, sailors on long voyages to Australia, colliers in the coal mines of Wales, schools in Canada, Jamaica and Belfast, and prisoners in Chicago. People all over the world, alone or in groups, felt comforted and encouraged by the idea of joining other Christians throughout the world in reading the same Bible passages. And they still do!

Today, over 135 years later, this rich history lives on, touching the lives of hundreds of thousands of people across the world. IBRA is now part of the Birmingham-based charity Christian Education and is working to continue the legacy, providing support to our global community of IBRA readers. Our aim is still to enable Christians from different parts of the world to grow in knowledge of and relationship with God through our international writers' and contributors' experiences of him.

The original mission continues today and will do into the future!

Winning and losing
1 Winning and losing in the Old Testament

Notes by **Mark Woods**

Revd Mark Woods is a Baptist minister and contributing editor for the online magazine *Christian Today* (www.christiantoday. com). He has previously worked for the *Baptist Times* and the Methodist Recorder. He is the author of *Does the Bible Really Say That?* (Lion Hudson 2016) and is on the leadership team of the church he attends in Cheltenham. Aside from reading everything he can lay his hands on, he enjoys walking, photographing birds and running, though more when it's over than when he's doing it. Mark has used the NIVUK for these notes.

Sunday 28 January
Moses' failure is Joshua's success

Read Deuteronomy 31:1–8

The Lord himself goes before you and will be with you; he will never leave you nor forsake you. Do not be afraid; do not be discouraged.

(verse 8)

This reading tells of the passing of authority from one of Israel's great leaders to another. Moses will not lead the people into the Promised Land; that task falls to Joshua.

These few verses address the twin themes of winning and losing. There's a sense in which Moses is the loser. After his faithfulness and leadership throughout the years of Israel's wandering, he will not receive the crown of victory because of a previous act of disobedience (Numbers 27:13–14). It is Joshua who is promised the presence of God in the forthcoming campaign.

But Moses shows no signs of disappointment or bitterness. He accepts what is happening because he knows that God will still fulfill his purposes – just not through him.

There's often a temptation to put too much weight on our own contribution to what God is doing and to imagine it all depends on us. When it goes wrong – perhaps when a church leader loses the confidence of the people, or a project fails or we make a costly mistake – we can be cast down and distressed. But God sees winning and losing in a different way. He requires faithfulness of us, not success.

† God, guard us from thinking too much of ourselves, and give us the grace to give up when others can do better than we can. Amen

Thursday 8 February
Gains and losses

Read Philippians 3:4b–11

More than that, I regard everything as loss because of the surpassing value of knowing Christ Jesus my Lord. For his sake I have suffered the loss of all things, and I regard them as rubbish, in order that I may gain Christ.

(verse 8)

Hyperbole is a powerful and effective tool for writers and speakers. When Jesus talks about cutting off a hand which leads you astray or removing a plank from your eye before dealing with the speck in someone else's, the exaggerated dimensions of offence and solution make the point very well. Like most sharp and incisive tools, it needs to be handled with care – and it is with care that we need to hear Paul's hyperbole when, in his marvellous enthusiasm for his new life in Christ, he appears to consign all of his previous life as a diligent Jew to the rubbish bin. In times of serious world conflict on real or supposed religious lines we need to be wary of the misuse of such texts.

Jesus never rejected his national, cultural and religious identity; he declared his desire *not* to reject the Law of Moses and indeed to *fulfill* the Law in his life, love and perfect integrity. That being so, maybe it is wise, when reading Paul, to let the initial blast of enthusiastic rhetoric blow through in order that the real gold of his writing might be discerned.

When you listen patiently to Paul, instead of what can almost sound like music to anti-Semitic ears, you hear an extraordinarily alive individual brimming over with excitement that the 'head understanding' of his upbringing had been overwhelmed and overtaken by his 'heart encounter' with Jesus. Listen wisely to Paul, but with a heart open and ready to be stirred by his infectious enthusiasm.

† Dear God, when I am clumsy in dealing with others' religious experience, give me sensitivity; when I am cautious about what you give, free me to delight in you. Amen

For further thought

• Avoid discarding other peoples' views or beliefs as 'rubbish'. Instead, listen out for truth in unfamiliar places.

Friday 9 February
Press on to win – against whom?

Read Philippians 3:12–16

… but this one thing I do: forgetting what lies behind and straining forward to what lies ahead, I press on towards the goal …

(verses 13b–14)

Listening this week to Paul it must have often felt that we have been in the presence of a dauntingly pumped-up athlete at the peak of his fitness, and we have witnessed him, every muscle, sinew and pulsing vein, launching himself towards the finish line. But here's a question to ponder – whom is he racing against? There were those in the early Church (look at 1 Corinthians 1 for a glimpse of this) who would have liked to have fragmented the Church into competitive groups, each following a different leader. Paul argues against that – instead, when you listen to this extraordinary, inspirational, sometimes disturbing person, the 'other' competitor in Paul's life race is, invariably, himself. Constantly, he tries to master the legalism and control of his former life as it wrestles with the Spirit-fuelled, bareback ride which has followed his encounter with Jesus on the Damascus Road. No wonder the poor man sounds extreme at times!

As a counterpoint to Paul's energy and drive, I remember watching severely disabled participants in the 2016 Rio Olympics compete in the sport of Boccia. As with bowls or curling, competitors aim to place leather balls as close to a jack as possible. Some throw conventionally, others push with a variety of limbs which are mobile and have control. Progress is often slow and painstaking.

Listening to Paul, watching the Boccia competitors, I realise that 'winning' in God's terms is not about becoming a spiritual superstar but simply using whatever gifts and opportunities we have to live the life of God's kingdom where and how we are.

† Loving God, take my strength and talents;
  take my past journeying;
  take my future days and let me serve you well. Amen

For further thought
• What ambitions drive, frustrate or energise your life?

Saturday 10 February
It's time to get fit

Read 1 Timothy 4:1–10

Train yourself in godliness.

(verse 7)

A friend recently posted on the internet his enthusiasm for a particular diet. Despite being inexplicably overlooked by the medical establishment, this diet could be, in his opinion, the salvation of the whole (obese) world. Perhaps it might, but it will have to compete with myriad diets, yoga methods and 'mindfulness' exercises, all of which promise something similar. Western culture currently seems fixated on escaping the empty promises of consumerism but often seems only to succeed in enlisting the support of yet another consumer product.

This reminds me of the gospel story of a rich man who asked Jesus for a method by which he might 'inherit eternal life'. Jesus' reply undermines the man's acquisitive mindset, by suggesting that he needed to do nothing more to achieve his desire. On the contrary, he needed to do less. 'Get rid of your wealth and its associated anxiety and false security,' says Jesus, 'and you will find that you already have what you seek' (Luke 18:18–30).

When Timothy is encouraged to 'train in godliness' I suspect that what was required of him was less about the taking on of rigorous study and elaborate prayer techniques, and much more about learning to rest in the security of God's provision, moment by moment, day by day. Once he had accomplished this resting upon God, he, like Paul, would be free to take on the demands and opportunities of life with equal confidence and resourcefulness.

† Dear God, teach me the discipline of simple offering. At work, in my walking, in what I build, and in the problems I dismantle, may I find you, know you and serve you. Amen

For further thought

• When faced with a fresh challenge, before rushing to acquire additional resources – time, money, skills – consider decluttering as a way forward.

Winning and losing
3 Endurance

Notes by **Ian Fosten**

See p. 36 for Ian's biography. Ian has used the NRSVA for these notes.

Sunday 11 February
Perseverance, character, hope

Read Romans 5:3–7

We also boast in our sufferings, knowing that suffering produces endurance, and endurance produces character, and character produces hope.

(verses 3b–4)

As a child my daughter didn't always seem to have a great deal of physical or social stamina. On a cycle ride she would walk up any uphill section. In social gatherings she would often prefer to read rather than deal with new people. I encouraged her to try a bit harder, especially at challenges which, I promised her, would be 'character-building'. With the years she gradually found more resources, and then came the time when, for several months, she became the carer of a severely disabled young woman. When I visited and saw how steadfastly she dealt with demands which would easily have defeated me, I realised with amazement and delight that the 'character-building' mantra had become redundant.

Paul's words to persecuted Roman Christians are not the advice of a 'spiritual hard man' who sought out difficulties in order to prove the virility of his faith; rather, they reflect the empathetic experience of someone for whom faithful living has led to trials and conflict. He had discovered that uninvited hard times had taught him, especially when his own strength had gone, to trust and be sustained by God. Endurance, character and hope are not earned, but given.

† Teach me, dear God, not to seek to be a stoic or a hero but to accept your gracious gifts of endurance, character and hope. Amen

Monday 12 February
Holding on by letting go

Read Philippians 4:8–13

... for I have learned to be content with whatever I have ... I can do all things through him who strengthens me.

(verses 11, 13)

A woman was admitted to hospital due to complications with her pregnancy. The doctor explained what was happening, what action would keep both mother and baby safe, but then asked, 'So, what would you like us to do?' The woman was baffled – hadn't the doctor just explained how the crisis could be averted and a safe birth follow? 'Ah,' said the doctor, mindful of the risk of possible complaint and litigation if anything went wrong with the procedure, 'the choice to proceed or not has to be yours, the patient.'

In many places today a rampant, destructive 'blame culture' is prevalent. Anyone who provides goods or services needs to be vigilant lest a patient or customer choose to blame the provider for contributing to their misfortune or loss of happiness. Consequently, social workers, teachers and grocery store owners can only give part of their attention to serving well, the rest of their efforts needing to be focused on avoiding opportunities for blame. Such an atmosphere is at best distracting; at worst, it can be utterly dispiriting to good and caring practitioners.

Such an inclination to blame our way through misfortune is not new – look at Job's so-called friends in the Old Testament – nor is it alien to Paul's experience at the hands of other people. However, knowing the corrosiveness of blame culture, Paul urges his listeners to face misfortune not with petulance but with spiritual maturity. Rather than seeking blame and retribution he tells us to learn instead to 'be content' and rest upon the ever-sustaining grace and power of God's love in Jesus.

† Cultivate within me, dear God, a readiness to overlook the faults and failings I see so easily in others, that I may see more eagerly that which is positive and good. Amen

For further thought

• In what practical ways might you roll back the blame culture and replace it with attitudes of understanding, generosity and forgiveness?

Tuesday 13 February
Win honestly – or lose integrity

Read 2 Timothy 2:1–7

And in the case of an athlete, no one is crowned without competing according to the rules.

(verse 5)

Sport can be a wonderful means of self-expression for individuals. Sport can exemplify fine examples of human collaboration and community. Many youngsters who may have struggled in the classroom or with a difficult home life have found tremendous fulfillment in their prowess on the track or pitch. And yet, sport can also provide the stage on which darker, more sordid aspects of humanity can be played out: doping allegations mar the Olympic ideal, cricket matches are 'thrown' to make money unfairly from betting and soccer players dive and feign injury in order to deceive the referee.

One summer, I played tennis with a friend. After a few sessions I realised that he cheated by frequently awarding himself points he had not won. Though we were evenly matched, on a couple of occasions when my lead couldn't be denied, he made an excuse and ended the game prematurely. I enjoyed playing tennis, but since he cared more for winning at all costs than he valued our friendship, our tennis-playing ended.

In advocating a 'clean' approach to sport, as in the whole of life, Paul is looking to a prize which is greater, deeper and richer than any medal or winner's bounty. What Paul has in mind we might call integrity – that clearly visible link between intention, application and outcome. Integrity, ultimately, always outperforms mere winning. You may hoodwink the referee, you may outwit the anti-doping agency, you may yearn passionately for your team to come out on top, but you can never fool God – nor can you ever outrun your conscience.

† Thank you, dear God, for sporting skills, commitment and prowess: and, win or lose, for great achievement and for games won well. Amen

For further thought

• Take game-playing seriously, especially with the youngsters you know. Teach them, by example and because you love them, that playing honestly and well is the only way to go.

Leadership
1 Servant leadership

Notes by **Nathan Eddy**

Nathan is editor of *Fresh from the Word*, a parent, a novice roller skater, exile from snowy mountains, and lover of the poetry of the Bible. He is ordained in the United Church of Christ (USA) and has served as a minister in the United Reformed Church. He loves empty holy places like pubs on a Saturday afternoon, and taking the long way through the park. He is finishing a PhD in the Psalms (honest!) and looks forward to what comes next. He lives in London with Clare, Mahalia and Elise. Nathan has used the NRSVA for these notes.

Wednesday 14 February (Ash Wednesday)
Leading and loving

Read Isaiah 41:25—42:4

Here is my servant, whom I uphold, my chosen, in whom my soul delights.

(verse 42:1)

Today, Ash Wednesday, we begin our series on Lent, focused this year on the theme of leadership. You've probably also noticed that, at least in most areas of our readership, today is Valentine's Day. So, go on: open a Valentine's card from God today: God delights in you.

The reading today, as well as many other passages in the Old Testament (e.g. Psalm 2 or Isaiah 11), says loud and clear that God delights in human leadership (verse 1). Leadership in the church is sometimes portrayed as a conflict between God's will and ours. There will sometimes be conflict, as there is in any relationship. But God views humanity as a partner in God's establishing of justice in the world (also verse 1). God doesn't simply tolerate human leadership, God desires it, even on Ash Wednesday; even given all the ways we mess things up.

This week, as we begin our Lenten journey together, I invite you to return to the idea that God takes delight in robust, creative, independent leaders. God believes in our leadership and delights in us. What better Valentine's Day or Ash Wednesday message do we need?

† Loving God, let me rest awhile in your gaze of love and delight. Thank you for delighting in all I am, and all I can be. Amen

Thursday 15 February
A life worth living

Read Ezekiel 34:11–16

'I will feed them with good pasture, and the mountain heights of Israel shall be their pasture; there they shall lie down in good grazing land, and they shall feed on rich pasture on the mountains of Israel.'

(verse 14)

The book *The Shepherd's Life: A Tale of the Lake District* by James Rebanks was a surprise bestseller a few years ago. In the book, Rebanks tells of this family's generations-long commitment to the wild countryside in the north of England, and his own decision to return to his family croft after university. As God promises to lead Israel to mountain pastures, Rebanks reflects movingly on his favourite time of year: the spring, when he can lead his animals up the mountains to the high pasture. The book ends with a strikingly biblical image: Rebanks lolling in the sun with his dogs by a high mountain stream, grateful for the turn of seasons and for his place in it.

The image of the shepherd is one of the most familiar from the Bible, but I'm not sure we appreciate its seasonal aspect. A shepherd is a leader who is tune with the cycle of nature, with the life that pulses in the animals, with the warming sun and cooling waters. As leaders, can we be in tune with the earth and its creatures, the way God is?

My family and I have a small garden with apple trees and vegetable beds. Whenever I spend more than a few minutes outside in it, I'm struck by the changes in the sky and weather, even though we live in the middle of a big city. Recently while I was weeding and my seven-year-old was climbing the tree, a hailstorm blew through. The hail stung my bare arms and my daughter and I laughed. We were grateful for our place in the world.

† Guide us, Redeemer God. Lead us beside still waters and restore our souls. Amen

For further thought
- What traditional ways do people use to stay close to the land where you live?

Friday 16 February
Upended

Read Matthew 20:20–28

'... *whoever wishes to be great among you must be your servant, and whoever wishes to be first among you must be your slave.*'

(part of verses 26–27)

In 2016 the Tate Britain gallery in London erected a Christmas tree. Nothing too shocking in that, except this one was different: it was suspended upside down from wires in the foyer of the grand building. At the top (bottom) of the tree, its roots were carefully cleaned of dirt and covered in gold foil. Artist Shirazeh Houshiary had the vision to 'bring earth to heaven', according to the museum's description of the sculpture.

In today's reading, we see the mother of James and John (not James and John themselves, as in Mark's version) asking Jesus for places in glory for her sons. Those seats could be seats in the judgement court envisioned in the previous chapter in Matthew (19:27–30) or they could be related to another text such as Psalm 110. At any rate, the request is inappropriate. Jesus' followers are supposed to serve the least, not elbow their way to the top seats. Jesus' response flips their request on its head, like the tree. Jesus doesn't reject power and leadership outright; rather he challenges them to direct it in ways that challenge conventional order. Leadership is not to be handed out from a CEO-like Jesus, but practised in their own lives. It must be practised with the least, and practised in ways that might lead us to suffering and rejection: at the end of the story, the only ones appearing to Jesus' right and left are criminals crucified with him (Matthew 27:38).

Followers of Jesus are to be a bit like that tree: its roots spread out strangely but beautifully in the air, glinting with gold. We, too, are to work the earth around us and offer our rootedness to heaven.

† God of the least, upend my vision today. Root me in your goodness, that I can serve others with my heart brimming with joy. Amen

For further thought

• How can this passage broaden and challenge what Eucharist or the Lord's Supper (with its shared cup, as in verse 23) and baptism mean to you?

Saturday 17 February
Heaven's dirty dishes

Read John 13:3–17

'So if I, your Lord and Teacher, have washed your feet, you also ought to wash one another's feet. For I have set you an example, that you also should do as I have done to you.'

(verses 14–15)

The last verse of the reading for today, the foot-washing scene from John, captures a great deal about leadership, and about John's portrait of Jesus: 'if you know these things, you are blessed if you do them' (verse 17). Leadership, including servant leadership, is about what we do with our time, our bodies, our hands and our feet. And that physical presence and service is something all who follow Jesus are to emulate. Good intentions and friendly smiles are lovely, but aren't enough.

Once when I worked as a university chaplain I was trying to get to know the staff who cleaned one particular group of halls. I lingered near their tea break rooms, introduced myself and made an effort to get to know them. But I didn't really begin to establish relationships until I volunteered for a few days on some of the cleaning and cooking shifts. I cleaned an oven or two, hoovered up a hallway, mopped a stairwell, did a shift on pot-washing duty and served up vegetables in the dining hall. It was only a few days of my time, but it was a sign of my commitment and at last I felt I earned the trust of the staff.

The ways we exercise this leadership will vary, but all who follow Jesus are called to give their time and use their bodies as they are able in ways that benefit others. Some things have to be done stair by stair, shift by shift, oven by oven and person by person. Any cleaner knows that. Jesus knew it – and tells us we are blessed if we do it.

† God of dirty feet, wash me that I might be clean, and have the energy to do the same to others. Amen

For further thought
- After a long day, what aching part of your body would Jesus seek to touch and wash?

Leadership
2 Leadership in the Old Testament

Notes by **Alexandra Wright**

Alexandra Wright is Senior Rabbi of The Liberal Jewish Synagogue, London. She studied at Leo Baeck College, London, where she also taught classical Hebrew after ordination in 1986. She was volunteer chaplain at the North London Hospice and is drawn particularly to accompanying those who are journeying towards their final days – which really includes all of us. Alexandra has used her own translation for these notes. Verse numbers are according to the NRSVA.

Sunday 18 February
Qualifications of a leader

Read Exodus 18:17–23

You shall also seek out, from among all the people, capable individuals who fear God – trustworthy ones who spurn ill-gotten gain … Make it easier for yourself by letting them share the burden with you.

(verses 21–22)

When Moses' father-in-law, Jethro, arrives at the Israelite camp at Sinai, he tells Moses he must find others to share in his leadership. Jethro sets four criteria for the applicants: they are to be *anshey chayil* – people of strength. 'Strength' here refers not only to military prowess, although the word *chayil* is certainly used in that context, but to individuals with clear moral values, as in *eshet chayil* – the 'woman of worth' in Proverbs. Secondly, they are to revere God – setting above themselves a supreme and moral arbiter of justice. Reverence for God removes the possibility of narcissism – that everything we do is for the glorification of ourselves at the expense of others. Thirdly, they are to speak truth to power – *anshey emet* – as people of integrity, faithfulness and truth. And fourthly, they are to reject any personal profit – monetary or otherwise – from their roles as leaders. Three times the text uses the word *anashim* – 'men' or 'people'. And perhaps in the repetition of this word as well, there is a clue to a fifth quality in the leader – humanity. Jethro implies that the magistrates must share Moses' humaneness, his empathy and understanding of the people.

Jethro's qualities serve as a good introduction to our theme this week, and in the weeks to come.

† May God grant us wisdom and understanding in our role as leaders of our community and so help us to contribute to the well-being of society. Amen

Monday 19 February
Integrity

Read 1 Samuel 12:1–5

'Here I am! Testify against me, in the presence of the Eternal One and in the presence of His anointed one: Whose ox have I taken, or whose ass have I taken? Whom have I defrauded or whom have I robbed?'

(verse 3)

Now an old man, Samuel yields his authority to Saul, the first king of Israel. Yet it is not without a degree of reluctance – for since childhood it has been his vocation to serve God and lead God's people. 'Have I acted corruptly or for my own profit?' he asks the Israelites?

'Whom have I defrauded or whom have I robbed?' The Hebrew of this sentence suggests a greater violence than the English translation; rather 'Whom have I oppressed or whom have I crushed?' The great mediaeval French commentator, Rashi, notes that whenever these two Hebrew verbs, *ashak* and *ratzaz*, occur together in the same sentence they imply violation of the most vulnerable members of society, particularly the poor.

Those of us who live in comfortable houses, with warmth, water and light, in cleanliness and with enough food to eat, have a responsibility not only to speak out against injustice and unfairness, but to embody the teachings of our traditions in what we do on a daily basis.

The test of true leadership is integrity; the good leader is the individual who is not afraid to address the truth and to act nobly and honestly for the cause of the well-being of others. In Jewish tradition, rabbis could be critical of those who failed to speak out. In a *midrash*, or ancient commentary on the Bible, the rabbis taught that one who withdraws from public life, and says, 'What have I to do with the burdens of the community, or with their disputes; why should I listen to them? Peace to you, O my soul – such a person destroys the world' (*Midrash* Tanchuma, *Mishpatim* 2).

† O God: we are not required to complete the work, but neither are we at liberty to abstain from it. Amen

For further thought
• Seeking out those who do not have the same privileges as we do is a way of offering friendship and giving immediacy to their stories.

Tuesday 20 February
God looks at the heart

Read 1 Samuel 16:1–13

So they sent [for David] and brought him. He was ruddy-cheeked, bright-eyed, and handsome. And the Eternal One said, 'Rise and anoint him, for this is the one.'

(verse 12)

It seems ironic that the very first thing we learn about David is about his appearance: he is handsome, rosy-cheeked and has beautiful eyes. Ironic, because in searching for a successor to Saul, God has already told Samuel, 'Pay no attention to appearance or stature … for God does not see in the same way as a human being sees; a human being sees only what is visible, but the Eternal One sees into the heart' (verse 7).

In turn, each one of David's older brothers is rejected. 'Are these all the boys you have?' asks Samuel of their father. He replies that the youngest is tending the flock.

Succession is urgent; just after the passage in today's reading, we hear that the spirit of God has fled from Saul and 'an evil spirit from God begins to terrify him' (verse 14). Once upon a time, we would have said that Saul had gone mad, but I wonder what it was that really terrified him. Did he hear voices? Was he delusional or deeply depressed? Did he suffer from a paranoia that made him lash out against those who were dear to him? Perhaps it was early onset dementia, and only music – the music of David playing his lyre – could calm his anxious spirit.

Sometimes, when we are in the presence of those who suffer from mental illness, we forget to look beyond the visible – to see the person they really are, to quell our own fears of the unknown and awaken our compassion for them by seeing into the heart. But the story of David's selection urges us to look beyond the appearance or stature of those who God might have chosen for great things. Leaders, we learn, come in all shapes and sizes – in God's eyes, at least.

† Open my heart, O God, to your teaching and help me to discern the goodness and feel the anguish of those in pain. Amen

For further thought

• Listening for the underlying meaning of those who speak in 'riddles' or confusion can help us discern what their fears and hopes might be.

Wednesday 21 February
Love and leadership

Read 1 Samuel 18:1–9

When David finished speaking with Saul, Jonathan's soul became bound up with the soul of David; Jonathan loved David as himself …

(verse 1)

It is not only Jonathan who is drawn to David; all Israel and Judah are said to love him because of the success of his military campaigns. Saul's daughter, Michal, is to fall in love with David – although how much that love is reciprocated is unknown. Saul enjoys a conflicted relationship with the man who soothes his turbulent spirit with music and looks as though he is going to usurp him. Even Saul's courtiers seem to be in love with this ruddy-faced, handsome, courageous man.

Jonathan's love is unusual; his soul becomes bound up with the soul of David. It is perhaps like the love of one brother for another; or the love that exists between soldiers, sharing the intimate and fearful moments in the midst of war. The love is sealed by a pact, a covenant between the two, elevating it to the paradigmatic level of God's love for Israel. The cloak, and battle garb – the sword, his bow and his own belt – that he removes from himself and hands over to David, are a symbol of Jonathan's acknowledgement that David will be king. It is only after Jonathan's death that we learn of David's own love for his friend: 'More wondrous your love to me than the love of women' (2 Samuel 1:26).

David, for all his faults, shows that love and friendship can be a part of healthy leadership. But Saul shows that the opposite is also true. Saul is jealous of David's success, getting angry (verse 8) and viewing David as a rival to the throne from that moment on (verse 9). If love and friendship can be part of leadership, jealousy and vindictive anger cannot.

† Great is your love for us, Eternal God, and abundant your compassion – in love you call us to serve you. Amen

For further thought
• Even when God's love feels remote from us, let us feel and reciprocate the love of those dear to us.

Thursday 22 February
Diligent in preparation

Read Nehemiah 2:1–8

The king said to me, 'What is your request?' With a prayer to the God of heaven, I answered the king, 'If it please the king, and if your servant has found favour with you, send me to Judah, to the city of my ancestors' graves, to rebuild it.'

(verses 4–5)

Nearly 50 years have passed since the exile of the Israelites from Jerusalem. Nehemiah, cupbearer to the Persian king, requests that he might return to Judah to begin the work of rebuilding the city. The king agrees and, with letters allowing him passage through neighbouring territories and army officers and cavalry accompanying him, he arrives in Jerusalem.

Three days after his arrival, he gets up at night and, riding his animal, goes out by the Valley Gate towards the Jackal's Spring and the Dung Gate, there to survey the walls of Jerusalem – broken and consumed by fire. Who knows what was in his heart – dismay that the great edifice built by Solomon had been destroyed? But also resolve to rebuild the walls of Jerusalem, 'to suffer no more disgrace' (verse 17).

When foreign or civil wars oppress populations, forcing them out of their homeland and leaving rubble and ruin in their wake, what is it that stirs people to return and rebuild what has been lost? For Nehemiah, it is faith in God's benevolence, but also the compassion of a king who could see the heartbreak in his cupbearer's countenance – 'How is it that you look bad, though you are not ill? It must be bad thoughts' (verse 2).

Refugees who return to their homeland are often disillusioned. Their homes lie in ruins and the future is far from secure. Faith can offer resilience, but it is the support of other individuals and the organisations they represent that can help them achieve practical outcomes. Leadership in this mould is courageous after defeat and brave in the face of huge obstacles. Yet this leader knows, too, that one person cannot rebuild a nation, and thus looks for the benevolence of others.

† Help us, O God, to embody the teachings of our faith: 'to seek justice, relieve the oppressed, defend the orphan, plead for the widow.' Amen

For further thought

• Seek out ways to alleviate the suffering of victims of war – through charity and supporting organisations that reach out to the most vulnerable.

Friday 23 February
Overcoming opposition

Read Nehemiah 4:1–23

And so we worked on, while half were holding lances, from the break of day until the stars appeared.

(verse 21; Hebrew verse 15)

While Nehemiah and those who have returned to Judah work on repairing the walls of Jerusalem, the local people are angered and come together to create confusion and opposition. Nehemiah's response is filled with faith: 'Because of them we prayed to our God' (verse 9).

The workers are dispirited by relentless harassment from their enemies. 'Do not be afraid of them,' says Nehemiah. 'Think of the great and awesome Lord, and fight for your brothers, your sons and daughters, your wives and homes' (verse 14).

But Nehemiah is also pragmatic. While half the workers are set to work on the walls, the other half, carrying weapons of defence, are placed as guards to deter the enemy and so they are positioned from morning until darkness descends.

Perhaps it is not such a strange thing that the Talmud, the ancient compilation of Jewish teaching, uses this verse centuries later to define when evening starts and therefore the time from which the evening prayer may be recited. Evening is not simply when the sun begins to set, but when the stars appear in the sky.

There is a time for work, but there is also a time for *God's* work, and prayer can often provide the undergirding strength in times of obstruction and challenge. The faith-filled, yet pragmatic leadership of Nehemiah models this.

† May the words of my mouth, and the meditations of my heart, be acceptable to You, O God, my Rock and my Redeemer. Amen

For further thought

• We cannot change things through prayer, but we can pray for courage to do and become something more than we thought we could be.

Saturday 24 February
Victory through advisors

Read Proverbs 11:7–14

In an abundance of counsellors there is deliverance.

(verse 14)

This reading from Proverbs suggests something about leadership that we have observed all week: that a leader must seek wise advice in order to prosper. No leader can go it alone.

Notice the different advisors we've seen gathered around the leaders in our readings: on Sunday, we saw that Moses needed strong, reverential people around him in order that Moses could share out his leadership. On Wednesday, it was Saul who sought to eliminate opponents, and David who, by contrast, built friendship with Jonathan and led his own fighters effectively. On Thursday, we saw that Nehemiah was one who trusted in the benevolence of the Persian king who sent him back to Jerusalem to rebuild. And yesterday we saw that Nehemiah balanced his faithful leadership with common sense, listening to the issues raised by the people struggling in their work of rebuilding the wall.

Leadership in these passages is about trusting in God above all, but leadership is also about trusting that God has set others around us to guide us. According to Proverbs, the wise leader must trust his or her wise counsellors. And the alternative? The 'hopes of the wicked' are doomed and will amount to nothing (verse 7).

† Spread over us the shelter of your peace, Eternal God, and guard our going out and our coming in, that now and always we may have life and peace. Amen

For further thought
• Who are the trusted advisors around you, whom you can seek out for advice?

Leadership
3 Leadership in the New Testament

Notes by **Mark Woods**

See p. 29 for Mark's biography. Mark has used the NIVUK for these notes.

Sunday 25 February
Why Jesus called for childlike leadership

Read Matthew 18:1–10

He called a little child to him, and placed the child among them. And he said: 'Truly I tell you, unless you change and become like little children, you will never enter the kingdom of heaven. Therefore, whoever takes the lowly position of this child is the greatest in the kingdom of heaven.'

(verses 2–4)

I'm writing these notes part way through the UK TV series *The Apprentice*. Another group of hopefuls is out to impress top businessman Lord Sugar with their abilities. They are highly competitive and some of them are rather ridiculous. They are convinced of their own brilliance and continually tell the world how wonderful they are.

When *The Apprentice* starts to look like the Church, there's a problem. Jesus said those who are 'greatest in the kingdom of heaven' are those who are most like children. What he seems to mean is that they know they are powerless and vulnerable. They don't seek to impress by how capable they are. They are dependent on others rather than seeking to dominate them.

Jesus' teaching about the value of children, in which he says it would be better for someone to be drowned than cause one of them to 'stumble', does refer to children. But it also refers to Christians of any age. The spiritual consequences of Christians playing the world's games of domination, aggression and control are dreadful. Whatever it costs – and Jesus uses some vivid and horrifying imagery about maiming ourselves – this perversion of the faith is to be shunned. As we will explore this week, we are to be like children in our leadership and in all our lives.

† God, help me to resist the temptation to live as the world lives. Help me to find my worth in serving you, not in dominating others. Amen

Monday 26 February
Leading in a world turned upside down

Read Luke 22:24–27

The greatest among you should be like the youngest, and the one who rules like the one who serves. For who is greater, the one who is at the table or the one who serves?

(verses 26–27)

One of the ways in which the gospel challenged the ancient world was in how it conceived of leadership. The world in which it took root was rigidly stratified. Everyone knew their place. For a person of status, honour was everything. A noble would not serve his own servants, or a teacher his pupils.

In Jesus' new kingdom, though, there was to be a different type of leadership. It was not going to be based on inherited status, or money, or political power; the standards were to be entirely different. Christians were to be taught that they should honour those who *served*, rather than those who *dominated*. We should not seek praise or recognition. There is nothing wrong with being humble, as the ancient world would have thought; it is Christ-like.

We have not always done this very well. Some churches have elaborate hierarchies and their leaders have to struggle with the temptation of all-out career ambition. Those whose leaders wear suits and ties, or casual clothes, rather than elaborate robes and vestments, are just as vulnerable. Leaders get put on pedestals, and some of them rather like it there.

Church leaders have a heavy responsibility not to take themselves too seriously. Partly they should do this by cultivating a healthy prayer life and the habit of self-criticism. Partly they can be helped by personally engaging with their congregations rather than remaining remote from them, just as Jesus personally served his disciples. And congregations can help by remembering their leaders are human, and reminding them of it occasionally.

† God, forgive me if I have sought praise instead of just doing right. Help me to have a right view of myself and others and to remember each of us is equal in your sight. Amen

For further thought
• How do I form my opinion of other people? Do I look at their status, or their character and godliness?

Tuesday 27 February
Who cares who wins? Leading in God's way

Read Romans 12:3–8

For by the grace given me I say to every one of you: do not think of yourself more highly than you ought, but rather think of yourself with sober judgment, in accordance with the faith God has distributed to each of you.

(verse 3)

Youth is often a golden time, when we're testing our limits and working out what we're good at. If we're fortunate, we find our way into a life that enables us to reach our maximum potential. Not all of us do, by sheer force of circumstance, but all of us, no matter how gifted we are, have to learn to accept our limitations. There will always be people smarter or better-looking or richer than we are.

What Paul says in this passage is very important for all Christians, but especially for Christian leaders. Paul is clear: the fact that some are more talented or more successful than ourselves doesn't ultimately matter.

The urge to compete is built in to human beings. This drive to excel has made wonderful achievements possible. We are gripped by races and tennis or football matches, and there are many great Christian athletes. But in the realm of Christian relationships, competition is outlawed. We are to think of ourselves with 'sober judgment', says Paul, and not to worry if someone else is better at something than we are. We are not just individuals striving for dominance; we are part of a whole body.

When we're young, it can be hard to grasp that there are things we just aren't going to be able to do. Maturity comes when we focus on the things we can do, and learn to give God the glory for them. Wise leaders know their limitations, and rejoice in the gifts of others; it's the contributions of everyone working together that make up a healthy congregation.

† God, I am not as wise or as strong, as clever or as kind as other people. Help me to do my best as I am, without being bitter or resentful about what I'm not. Amen

For further thought

- Shakespeare talked about 'desiring this man's art, and that man's scope'. Am I jealous of other people's talents and skills?

Wednesday 28 February
The really important thing about Christian ministry

Read Ephesians 4:11–16

So Christ himself gave the apostles, the prophets, the evangelists, the pastors and teachers, to equip his people for works of service, so that the body of Christ may be built up.

(verses 11–12)

One of the most interesting questions I've ever answered as a minister was also the simplest and most obvious. Someone who was not a churchgoer asked, 'What exactly does a minister do?' More than just wanting to know about how much of my time I spent on weddings and funerals, she wanted to know what I was for.

The answer is here in Ephesians and it is challenging not just for church leaders but for congregations. Leaders and teachers are to equip Christ's people for works of service. It is through doing that we become spiritually mature, not just by talking or thinking. Contemplation and study are good, but they must not be divorced from the life of the Christian community. It's in our relationships of love and service that we grow into unity and become mature. It's when we separate ourselves from one another that we lose our spiritual moorings and are 'tossed back and forth by the waves' (verse 14). The cure for that is 'speaking the truth in love' to each other (verse 15), being accountable to one another and involved in each other's lives.

The minister can't be a distant or detached figure. He or she must be part of the congregation, sharing their joys and their sorrows and allowing them to share his or her own. But there must also be a single-minded commitment to building up the church and enabling growth into Christlikeness among its members. Something like that is how I answered my questioner.

† God, keep me connected to my brothers and sisters in the faith. Help me not to become proud of the books I've read or the things I know. Help me remember we are one body. Amen

For further thought
• Do I think and talk about the things of faith rather than actually doing anything about them? What are my 'works of service'?

Thursday 1 March
The really essential qualification for ministry

Read 1 Timothy 3:1–7

Here is a trustworthy saying: whoever aspires to be an overseer desires a noble task. Now the overseer is to be above reproach, faithful to his wife, temperate, self-controlled, respectable, hospitable, able to teach.

(verses 1–2)

Paul sets high standards for 'overseers' – the word is the one from which 'bishop' comes, but he probably means what we would call a pastor. And the interesting thing is that he is hardly concerned with their abilities at all. He is much more worried about their character. He wants the Church to be led by people who are morally admirable. They must be personally upright, but upright in their family lives as well. And they must be experienced Christians, not recent converts. No one should become a pastor as a career move.

He writes in a context where a husband had unquestionable authority over his wife and children, and any failing in his family could be assumed to be his fault. Our society is very different. We should not attempt to blindly replicate the first century in how we do family life, and we should not judge a pastor unqualified for office if his (or her – another difference) children go off the rails. But we can learn from what Paul says anyway. He says an overseer should see that his children obey him 'in a manner worthy of full respect' (verse 4) – that is, kindly rather than harshly or cruelly. This fits the pattern of the godly pastor he's drawing in this passage.

In our own day, congregations might expect their ministers to be able to do everything from preaching like Spurgeon to fixing the church roof. Paul would ask different questions: what is their character? How are they before God?

† God, help me to think less about what a person can do and more about who they are. Teach me patience when people fail and humility before those whose Christian character is better than mine. Amen

For further thought
- Do we expect the wrong things of our ministers? How high up on their job specification are prayer and spirituality?

Friday 2 March
Why character matters

Read 1 Timothy 3:8–13
In the same way, deacons are to be worthy of respect, sincere, not indulging in much wine, and not pursuing dishonest gain. They must keep hold of the deep truths of the faith with a clear conscience.

(verses 8–9)

The early Church was a fast-growing movement in which things were still being tried out. It looks here as though there were servants – the meaning of the word 'deacon' – of Timothy's church whose responsibility was not teaching. Among them were women (verse 11). There is a female deacon, Phoebe, mentioned in Romans 16:1.

The qualifications for being a deacon are much the same as they are for 'overseers'. Their spiritual qualities are what matter, and this is important. This was a long time before there was an elaborate hierarchy, as many churches have now. But the principle is the same: how the leaders conducted themselves and what they believed mattered because it affected the rest of the church.

Church leaders, whether they occupy a pulpit or not, are in a position of great influence. Their example can set the tone for a whole congregation. Their teaching can build a church up or tear it down. If they stray away from biblical orthodoxy they can do enormous damage. And this concern for character and integrity goes right through what we might now call the leadership team: Timothy is not to go easy on someone because they have a gift or skill that's particularly useful to the church.

The picture we have in 1 Timothy is of a group of church leaders who are to be accountable to each other and to the congregation. Leadership is a responsibility and a privilege, because it affects the body of which Christ is the head.

† God, help me to realise how much what I do affects other people. I value it when others play their part in the life of the church; help me to play mine too. Amen

For further thought
• Are we just so grateful when people want to help at church that we overlook serious character flaws that should be lovingly challenged?

Saturday 3 March
What elders are really for

> **Read Titus 1:5–14**
>
> *[An elder] must be hospitable, one who loves what is good, who is self-controlled, upright, holy and disciplined. He must hold firmly to the trustworthy message as it has been taught, so that he can encourage others by sound doctrine and refute those who oppose it.*
>
> *(verses 8–9)*

Elders in Paul's letter to Titus are the same as overseers in his letter to Timothy. He says much the same things about them, but the context is different. In Crete, where Titus lived, the church was in disarray. It needed leaders who could confront false teaching. We don't know the details exactly, but Paul's reference to the 'circumcision group' (verse 10) and to 'Jewish myths' implies they were teaching that (Gentile) Christians had to obey the Jewish law and that the men had to be circumcised.

This is a problem the early Church had to deal with at various times. Behind it lay a deep question: was faith in Christ sufficient, or did God want more? In the end, the answer was that yes, Gentiles did not need to live as Jews in order to be Christians (Acts 15).

That particular question has long been answered, but it keeps coming back in other forms. Whom will we recognise as fellow believers? It ought to be all those who have faith in Christ. But we have a nasty habit of limiting fellowship to people who think like us, talk like us or even dress like us. We preach our own brand of Christianity rather than Christ crucified.

So Paul's command to Titus about his elders is vitally important. They needed to keep the eyes of the people on Christ rather than letting their faith be diluted or compromised by a different message. Good leaders challenge us to be purely Christian, rather than Christians and something else.

† God, there are probably things in my life that get in Christ's way. Show me what these are and help me to deal with them, so that faith can be all about him.

For further thought

• What are the things we've added to the faith out of habit or prejudice? What gets in the way of Jesus?

Leadership
4 Leadership qualities part 1

Notes by **Bola Iduoze**

Bola Iduoze is a qualified accountant with over 25 years' experience in the marketplace. She has worked in many industries, including business consultancy. She is now a home business entrepreneur and an Associate Pastor with Gateway Chapel, UK. Bola is an inspiration to many through her home business coaching and weekly blog. She is married with two children. Bola has used the NIVUK for these notes.

Sunday 4 March
God meant it for good

Read Genesis 50:15–21

You intended to harm me, but God intended it for good to accomplish what is now being done, the saving of many lives.

(verse 20)

My mother's mother in Ibadan in Nigeria, who was a very devoted Christian, came to live with us towards the end of her life. She used to sit us down and tell us stories of how she was wronged by different people at different times and how God used such incidents to provide her with great opportunities for growth. She then referred back to Joseph's story and how God is capable of bringing good out of negative circumstances.

Life sometimes throws difficult situations our way. Though we don't plan for these events nor typically appreciate them, we can use them to learn a good lesson about ourselves and about other people around us. And leaders who are able to reflect on setbacks and pain are able to lead with more humility and compassion.

In the story today, Joseph's brothers show fear after their father died, thinking Joseph would retaliate. It is a story of human expectation overturned. Joseph's brothers expected revenge but Joseph decided to exhibit forgiveness as a leader.

Although he was betrayed by his brothers, Joseph was able to see the hand of God in his situation, leading to his promotion and not destruction as his siblings had intended. This helped him put into perspective his previous experiences. My grandmother would have approved.

† God, help me to recognise that you are at work in every situation. May I live a life of forgiveness at all times. Amen

Monday 5 March
Anger is expensive

Read Numbers 20:2–13

[Moses] and Aaron gathered the assembly together in front of the rock and Moses said to them, 'Listen, you rebels, must we bring water for you out of this rock?'

(verse 10)

As a young girl, my older sister used to have major problems with her temper. Every time she got angry in her secondary school days, she would say the wrong thing to her friends and end up losing one friend after another. As we grew up, we all learned the lesson that anger is very expensive. Eventually my sister had to weigh the cost of her anger with the benefits she enjoyed on the back of the outburst. This led her to make up her mind to try to drop this dangerous element of life and start living her life differently.

Moses' anger with God's people led him to say some extremely harsh words to the Israelites. Even though Moses' frustration seemed logical, it still led him to say the wrong things and sin against God. According to verse 12 in today's reading, the ultimate result of the anger was the loss of a bright future assignment and the ability to enter the Promised Land.

From my perspective, this story from Numbers is one of the saddest in the Bible. It shows how a great leader lost everything because he could not manage his emotions.

Anger is a very expensive emotion and needs to be managed by every one of us – especially those of us in leadership of any kind – lest it take us away from what God has planned for us!

† God, please help me manage my emotions daily. Grant me equanimity and wisdom today and all the days of my life. In Jesus' name. Amen

For further thought

• Why do you think God punished Moses and Aaron in the way that he did? The Bible has several answers but not, seemingly, a clear one; see also Deuteronomy 32:50–52, Psalm 106:32–33 and Numbers 27:14.

Tuesday 6 March
I will be with you

Read Joshua 1:1–9

No one will be able to stand against you all the days of your life. As I was with Moses so I will be with you; I will never leave you nor forsake you.

(verse 5)

My teenage years were a time of interesting discoveries. My family and I used to attend a small Baptist church. Every year we had our Baptist Home and Foreign Mission Week. I vividly recall the sermons in that week, all related to the fact that every missionary, pastor or Christian leader is called by God. 'The call' differs from person to person, but each of the called have a message to go and proclaim for God. These leaders need us, the church, to support them with our prayers and money.

Every leader in God's kingdom is called by God to do specific things, and they need the backing of God to fulfill this call faithfully. As it happened to Joshua in today's scripture, the biggest part of the call is the presence of God. The assurance of God's support, backing and presence is what gives boldness to any leader to keep pushing forward, knowing that they are not alone.

The call of God in our lives, however, requires us to be bold and courageous because there will be things that will happen to create fear or discouragement. But a leader who is truly working and walking with God must also have roots deep in the word of God which gives the plan, provision, protection and the prosperity which God has ordained for his own.

God calls, backs and helps everyone he has called to fulfill the purpose of the call.

† Father, help me to hear your call, respond to it and be conscious of your presence with me at every stage of life. In Jesus' name. Amen

For further thought

- Each of us is called to work wherever we live. How would you describe your call?

Wednesday 7 March
Prophet, leader, woman, wife

Read Judges 4:1–16

Then Deborah said to Barak, 'Go! This is the day the Lord has given Sisera into your hands. Has not the Lord gone ahead of you?' So Barak went down Mount Tabor, with ten thousand men following him.

(verse 14)

Deborah was a prophet. She judged the people and also heard from God in order to warn and give direction to God's people.

The Old Testament tells of different leaders who are chosen and given specific assignments for a period of time, for a specific people. This is true of Deborah, as well; when the children of Israel cried out to the Lord in the midst of an oppressive period, God called her. For 20 years, the people of God were under severe oppression and God sent them what was for the time an unusual solution to their problems: a woman, a wife and prophet of God was to be judge for God's people. This leader had a lot of roles to fulfill and never dropped the ball.

After she became a leader, Deborah was not shy to give instructions according to what she had heard from God. Barak decided to go with her to Mount Tabor, and with her help the children of Israel were successful in battle.The success was not just attributed to Barak, but also to Deborah who was confident enough to fulfill her call and give the instruction God had called her to deliver.

It is important to note that a sent leader should focus on the one who gives the message and on the people to whom the message is sent. God can use anyone, as long as we make ourselves available!

† Lord, I pray that you make me useful for you today. May I deliver your message without fear or personal limitations with the assurance of your help. Amen

For further thought

• God has no stereotype when it comes to leaders. How do God's choices compare to the choices of major corporations near you in their choosing of executives?

Thursday 8 March
The fall of Saul

Read 1 Samuel 15:10–26

But Samuel replied:

> *'Does the Lord delight in burnt offerings and sacrifices*
> *as much as in obeying the Lord?*
> *To obey is better than sacrifice,*
> *and to heed better than the fat of rams.'*

(verse 22)

In the quoted verse, we see that God's concern for obedience is a big part of how God values his chosen leaders. God delights much more in our obedience than he does in our sacrifices.

My mum used to repeat to us the value of obedience. I remember her saying, 'We should not only choose to obey, but always obey on time and unreservedly.' She used to say, 'Delayed obedience is disobedience.' How much more is God grieved by disobedience and partial obedience?

The people of God asked God for a king like other people had. It grieved God to yield to his people, as God considered it rejection, but God still told his servant Samuel to get the people a leader based on their request. Saul was chosen to lead and given instructions by God, but Saul failed in this task and didn't remain obedient. This, too, upset God and he sent Samuel to deliver his disappointment to Saul. It grieved God and also Samuel that Saul disobeyed God. Instead of owning up to the error, Saul defended his actions and gave excuses about his actions.

It is our job as Christians and leaders to ensure we walk in obedience to God's instructions daily, as far as we are able.

† Lord Jesus, help me to be faithful in obeying your instructions fully. Please also give wisdom to the leaders of the world, that they can give justice. Amen

For further thought

- When does leadership require breaking the rules? What, then, do you make of this story?

Friday 9 March
Taking the right advice

Read 1 Kings 12:1–1

But Rehoboam rejected the advice the elders had given him and consulted the young men who had grown up with him and were serving him.

(verse 8)

My husband comes from a part of Nigeria called Benin City. It has a monarchy and adjoining villages with chiefs who report to the Benin king. A few years ago, one of these chiefs died and, by rights, the son took over the rulership of the village. The boy was young and his uncle became the prince regent. The whole city and region watched the young prince grow and eventually he took his place as the king when he turned 18. After ascending to the throne, he still needed his uncle and other palace advisers on a regular basis because they were experienced in the role and had the interests of the people at heart.

As I read the story of Rehoboam, I remembered this incident and was not surprised that the new king needed advisers. The problem, however, was that he decided to listen to the advice of both the older and the younger ones. He eventually went for the advice of the younger ones and created chaos in the land. Every leader needs advisers, but not all have access to godly advisers.

Rehoboam made a bad choice and his actions caused revolt in the land. Bad advice today can still create chaos in any church or organisation. We have the responsibility of seeking counsel from God first, and then the right and wise people God has put around us. Even after this we should still take it back to God before we make our final decisions.

Seeking counsel is excellent, but we need to ensure we do it from the right people, and at all times.

† Gracious God, help me to listen to your instructions daily. Also help me seek counsel from the right people and listen to the voice of wisdom in all I do. In Jesus' name. Amen

For further thought

• Have you ever taken a decision without seeking out the advice of those you trust? What did you learn from the experience?

Saturday 10 March
Don't be discouraged

Read 1 Kings 19:1–18

There he went into a cave and spent the night. And the word of the Lord came to him: 'What are you doing here, Elijah?'

(verse 9)

A few years ago, I was with a friend. After about 15 minutes, she broke down in tears and was inconsolable. I later discovered that her pastor had decided to quit pastoring. As I inquired further, I realised that he had been pastoring for years, but due to a series of incidents, he felt so down that he tendered his resignation and left the sheep and pastoring completely to go and pick up a new career. This hurt his congregation, but I spent more time thinking of how bad things must have gotten for the leader to get so discouraged.

In our story today, Elijah felt discouraged. Perhaps he simply got exhausted and began seeing himself as inadequate to face the next phase of life. His discouragement got him complaining about his life and his God. This led to him just lying down to sleep, the classic reaction of a severely discouraged person.

The beauty of working with God is reflected in our scripture today: the angel of the Lord came and ministered to Elijah in the midst of discouragement. God always cares for us even during the tough times of life. As Elijah lay in the cave, God's word came to meet him just where he was.

God's word is still active and powerful and can surely send help and strength at the time of need in every area of our lives. Do not be discouraged; take the promises God has for you, even when they seem very far away.

† Father, I pray for every discouraged leader, and I ask you to provide for them. Speak to them even when they hide in the caves of life, and don't let them miss your word of encouragement. Amen

For further thought

• What has helped you get through times of discouragement in the past?

Leadership
5 Leadership qualities part 2

Notes by **Jan Sutch Pickard**

Jan Sutch Pickard is a writer and storyteller living on the Isle of Mull, and a former warden of the Abbey on Iona. In the last few years she has served twice with the Ecumenical Accompaniment Programme in Palestine and Israel, based in small West Bank villages but with a chance to spend time in Jerusalem and reflect on its divisions today. A Methodist Local Preacher, she leads worship for the Church of Scotland on Mull. Jan has used the NRSVA for these notes.

Sunday 11 March
The power of mercy

Read 1 Samuel 24:1–15

'… the Lord gave you into my hands in the cave. Some urged me to kill you, but I spared you; I said, "I will not lay my hand on my lord, because he is the Lord's anointed."'

(verse 10)

This week most of the Bible passages offer glimpses of leadership in the early Church, examples of how men and women embodied the qualities their congregations needed. But we start with two Old Testament stories about outstanding individuals.

Today, two men ranging about in a country at war come very close – a scene repeated over and over again in places we could name today, in an encounter that could be fatal. David and his soldiers have taken refuge in a cave. Saul arrives, and, in ignorance and in search of privacy, goes in there to relieve himself. Even great leaders have this basic need. Saul is at his most vulnerable and David is in the shadows with a drawn sword. Saul has wronged him, is his enemy, but is also the anointed king. Finding he has the power of life and death, David chooses to show mercy.

Then, coming out into the daylight, he shows the cut piece of the king's cloak as a sign of Saul's narrow escape, a sign of respect for the tradition of kingship and (most significant for us) a sign of mercy. In any leader, compassion is not a sign of weakness, but strength.

† Just and merciful God, may we distinguish right from wrong, and, when we think we're in the right, act with compassion. Amen

Monday 12 March
Ability and integrity

Read Daniel 6:1–14

Now when Daniel learned that this decree had been published, he went home … Three times a day he got down on his knees and prayed, giving thanks to his God, just as he had done before.

(verse 10)

David, in yesterday's reading, was a soldier: Daniel was a civil servant. He was also a man of courage. Though an alien, one of the Jews living in exile among their Persian conquerors, he had become a key member of society. King Darius valued his administrative skills and integrity and planned to put him in charge of the national economy. Daniel had enemies, though, who were prejudiced about him because he was an 'outsider', and probably jealous of his abilities. When they persuaded Darius to sign an edict which would criminalise Daniel for praying to his God, his response was to keep on praying – and to do so in a place where this could be clearly seen.

Recently, televisions round the world showed a small group of Christians standing in a ruined church, at last able to return to their home town in Iraq. Islamic State had just been driven out but there was still danger of snipers. Surrounded by rubble, questioned by reporters, what did these men do? They prayed.

It was not just Daniel's efficiency that was envied by his enemies and valued by Darius, but the quality he showed in this crisis – his integrity. When the king learned that his edict had been used to entrap Daniel, we are told that, in distress, he searched for a way to save this faithful servant.

† Strong and constant God, we thank you for being firm ground under our feet, loving hands that uphold us when we feel unsure or afraid. May we never forget the power of prayer. Amen

For further thought

• Think of someone you would describe as a person of integrity. Does it take courage? What enables them? If possible, ask them.

Tuesday 13 March
Hospitality

Read Acts 16:11–15

The Lord opened [Lydia's] heart to respond to Paul's message. When she and the members of her household were baptised, she invited us to her home. 'If you consider me a believer in the Lord,' she said, 'come and stay at my house.'

(part of verses 14 and 15)

In a town in the West Bank Palestinian territories lives Afaf, a retired school teacher, and her brother, their family long respected in the town. They're the last Christian family living there, the others having left because of the Israeli occupation. This family have chosen to stay on in their Muslim community. Respecting the Ramadan fast, Afaf prepares an *iftar* meal for their neighbours to share in the cool of the evening. They sit together on her terrace under a lemon tree, talking about things important to them all.

Outside the city gate, a group of women are sitting beside the river. If it were not the Sabbath they might have been gossiping while doing the washing or rinsing dyed cloth. But now they are gathered for quiet fellowship and prayer. A couple of strangers come and sit down with them. Backed by the sounds of the city and the river, their story unfolds. The women give it full attention. Both these true stories pivot on welcome, which takes different forms, some of which we may recognise from our own experience. In the modern-day situation, there's neighbourliness, respect for different beliefs, an open home and shared food.

In the story from Acts we see a gathered group who make space for strangers, and offer unprejudiced listening: the welcome of a heart opened to God and the church's welcome in baptism. And finally, the welcome to her home that Lydia, the convert, offers to Paul and Silas.

† O God, you welcome each of us into your world at birth, and into your Way as believers; may we learn to be open-hearted and may your churches be places of welcome. Amen

For further thought
- Reflect on the way that the fellowship of the Church is where hospitality can be both given and received: between human beings and between us and God.

Wednesday 14 March
Mentoring

Read Acts 18:24–28

[Apollos] began to speak boldly in the synagogue. When Priscilla and Aquila heard him, they invited him to their home and explained to him the way of God more adequately.

(verse 24)

This is a story about people on the move finding a welcome and sharing journeys of faith. Paul came from Tarsus but, by this stage in the story of the young and growing Church, had covered many Mediterranean miles by sea and land. Aquila and Priscilla, whose family business, like Paul's, was tent-making, were Jews who had been evicted from Rome by edict of Emperor Claudius. Apollos came from Alexandria.

From different communities, from places where the culture was different, where the gospel had been heard in different ways, they could both learn from each other and deepen each other's faith.

That was my experience as a mission partner in Nigeria many years ago. My husband and I, there to teach, were welcomed as part of the SCM Senior Friends group, meeting in homes on the campus of the university, theological college and Christian Council conference centre. Members from Nigeria, Ghana, the US and the UK shared their faith, questions and their radical understanding of the gospel.

We were not remote and intellectual theorists, but people still growing in our faith, hoping to encourage and be in dialogue with a new generation of Nigerian Christians, and to contribute to reconciliation, reconstruction and redevelopment in a nation that had been at war. Still young myself, I listened, learned and grew as we met together. I still thank God for those friends and mentors.

† God, our gentle teacher and encourager, help us to grow in understanding and in grace; and may we encourage others we meet along the way. Amen

For further thought

• Sharing questions and sharing meals are ways of sharing our faith, as well as preaching. Write down (or draw) what works for you.

Thursday 15 March
Justice and integrity

Read 2 Timothy 2:15–26

… pursue righteousness, faith, love and peace, along with those who call on the Lord out of a pure heart. Don't have anything to do with foolish and stupid arguments.

(part of verses 22–23)

We come back to this word 'integrity', another translation for the word 'faith' above. Once, in an organisation which had been through turbulent times, I heard a colleague describe new leadership committed to making peace as 'boring … it's fun to have leaders who stir things up a bit!'

On a campus during an election, as someone who has always valued the right to vote, I was astonished to hear students, a younger generation who would have been voting for the first time, saying, 'Why should we bother? Politicians are all the same. What difference will it make?'

More recently, like people all over the world, I watched, shocked and anxious, as those who wanted to lead a great nation contested for power. We all witnessed slander and insults, boasting and bullying. Yet these seemed to win the day.

Controversy, wild speculations, overstating the case and dwelling on the differences between 'us' and 'them' certainly liven up relationships – whether in a work setting, church, neighbourhood or national politics. We have probably all seen this happen, at some level, in the last couple of years. But is this responsible leadership?

Challenging intolerance isn't a sign of weakness, nor is peacemaking. Self-discipline sets an example which can help everyone to change. Good leadership can make a difference.

† God-with-us, help us to know good leadership when we see it; whether we are taking the lead, or casting our vote, may we act with integrity. Amen

For further thought

• Think of positive examples of good leadership, on a large or small scale. Thank God for these people, by name. How can you support them? Why not write about something that needs changing, to someone who has the power to do so?

Friday 16 March
Enduring hardship

Read 2 Timothy 4:1–8

But you, keep your head in all situations, endure hardship, do the work of an evangelist, discharge all the duties of your ministry.

(verse 5)

This letter from Paul to Timothy and through him to the church in Ephesus is brief but full of advice based on Paul's experience of hard work and hardship, of strenuous efforts to share the good news and to build up Christian community. This letter is also full of names, so that community comes alive for us: people whom Paul has found helpful and others who have found the challenges too great. With warmth he names Lois and Eunice, Timothy's grandmother and mother, who clearly have the apostle's deep respect. There are Priscilla and Aquila, whom we have already met and Luke and Mark, described as 'helpful in my ministry' (verse 11). It is a community of women and men, many of whom will have tasted, or face, similar challenges to Paul.

Paul is now in prison in Rome, writing to encourage them all, knowing that they too may have to face persecution from without and betrayal from those in their midst. Like Palestinian Christians in the land that today we call Holy (like Afaf and her brother), they may embody *sumoud* – endurance and steadfastness – in the face of many problems.

Paul is handing on the task, just as any leader needs to do. He himself is coming to the end – not of his tether, but of his life: 'I have finished the race' (verse 7). This was not a sprint, for Paul's ministry has covered a lot of ground over many years. He has needed the kind of stamina that keeps a marathon runner going. What has sustained him is the strength that comes from God.

† God of constant love and encouragement, we give thanks for the strength you give us to bear hardships – and to bear witness. Amen

For further thought

• What are the names of those who form your Christian community? This includes not only your local congregation and/or neighbours, but those in the past or at a distance. Say those names aloud – as though lighting a candle for each.

Saturday 17 March
Caring for the flock

Read 1 Peter 5:1–11

... be shepherds of God's flock that is under your care, watching over them – not because you must, but because you are willing, as God wants you to be; not pursuing dishonest gain, but eager to serve.

(verse 2)

It was lambing time when Ronnie had his heart attack. When the hospital sent him back to his small farm, his croft, he wasn't able to work with the sheep. Neighbours tried to help, including Jackie the postwoman, inspired by how, in a previous crisis, the minister had rolled up his sleeves. For weeks the red post van arrived at the croft and – after delivering letters and parcels all day – she got on with delivering lambs.

In this true story from the island where I live, neither Bill, the minister, nor Jackie the postwoman thought that their role set them above helping out on the croft. Of course it wasn't just about looking after the sheep – as good neighbours they were caring about a man's livelihood and helping him back to full health.

Is this letter of Peter addressed to church leaders who were more interested in status than down-to-earth caring? Peter himself had been a fisherman before he became a church leader. He failed to live up to the responsibility with which he'd been entrusted, three times denying Jesus before the crucifixion, but then found himself forgiven. John's Gospel describes a conversation between Peter and the risen Christ, who asks three times 'Do you love me?' and three times tells Peter 'Feed my lambs ... tend my sheep ... feed my sheep' (John 21:15–19). So is it surprising that in this letter he uses the rich biblical image of the shepherd caring for the flock – which had, for him, taken on a fresh meaning? It is not about status or control but responsibility and real caring.

† God, you are our shepherd: in your care we will never lack for love; we are guided and nourished, led through danger and distress to wholeness and healing. Amen

For further thought

• Continue to pray, asking God to bless those we know who are 'shepherds of the flock', recognising their human faults, respecting their task and naming them with love.

The lonely city (Lamentations)

Notes by **Lynne Frith**

Lynne Frith loves playing with words – whether writing poems or prayers, playing Scrabble or messaging friends – and has a secret longing to write on walls with a spray can. The rest of the time she is a Methodist Presbyter in Auckland, Aotearoa (New Zealand), where she is privileged to serve with an inclusive, welcoming congregation. Lynne has used the NRSVA for these notes.

Sunday 18 March
Bread for survival

Read Lamentations 1:1–11

How lonely sits the city that once was full of people! ... All her people groan as they search for bread; they trade their treasures for food to revive their strength.

(part of verses 1 and 11)

The book of Lamentations is a response to the destruction of the city of Jerusalem as a result of the Babylonian invasion from 589–587 BC. It could just as easily be a lament for war-torn Aleppo, or any other city in any part of the world.

Today's reading is a vivid description of the loneliness of the devastated city. The loneliness is compared to that of a widow, abandoned by those close to her.

It's a communal lament, describing misery and desperation, contrasting the past and the present.

Lament enables us to rail at God and each other, to give words to pain and suffering, to describe the horror of what we witness or experience.

Lament allows us to ask, without fear of judgement, why? For how long? What have we done to deserve this? Will no one come to our aid?

Lament is seldom included in the liturgies of the church other than during Lent. It's as if we are afraid of speaking the unspeakable, asking the unanswerable question, challenging the notion that suffering is somehow good for us and must be endured.

This week, we join our voices to the cries of all those whose lives, homes and lands are in ruins.

† Prayerfully begin making a collage of images and headlines that show the present-day devastation of cities anywhere in the world.

Monday 19 March
Does anyone care?

Read Lamentations 1:12–22

Is it nothing to you, all you who pass by?

(part of verse 12)

New Zealand poet David Merritt spends a lot of time on the streets of New Zealand cities.

He observes, in *First Friday Out* (LandRover Farm Press):

I am not hunting for anything here on a
cold and windswept and busy alleyway in
Christchurch.

The poet, ancient or contemporary, is intimately acquainted with suffering and voices desolation that is echoed around the broken community and the world.

The city streets will not deliver up any comfort or relief. Passers-by ignore the outstretched hands of the beggar.

The plea for compassion is heartfelt, the accusations against God intense, the anguish immense.

God is portrayed as an unrelenting abuser, and Zion as an abused woman. The one who was trusted has become the instrument of torture and suffering. Zion blames herself for all that has befallen her.

There is no consolation to be found, only more misery and betrayal of trust.

Images of the destruction and desolation of cities stream constantly across social and news media. earthquakes, tsunami, floods, fires and war wreak unspeakable havoc. We are more likely to hear the voices of news reporters and political commentators than of those whose lives are fragmented.

Destruction of the city, whether as a result of war or natural disaster, strikes at the heart of economic and political power, causes social disruption and dislocation. The consequences are relentless and hope is fragile.

Those of us who are privileged to live in places untouched by such catastrophe, may be horrified at what we see. Yet imagine how it must feel for the people, and for us to go on with our lives uninterrupted.

'What can we do?' we cry.

† Pray for those whose trust has been betrayed by community or political leaders, or by family members.

For further thought

• Continue to make your collage of images of devastation.

The lonely city – Lynne Frith

Tuesday 20 March
Daughters of despair

Read Lamentations 2:1–10

The elders of daughter Zion sit on the ground in silence; they have thrown dust on their heads and put on sackcloth; the young girls of Jerusalem have bowed their heads to the ground.

(verse 10)

The city is a place where extremes are found. On the one hand is economic, social and political power. On the other are disempowerment, alienation, marginalisation.

The city is an easy target. Not only is political power concentrated there, but also people, utilities, transport, hospitals.

The way to destroy a nation, to bring down a government, is to destroy the cities.

Today's reading is a recitation of despair, with its description of a new landscape that bears little resemblance to what people remember. Not only has the physical landscape changed, but also the social structures of festival and Sabbath that give meaning to the community and bind it together. My twenty-first-century mind will not allow me to attribute blame for such destruction to a divine being. Rather, I see the work of hostile political powers, of nation against nation, of political and religious factions and leaders jostling for supremacy.

Our screens continue to be flooded with images of terrified people, dispossessed, homeless, fleeing for their lives, saying goodbye to family members in expectation that they will never see them again.

No amount of petitioning to our governments seems to make any difference. In New Zealand our government seems more concerned to protect the conditions of trade agreements than to challenge inhumanity and breaches of human rights in countries who are potential trade partners. The 'super powers' appear to be interested only in protecting their own interests and access to resources.

† Pray today for the peacemakers of the world.

For further thought
• Make a donation to a humanitarian organisation today.

Wednesday 21 March
Feeling the rhythm of grief

Read Lamentations 2:11–22

My eyes are spent with weeping ... because infants and babes faint in the streets of the city.

(part of verse 11)

Forlorn with a heart full of lament
A song long unsung stirs
I feel the rhythm of grief

– David Merritt, *Taumaranui Railway Station #1*

A few months ago, in the city in which I live, homelessness was forced to the fore of the political agenda. This is not homelessness caused by war or by natural disaster, but by an ever-increasing gap between rich and poor, soaring house prices and a desperate shortage of rental accommodation.

A local *marae* (Maori community centre) opened its doors and its communal heart to provide temporary accommodation, food, medical care and social support through the winter months. There were heart-rending stories of families living in cars or vans, of a child whose family moved with her to the city for her to have cancer treatment and were unable to find affordable accommodation.

Now, as I write, the long queues of people waiting for food banks to open demonstrate that life is still a struggle for many families and individuals.

The city leaders had a slogan – to make it the world's most liveable little city. Most liveable for whom, I ask? For rough sleepers under bridges and in shop doorways, for children trying to do their homework in the back of a car? If only that were so.

Our cities, towns and villages need to be liveable for all their inhabitants. Jeremiah reminds us to seek the welfare of the city, for in its welfare we will find our own welfare (Jeremiah 29:7). When children are faint with hunger, when young and old alike are suffering, the whole community suffers.

† Pray for hungry children, and those who provide humanitarian aid that is focused on children.

For further thought

• Think about ways in which you might contribute to the welfare of the city, e.g. volunteering at a food bank or supporting community initiatives to end homelessness.

Saturday 24 March
A joyless existence

Read Lamentations 5

The joy of our hearts has ceased; our dancing has been turned to mourning.

(verse 15)

The lament begins with a demand that God remember the past and all that has happened. The present generation bears the consequences. The misery is intense. Social systems have been turned upside down. The atrocities continue and no one is safe.

The suffering at the hands of the oppressors is extreme.

The mere act of getting bread is perilous. Life is hard and joyless. People are struggling for survival.

The lamenting community turns inward, and, rather than direct anger at the foreigners who are causing such suffering, identify with the sinfulness of their forebears. The consequences of social and economic inequality and injustice are all too visible and are intergenerational.

There are similarities to the way in which victims of family harm and abuse blame themselves for the abuse that has been heaped upon them, such as a belief that if only they had behaved differently the violence would not have occurred.

It's an all too familiar picture.

David Merritt reflects:

> through the throng you notice the by
> Themselves, the alone, the desperate and
> the disparate, the malcontented, those way
> outside their comfort zone.

– David Merritt, First Friday Out

The fifth lament concludes with a sad cry that God appears to have forgotten the people, and even though time has passed by, the community feels forsaken. They plead with God to restore relationship, and so restore the people, but the doubt lingers.

† Pray for the lonely, the desperate and the forgotten people.

For further thought

• Share your collage as a focus for prayer with your study group, church or community of concern; and please share a picture of it on our *Fresh from the Word* Facebook group.

Holy Week and Easter with the Psalms
1 Songs of pain

Notes by **Ann Conway-Jones**

 Ann Conway-Jones is a freelance theologian, writer and teacher. Ever since she can remember, she has been fascinated by the Bible and involved in intercultural/interfaith exchange. She is a specialist in early Jewish–Christian relations and the beginnings of mysticism. She holds honorary research fellowships at the University of Birmingham and The Queen's Ecumenical Foundation. She has been elected Joint Honorary Secretary of the Council of Christians and Jews and she preaches in her parish church on an occasional basis. Ann has used the NRSVA for these notes.

Sunday 25 March
Blessed is the one who comes

Read Psalm 118:24–29

Save us, we beseech you, O Lord! O Lord, we beseech you, give us success! Blessed is the one who comes in the name of the Lord.

(verses 25–26a)

We journey through Holy Week with some of the psalms which inspired the New Testament writers as they meditated on Jesus' last days. These psalms of lament speak of suffering, pain, loneliness and betrayal – common human plights. So alongside Jesus' passion, we remember those people praying similar words today.

The Hebrew words for 'please save' in Psalm 118:25 are *hoshi'ah na*, which other languages turn into 'hosanna'. In Christian minds, the cry 'hosanna' is so associated with praise and acclamation of Jesus (see Mark 11:9) that we have forgotten its original meaning. But Psalm 118's combination of celebration and entreaty is particularly suitable for Palm Sunday. Churches start Holy Week on a festive note, processing together and enthusiastically waving palm crosses. A more sombre mood soon takes over, as Jesus' suffering and death become the focus for the week and we bring to mind the sorrow of the world Jesus came to save.

Each day's notes end with some lines from a traditional Holy Week hymn, illustrating how Christians have continued to reflect on the significance of Jesus' death.

† Ride on, ride on, in majesty! / In lowly pomp ride on to die!
　O Christ! Thy triumph now begin / Over captive death and conquered sin.

– H. H. Milman

Monday 26 March
Betrayal by a friend

Read Psalm 41

All who hate me whisper together about me;
they imagine the worst for me …
Even my bosom friend in whom I trusted,
who ate of my bread, has lifted the heel against me.

(verses 7, 9)

'They whisper behind my back. Spread malicious lies. Turn my foibles into jokes. Is it all my fault? Whom can I trust?' – such are the psalmist's inner thoughts. A bosom friend, with whom meals were shared and confidences exchanged, has gone over to the enemy. Caught in a web of doubt and deceit, there is no choice but to turn to God. God will deliver, protect, sustain and heal. Coming into the divine presence, however, requires truthfulness, even about disturbing emotions. Talk of 'enemies' and 'revenge' in the psalms makes us uneasy. Is God not a God of love? Are we not supposed to love our enemies? But precisely because that is so, the most helpful and courageous thing to do with a desire for revenge is to confide it to God, rather than allowing it to poison the soul. If vengeance belongs to God, it does not belong to us. Having surrendered the burden of inner turmoil, the psalmist ends with a blessing.

As the gospel writers thought about Judas Iscariot, it was this psalm they turned to – Mark alludes to it (14:18) and John quotes it (13:18). One of the 12, who has dipped his bread into the common dish, is to betray Jesus. The Greek verb translated to 'betray' simply means 'hand over'. Judas' role in the passion story is to hand Jesus over. In that moment, Jesus' life changes from active to passive, from working to waiting. Love manifests itself as surrender.

† Inscribed upon the cross we see
  In shining letters, 'God is love';
  He bears our sins upon the tree:
  He brings us mercy from above.

– Thomas Kelly

For further thought

• When have you felt betrayed? How did you manage those emotions?

Tuesday 27 March
Malicious witnesses

Holy Week and Easter with the Psalms – Ann Conway-Jones

Read Psalm 35:11–25

Do not let my treacherous enemies rejoice over me,
or those who hate me without cause wink the eye.
For they do not speak peace …
They open wide their mouths against me;
they say, 'Aha, Aha, our eyes have seen it.'

(verses 19–21)

If you were accused of a crime, would you expect a fair trial? Would the police behave correctly? Would the judge be impartial? Would the witnesses tell the truth? Or could you be convicted on the word of troublemakers? As Mark tells the story of Jesus' trial, we get the impression of a kangaroo court, hastily arranged by night. The procedure is illegal, whether by Roman or Jewish standards, reliant on false witnesses (Mark 14:56–57). In John's Gospel, as Jesus addresses his disciples during their last meal together, he claims that the world hates him, adding, 'It was to fulfill the word that is written in their law, "They hated me without a cause"' (15:25). 'The law' usually means the Torah – the first five books of scripture. But here the quotation comes from Psalm 35:19. In verse 11, the Psalm talks of 'malicious witnesses', and it goes on to paint a vivid picture of unjustified abuse. The psalmist does not seem to understand why people have risen against him (or her), repaying evil for good. The description of taunting and jeering is particularly compelling. Because the language is stylised, the imagery could apply to many different circumstances. The persecution could be real or imagined, the enemies could be external or internal. The gospel writers found echoes of Jesus' situation. The psalmist daringly calls on God to wake up, desperate that the ruffians, whoever they are, should not have the last word.

† Why, what hath my Lord done?
What makes this rage and spite?
He made the lame to run,
He gave the blind their sight.

– Samuel Crossman

For further thought

• Consider writing a letter or email in support of a prisoner of conscience. Go to www.amnesty.org.uk for suggestions.

Wednesday 28 March
Bearing reproach

Read Psalm 69:1–15

It is zeal for your house that has consumed me;
the insults of those who insult you have fallen on me …
I am the subject of gossip for those who sit in the gate,
and the drunkards make songs about me.

(verses 9, 12)

Psalm 69 is a dramatic personal lament. It is difficult to work out the psalmist's exact situation. Verse 4, for example, refers to an accusation of theft. Verse 8 talks of estrangement even from family. Today's extract begins and ends with the metaphor of drowning. The language is relevant to so many circumstances: illness, mental distress, overwork, persecution … That feeling of being overwhelmed, of having water up to one's neck, is one that many of us can identify with. Equally vivid is the imagery of being caught in a mire, in quicksand: the harder one struggles, the further one sinks. And all the while other people gossip – it's just a joke to them.

This is one of the psalms that New Testament writers were convinced spoke of Jesus. We get a glimpse of the process thanks to John 2:17. As the disciples reflected on Jesus' outburst in the Temple, trying to make sense of it, they remembered Psalm 69:9a, referring to zeal for God's house. And Paul drew on the second half of the same verse as he sought to persuade his Roman readers to put up with the failings of the weak: 'For Christ did not please himself; but, as it is written, "The insults of those who insult you have fallen on me"' (Romans 15:3). Psalm 69 gave early Christians the words they needed to express their belief that Jesus' suffering and death were part of a divine plan.

† O sacred head, sore wounded,
  Defiled and put to scorn;
  O kingly head surrounded
  With mocking crown of thorn.

– Paul Gerhardt

For further thought

• How does gossip manifest itself today, in the age of social media?

Thursday 29 March (Maundy Thursday)
Vinegar to drink

Read Psalm 69:16–21

Insults have broken my heart, so that I am in despair.
I looked for pity, but there was none;
and for comforters, but I found none.
They gave me poison for food, and for my thirst they gave me
vinegar to drink.

(verses 20–21)

In difficult situations, food and drink provide solace. In England, we have traditionally relied on cups of tea. Or we revert to favourite dishes from childhood. But for the psalmist, there is no comfort food. Only tormentors, who revel in providing poison for food and vinegar to drink. No one takes pity.

Today is Maundy Thursday, when Christians traditionally remember the last meal that Jesus ate with his disciples. That sharing of food in fellowship contrasts strongly with events less than 24 hours later, when Jesus is hanging on the cross, abandoned by most of his followers, and offered coarse, bitter wine from a sponge on a stick, held out by a stranger (Mark 15:36). Scholars are divided over how this action should be seen. Is it a gesture of pity? A drug to ease the pain? Proverbs 31:6 enjoins, 'Give strong drink to one who is perishing, and wine to those in bitter distress.' And the Talmud tells of the women of Jerusalem taking pity on those condemned to execution, providing for them a goblet of wine containing a grain of frankincense. The first offering of drink to Jesus mentioned in Mark's Gospel (15:23) should probably be interpreted along those lines – a mild anaesthetic. Jesus refuses it, determined to give himself fully to God's will. The second offering, however, in conformity with Psalm 69:21, is more likely to be mockery – vinegar to aggravate thirst (or possibly quench thirst and delay the end).

† See from His head, His hands, His feet,
  Sorrow and love flow mingled down!
  Did e'er such love and sorrow meet,
  Or thorns compose so rich a crown?

– Isaac Watts

For further thought

- What messages are encoded in the food and drink we give or receive?

Friday 30 March (Good Friday)
Why have you forsaken me?

Read Psalm 22:1–15

My God, my God, why have you forsaken me?
Why are you so far from helping me, from the words of my groaning?
O my God, I cry by day, but you do not answer;
and by night, but find no rest.

(verses 1–2)

Jesus' cry of dereliction on the cross is a quote from Psalm 22:1. After a lifetime of praying with the psalms, they provide him with the words to voice his desolation. Mark (15:34) and Matthew (27:46) suggest that he recited the verse not in Hebrew, the Jewish liturgical language, but in Aramaic, his mother tongue (*sabachthani* is Aramaic, the Hebrew is *azavtani*). It is an intimate expression of abandonment.

The psalm reflects an ongoing struggle between despair and faith. In the midst of anguish, there are two things that the psalmist tries to hold on to: the community's belief and personal experience of God's ongoing care. The initial howl turns into remembrance of ancestral faith: 'they trusted, and you delivered them' (verse 4). But this gives way to self-abasement – 'I am a worm' (verse 6), reinforced by the mockery of others. Then the psalmist brings to mind those first few precious moments of life, when the newborn baby is safely lifted up onto its mother's bosom. From that precarious beginning, trouble is always near, and each of us depends on the mercy of God. But those comforting thoughts don't last, and the desolation of the present moment once again becomes overwhelming. The wonder of birth does not erase the terrifying prospect of 'the dust of death' (verse 15).

Jesus' cry of dereliction was not the first or the last. There are many people in the world today for whom this psalm rings true. Pray for them this Good Friday.

† There is a green hill far away,
  Outside a city wall,
  Where our dear Lord was crucified
  Who died to save us all.

– C. F. Alexander

For further thought

• Write a lament psalm of your own and share it on our Facebook page today.

Saturday 31 March
Casting lots for garments

Read Psalm 22:16–31

My hands and feet have shrivelled;
I can count all my bones.
They stare and gloat over me; they divide my clothes among themselves,
and for my clothing they cast lots.
But you, O Lord, do not be far away!
O my help, come quickly to my aid!

(verses 16b–19)

The first verse of Psalm 22 is not the only one to feature in the narratives of Jesus' passion. There are reminders of the psalm in the jeering of the passers-by – their taunt that Jesus should save himself (Mark 15:29–32). And verse 18 plays an important role. All four gospels mention the dividing of Jesus' garments by lot (e.g. Mark 15:24). John 19:23–25 quotes the psalm verse and adds extra detail. The two halves of Psalm 22:18 echo each other, a feature of Hebrew poetry known as 'parallelism'. But in John's Gospel they are assumed to correspond to two different actions: the soldiers share out Jesus' clothes between the four of them, leaving the seamless tunic, for which they then cast lots. The Hebrew of verse 16b is uncertain, leading to many different translations. The NIV follows the Greek Septuagint (the Bible used by most early Christians) in translating it as 'they pierce my hands and my feet'. This would seem to fit the crucifixion, but interestingly is not quoted in the New Testament.

After all the anguished questioning and appeals for help, Psalm 22 ends with praise and thanksgiving. The psalmist promises to tell of God's name in the midst of the congregation. Deliverance is even proclaimed to a people yet unborn. This ending is not referred to in the gospels, but it may have been in the writers' minds. Jesus' cry of dereliction was not the end. Out of suffering came new life.

† Glory be to Jesus,
  Who, in bitter pains,
  Poured for me the life blood
  From his sacred veins.

       – Edward Caswall

For further thought

• Find an appropriate activity for this day of waiting – perhaps go for a walk.

Holy Week and Easter with the Psalms
2 Songs of praise

Notes by **Rachel Poolman**

 Rachel Poolman is a Minister in the United Reformed Church (UK). After service in a variety of contrasting settings in England she has settled on the Holy Island of Lindisfarne, a place of pilgrimage known as the 'cradle' of English Christianity. Here, as Warden of St Cuthbert's Centre, she engages with visitors from many places and backgrounds, plays her part in the island community, takes care of a nineteenth-century building regularly battered by North Sea gales and generally enjoys life. Rachel has used the NRSVA for these notes.

Sunday 1 April (Easter Sunday)
The name above every name

Read Philippians 2:5–11

Therefore God also highly exalted him and gave him the name that is above every name, so that at the name of Jesus every knee should bend, in heaven and on earth, and under the earth ...

(verses 9–10)

On Easter Sunday, where I live on Holy Island, we welcome a huge influx of pilgrims – far too many people to know individually, but each coming with their own story of physical and spiritual journeying. Wherever and however we observe Easter, the weekend can be a significant checkpoint on our own pilgrimage of faith.

Along with all those who share in the Christian pilgrimage, we can each name our own unique life experiences in the past and in the present. When we name our hopes and fears for the future, God hears us. At this point in the church year we can also name many emotions as we reflect on the stories of Christ's resurrection, and they won't all be ones of exuberant joy.

The hymn in Philippians reminds us that beyond all that we can name, there is, embodied in Christ Jesus, the mystery of resurrection and of eternal hope. There are always more steps to take on our pilgrimage and we do not travel alone.

† Above all, below all, within all, Christ is risen! Let resurrection continue for ever and ever!

Monday 2 April
I will sing to the Lord

Read Exodus 15:1–13

Who is like you, O Lord, among the gods? Who is like you, majestic in holiness, awesome in splendour, doing wonders?

(verse 11)

I live on a tidal island where one can't help but be aware of movement and change in our lived environment. Twice a day the road to the mainland is covered for five hours and our movements are governed by the North Sea. Each time the ebbing tide uncovers the causeway again the sands around it have shifted slightly and a new landscape is revealed.

Moses and the Israelites sing a love song to God with a fierceness that is perhaps alien in our eyes. They have faced a time of certain death and have then found themselves standing in a place of new life with all their foes vanquished. They rejoice in this gift beyond their imagining and speak not only of a God who is powerful and holy but who also gifts them steadfast and eternal love. Their landscape has changed, and in the early books of the Hebrew scriptures we follow their story as they journey on physically and in understanding of God.

As humankind we inhabit a vast canvas in time and space where themes of life and death can take years, decades or centuries to evolve. It is also true that on a daily basis sands shift around us and tides ebb and flow with rippling consequences. In the midst of it all we are invited to discern the narratives of a holy, life-changing God of love.

† This day, help me to be open to the gifts of renewal that are offered to me. May I receive them with grace and praise. Amen

For further thought

- Bring to mind the movement of water in the sea or swirled around in a bowl. What does it mean to 'go with the flow'?

Tuesday 3 April
My heart exults

Read 1 Samuel 2:1–10

There is no Holy One like the Lord, no one besides you; there is no Rock like our God.

(verse 2)

Hannah's experience of resurrection comes after years of heartache and stigma. She is carrying new life, but her child was conceived after she had known deep sadness and despair.

The praise that bursts forth from her heart acknowledges the light and shade and darkness of human existence. It is a song of gratitude, and a song of hope. It is a prayer not just for herself, but also for those who live in barren places and for those who know first-hand the unfairness of the world.

Against this backdrop Hannah wonders at the holiness of God and at divine mysteries beyond our understanding. God is her rock, a still and immovable presence in all the changing scenes of life.

Her certainties about God are not untested ones; they do not dictate that, if only people believe, they will be all right. Rather her faith and exultation are forged on an anvil of suffering, a profound appreciation of the gifts she has received and a longing for others yet to receive a similar depth of blessing.

Whether we are in a place of blessing, or a place of struggle, or somewhere in between there is much that we can learn from Hannah's prayer song, which embraces not just herself but also the needs of others.

† O God who inhabits light and shade, help me this day to give thanks, to name my struggles before you and to reach out to others. Amen

For further thought

• What is your unique prayer of exultation right now? Jot down some thoughts, or find words and music from elsewhere, and voice your prayer song aloud.

Wednesday 4 April
Let earth rejoice

Read Psalm 96

Let the heavens be glad, and let the earth rejoice; let the sea roar, and all that fills it;
let the field exult, and everything in it.

(verses 11–12a)

Over the last ten years I have lived in two of the most rural parts of England – in Cumbria in the north west, and in Northumberland in the far north east. In English terms these are sparsely populated areas at the mercy of the elements, although there are plenty of people in other parts of the world who would smile at this description! Nevertheless, in each location, I have seen examples of how visitors can be oblivious to the power of nature. Mountain rescue, coastguard and lifeboat volunteers all have many tales to tell of being called out to people who haven't realised that a mobile phone is of limited help when the fog descends on the Lake District fells, or that a four-wheel drive vehicle is not enough to combat the North Sea when it floods the Holy Island causeway.

In Psalm 96 the author is well aware of the power of nature, of necessity being much more affected by its vagaries than we usually are in the twenty-first century. In catching up the sea, the fields and the trees in this song of praise there is a recognition of our interconnectedness with the whole created order.

The psalm reflects awe at the beautiful gifts of creation that we have done nothing to deserve as well as respect for the power of nature. We are reminded to sing new songs, in harmony with all things, in praise of God who sits beyond and above us all.

† As the seasons of life, and death and resurrection turn beyond our control, may we listen for the eternal heartbeat. Amen

For further thought

• Find something that nature alone has had a part in creating, sit with it and wonder at how beautifully it is made.

Holy Week and Easter with the Psalms – Rachel Poolman

Thursday 5 April
Reap with shouts of joy

Read Psalm 126

Those who go out weeping, bearing the seed for sowing, shall come home with shouts of joy, carrying their sheaves.

(verse 6)

Easter celebrations can be difficult if you are living through a painful season in your personal life. I remember when I was a young minister leading the congregation of my first church in the traditional Easter responses 'Christ is risen! Hallelujah!' As we shared in those words of praise I caught the eye of a woman who I knew to be bereft following a recent family tragedy. Seeing her pain, I wondered how I could expect her to be singing 'hallelujahs' in worship.

That Easter Sunday I received a lesson that one person's joyful Easter service can be a bewildering and hurtful experience for those who feel they have nothing to celebrate. Good Friday is always part of Easter Sunday.

Psalm 126 is full of joy at a successful harvest and tells of laughter on receiving God's provision after a time of national heartache. In the midst of jubilation though there is still a sensitivity to those whose weeping continues.

In the psalm there is a yearning for ultimate hope for all who suffer, and the insight that even those who weep can carry seeds, which, when sown, will be a source of new growth. Resurrection isn't a one-off universal experience, but rather something which we will each experience in different ways in different seasons of our lives. Similarly, our Easter praise is not meant to be a triumphalist song that excludes those who suffer, but rather, a declaration of hope that one day the song will ring true for all of us.

† Loving God, help me to cherish the joyful times in my life, and to be aware of your presence in the painful seasons, and help me too to extend your sensitivity to others. Amen

For further thought

• Bring to mind anyone you know who has experienced heartache in the last year. What tangible action can you take to show that their sadness is not forgotten?

Friday 6 April
The garments of salvation

Read Isaiah 61:10–62:3

You shall be a crown of beauty in the hand of the Lord, and a royal diadem in the hand of your God.

(verse 3)

A good friend of mine frequently uses the phrase, 'Remember, you are a beloved child of God.' I have adopted that line, and when giving spiritual direction or leading a retreat sometimes invite people to say to themselves or to each other using their first name, '… you are a beloved child of God.' They are then invited to sit quietly with that truth and allow it to be absorbed into their hearts. This is quite a powerful exercise, as it can release a range of emotions, so it should be used sensitively depending on the individuals and the context, but these are words we should heed if we proclaim a God of love.

On the Christian pilgrimage we can be so caught up with journeying ever onwards that we forget to pause long enough to receive the gifts of God. Sometimes we only hear the challenges of scripture, the calls to change and to grow, or we become overburdened by what we are failing to achieve. In the midst of all this we can lose out on an awareness of all that we are and all that we do that already gives God pleasure.

The book of Isaiah isn't short of calls to repentance and of passages where we hear God lamenting the recalcitrance of the people of Israel. Yet God's love is always made explicit too. These demanding and exasperating children are treasured by God; God longs for them to recognise their true beauty and for them to let their light shine before others, for they, like us and all humanity, are beloved children of God.

† Today, I receive your unconditional love, O God. Help me to recognise my gifts as well as my weaknesses and to enjoy them to the full this day and this night. Amen

For further thought

• Try the exercise mentioned above. Repeat to yourself, whatever you are doing, 'I am a beloved child of God.'

April

Holy Week and Easter with the Psalms – Rachel Poolman

Saturday 7 April
Holy, holy, holy

Read Revelation 4

Holy, holy, holy, the Lord God the Almighty, who was and is and is to come.

(verse 8b)

When you minister in a place called Holy Island, people expect you to know a thing or two about holiness. On occasion, I have found that people not only expect me to be an expert on the subject, but also expect me to embody holiness at all times and in all places – this would be a challenge for me, and I suspect for all of us!

Holiness is, by definition, beyond our understanding. To stand on holy ground is to visit a place of mystery where we experience the divine in a way beyond words and logic.

Revelation 4 is redolent with imagery that speaks to this. I can't believe that the passage is meant to be a detailed description of what heaven looks like, rather the writer is invited to a place that transcends human experience, where all the senses are engaged until one can't help being fully caught up in the eternal song, 'Holy, holy, holy, the Lord God the Almighty, who was and is and is to come.'

We have yet to be translated to a state where we permanently experience holiness, but we are gifted with places and moments where we can experience that peace that passes understanding, where our only response is awe and wonder. We may seek out places where our prayers are layered on those of generations that have gone before, or places of natural beauty. However, we can also have fleeting moments in our day-to-day context where we know heaven touching earth. Often, the challenge is to still our souls enough to allow them to be open to divine moments and to receive unexpected gifts.

† O God, holy beyond our understanding, yet made incarnate in human flesh, touch and transform me through your Spirit this day as you walk through it alongside me. Amen

For further thought

- Look at your diary – when and how can you make head and heart space to encounter holiness?

Hebrews
1 Jesus the true High Priest

Notes by **Catrin Harland**

Catrin Harland is the Methodist chaplain to the University of Sheffield, where she spends her time discussing life and faith with students and staff, usually over a coffee and a slice of cake. She has a doctorate in New Testament studies, a passion for reading, walking and comedy (watching, rather than performing, much to the relief of those who know her) and three children who fill her time fairly effectively between them. Catrin has used the NRSVA for these notes.

Sunday 8 April
Singing a song of praise

Read Hebrews 1

He is the reflection of God's glory and the exact imprint of God's very being, and he sustains all things by his powerful word. When he had made purification for sins, he sat down at the right hand of the Majesty on high, having become as much superior to angels as the name he has inherited is more excellent than theirs.

(verses 3–4)

Patterns of Christian worship vary enormously, from the very liturgical to the very free. But almost all begin in praise, inspired by the love and grace of Christ, in whose name we gather.

The letter to the Hebrews is in many ways a devotional text. It is most likely written to a community of Jewish Christians, steeped in Jewish traditions, theology and liturgy, but regarding Jesus as the fulfillment of the Jewish Law.

Hebrews opens with a call to worship – a reminder of all God has done for us in Christ, inviting us to praise. Then come several snippets of scripture, singing of Christ's superiority over other heavenly beings, Christ's eternal reign and Christ's divine Sonship. Most of these are from the Psalms – they are songs of praise from deep within Jewish worshipping tradition.

Many of us will join in public worship today. As we do, most of us will begin with hymns or songs of praise. Some will be ancient, some very new. But all will share in praising together the One who lived and died for us – who is 'as much superior to angels as the name he has inherited is more excellent than theirs' (verse 4).

† Offer a prayer of praise in your own words or using a hymn or song. Why not also pray for those who cannot praise God?

99

Monday 9 April
Confession and forgiveness

Read Hebrews 2

But someone has testified somewhere, 'What are human beings that you are mindful of them, or mortals, that you care for them? You have made them for a little while lower than the angels; you have crowned them with glory and honour.'

(verses 6–7)

A confession: I've never really warmed to romantic poetry, even by the great romantic poets. When I first encountered such poems, as a cynical 14-year-old, I found the seemingly endless stanzas about the loved one's perfection somewhat nauseating. In fact, the only thing worse was the poet's own declared unworthiness of her love. Both sentiments seemed utterly overblown. No one is that sickeningly perfect, and I suspected that the self-abasement was little more than eloquent attention-seeking. The romance was sadly wasted on me.

But a similar instinct is a central part of most of our worship. Yesterday, we reflected on the impulse to praise and worship God. If praise leads us to think about the nature of God, and if that nature is perfection, then how can we not be painfully aware of our own imperfection?

So, time and again, praise and adoration lead us into confession. And Hebrews, too, flows naturally from the relationship between the Father and the Son to the relationship between God and humanity, with recognition that we have not deserved God's love.

But when we make our confession, the point is not to indulge in a time of breast-beating self-loathing. Rather, it's to recognise the full glory of God's saving grace. If we were perfect, God's love for us would be rather less amazing. But we are not, and yet God loves us still! How can we not be awestruck and humbled that we, imperfect as we are, are worth God's care and love?

† Offer to God the ways in which you have fallen short of perfection. Sit in silence for a while, allowing yourself to feel God lifting the burden of imperfection and to feel yourself completely loved.

For further thought

• Through this week, look for God's image in the people you encounter. Remember that even though that image is tarnished, God's love is perfect.

Living faithfully as members of the household of God

Read Hebrews 3

For we have become partners of Christ, if only we hold our first confidence firm to the end. As it is said, 'Today, if you hear his voice, do not harden your hearts as in the rebellion.'

(verses 14–15)

It is probably an eternal truth that siblings will squabble and fight, and my children are no exception to that rule. It seems to be their mission in life to annoy and aggravate one another (and me) as much as possible. But there is another side to their relationship – when one of them is in trouble, the others will move heaven and earth to help out. They will defend each other against all external threats, and would share their last penny with each other if it really mattered. Then they go back to the arguments and the bickering …

The writer of Hebrews paints a picture here of a family community. The family, or household, in Greek and Roman society, included more than parents and siblings. The extended family might be included, along with servants and slaves. Some of these household communities could become quite large, and everyone had a place (high or lowly) within it.

So, drawing on this image, Hebrews offers us the example of the faithful servant (Moses) and the faithful son (Jesus) – and the counterexample of the unfaithful people of Israel, at the time of the Exodus. We are invited to be part of the household of God, but if we accept, we are asked to pledge our loyalty to the head of that household, and to the Son. God is utterly faithful to all members of his family, and has granted us the honour of being on the receiving end of that faithfulness. Will we, in turn, be faithful members of the family or household of God?

† God of love and community, thank you for the privilege of belonging to your household. Make me faithful to my brothers and sisters, and to you who welcomes us in. Amen

For further thought

• What does it mean to be loyal or faithful to God? What are the characteristics of faithful members of the household of God?

Wednesday 11 April
Rest in the arms of God

Read Hebrews 4

For we do not have a high priest who is unable to sympathise with our weaknesses, but we have one who in every respect has been tested as we are, yet without sin. Let us therefore approach the throne of grace with boldness, so that we may receive mercy and find grace to help in time of need.

(verses 15–16)

You don't get anywhere without hard work. That's what we're taught from a very early age. Perhaps that's why society's reaction to those claiming welfare benefits (or inheriting a fortune) is frequently so hostile. We are suspicious of those who get rewards that we deem not to have been earned. It also explains the superstar status which successful sportspersons often enjoy; we are fascinated by the struggles, sacrifices and sheer single-minded focus behind that gold medal or world record.

But while we make a virtue of getting the rewards we deserve, the Christian gospel proclaims a different message. The life, death and resurrection of Jesus is fundamentally a story of unearned forgiveness. Jesus offers healing, love and compassion, without pausing to enquire whether it has been earned. Sometimes, these gifts are offered precisely where they're not deserved. All he seems to ask is a heart willing to receive them. Zacchaeus is not loved and accepted because he has made amends; rather, he makes amends because he has experienced Christ's accepting love.

Similarly, the writer of Hebrews isn't telling his readers to work hard and earn their way to a reward. He's not telling them to strive for perfection. Rather, he's telling them to listen to the voice of God and to open their hearts, learning to rest in God's love. We're judged not on our pious achievements, but on the strength of our desire to enter God's eternal rest. And we're judged with compassion, and with the desire to offer to us what we haven't deserved.

There's a word for that. Grace.

† Instead of offering prayer to God in words, find somewhere quiet or calming and spend some time listening for the voice of God. Focus your thoughts on God, and just be still and open.

For further thought

- Of course, like Zacchaeus, we sometimes are called to hard work and struggle. How do you allow your faith to equip you for that?

Thursday 12 April
The qualities of a priest

Read Hebrews 5

Although he was a Son, he learned obedience through what he suffered; and having been made perfect, he became the source of eternal salvation for all who obey him, having been designated by God a high priest according to the order of Melchizedek.

(verses 8–10)

To summarise the writer Douglas Adams, on finding a good leader: those who most want to lead are by definition least suited to it. In other words, there is a real danger that those who seek power are motivated by the desire for power, rather than the desire to serve.

I suspect that the writer of Hebrews may have been very aware of this danger. He is clear that a good high priest is aware of his own sinfulness, humble enough to recognise his own need for atonement. A good high priest is motivated not by a sense of his own superior holiness, but by a feeling of solidarity in weakness.

A good leader, not least a good religious leader, is driven less by ambition than by a desire to learn. She will be humble and aware of how little she knows. She will have responded to a call to leadership, but not desire it as an end in itself.

In this, of course, we have a model in Christ himself. He, we are told, is appointed high priest for all time, but not through seeking it for his own glory. Rather, he set out to serve and was willing to suffer and be humbled. He practises what he preaches – that anyone called to lead must do so by serving (Matthew 20:24–28).

His calling to the high priesthood is a sign that he lived this to the utmost.

† God, guide those who lead in church and society, that they may be motivated by the desire to serve. Give compassion to those they serve, to expect humanity, not perfection, in their leaders. Amen

For further thought

• Where do you see abuses of power in leaders? And where do you see unrealistic expectations of leaders? How can you challenge this?

Friday 13 April
Perfected in love

Read Hebrews 6

And we want each one of you to show the same diligence, so as to realise the full assurance of hope to the very end, so that you may not become sluggish, but imitators of those who through faith and patience inherit the promises.

(verses 11–12)

Apparently, a little knowledge is a dangerous thing. But in many areas of life, a little knowledge is probably all I'm going to be able to gain, and I just have to hope that it's better than no knowledge at all. I'm not a human biologist, but I know a little about how to keep my body healthy. I'm not a computer scientist, but with a little knowledge (and a search engine), I can resolve most minor software issues. Life is too short to become an expert in everything. I combine a little knowledge with gratitude for other people's expertise.

But of course we do typically gain expertise in some fields. We may be qualified in a trade or profession, or skilled at catering for our family. We may hold an encyclopaedic knowledge of our children's social and educational commitments, or know exactly how to reassure an anxious friend. In some things, it's enough to know a little, while in others we strive for perfection.

One area in which we should all be aiming to grow in expertise is in our relationship with God. Hebrews has already reminded us that God's love isn't dependent on our achievements, and that we are judged on our openness to his grace, but this doesn't absolve us from the call to respond to God's love. God's love makes us long to know God better, and aspire to perfect love of God and our neighbours.

We don't need to be perfect to be loved by God, but God's love inspires us to aim for perfection.

† God of perfection, make us dissatisfied with passionless half-commitment, and not content to rest on the laurels of your grace. Instead, inspire us to go on towards perfection in our love of you. Amen

For further thought

• Do one thing in response to God's love, such as spending time in prayer, showing love to someone or practising a skill to serve God.

Saturday 14 April
Time and tithes: supporting the work of God

Read Hebrews 7:1–14

This 'King Melchizedek of Salem, priest of the Most High God, met Abraham as he was returning from defeating the kings and blessed him'; and to him Abraham apportioned 'one-tenth of everything'. His name, in the first place, means 'king of righteousness'; next he is also king of Salem, that is, 'king of peace'.

(verses 1–2)

Tithing is a controversial practice. Churches which tithe tend to have plentiful financial resources and a habit of instinctive generosity. They argue that everyone giving the same proportion of their income (a tithe, or tenth) is a fair way of spreading the cost of church life and Christian witness. Others argue that it can place unfair expectations on those on a low income, and allow others to be ungenerous or legalistic in their giving. It also tends to emphasise giving specifically to the church, perhaps not recognising other acts of generosity which may be as much a part of Christian witness.

However we may feel about tithing, giving has always been a part of Christian living. In this passage, we see Abraham honouring the priest Melchizedek, by giving him a tithe of his property.

So is giving out of our wealth or income an appropriate way of showing respect to those who are chosen by God for religious office? Perhaps so, or perhaps by sharing our wealth in this way we are showing our love and respect for Christ, the one given eternal priesthood, 'according to the order of Melchizedek' (6:20).

In giving to the church, to support those giving their time and talents, we are enabled to be a part of the church's witness. Some have time and gifts to give, while others have financial or material resources. Many of us will have a combination of gifts to offer. But to give what we have, freely and generously, as an act of faith and love, is part of our calling to Christian life.

† Generous God, giver of good things; help me in gratitude to offer back to you all that I have, all that I am, and all that, through your grace, I may become. Amen

For further thought

• What do you think about tithing? What do, or can, you give (remembering that giving is not always financial)? Where do you direct your giving?

Hebrews
2 The new covenant

Notes by **Abraham Mathew**

Abraham Mathew is an ordained minister of the Mar Thoma Church, which belongs to the Reformed Orthodox tradition. He is vicar of Immanuel Mar Thoma Church in Noida, India, and has a doctorate in Mission studies from Bristol University, UK. He teaches at Dharma Jyoti Vidya Peeth, a seminary in Faridabad, India and he has worked in several mission fields. He enjoys reading, writing, painting and preaching. He and his wife Elizabeth live in Noida with their two daughters. Abraham has used the NRSVA for these notes.

Sunday 15 April
Self-sacrificing priest

Read Hebrews 7:15–28

Unlike the other high priests, he has no need to offer sacrifices day after day, first for his own sins, and then for those of the people; this he did once for all when he offered himself.

(verse 27)

The word 'covenant' refers to an agreement between two parties which involves promises to be kept by both. The concept of a covenant between God and human beings is one of the central themes of the Bible. In the Old Testament we read of God's covenant with Noah, Abraham, Jacob and the people of Israel. God through Moses established the Sinai covenant and promised to lead the Israelites if they observed it diligently. The High Priests were to offer sacrifices as atonement for sin and as part of some other rituals.

In the New Testament, Jesus, through his self-sacrifice, has established a new covenant by which our sins are forgiven. It is not our efforts or good works that enable us to maintain this covenantal relationship but our dependence on the grace of Christ.

We are called to follow Jesus' example of self-sacrifice in our life in this world today to exemplify God's redemption from structural sin. There is need for empowerment of the downtrodden and marginalised who have for generations been sidelined. Are we willing to sacrifice our resources and possibilities so that they can have a taste of life in abundance?

† O Lord, who guarantees a better covenant, thank you for the redemption we have in you. Help us to offer ourselves as living sacrifices for your kingdom. Amen

Monday 16 April
New way of living

Read Hebrews 8

But Jesus has now obtained a more excellent ministry, and to that degree he is the mediator of a better covenant, which has been enacted through better promises.

(verse 6)

Though the old covenant had the best of intentions, the people failed to keep their part of the agreement as they disobeyed God's laws. So God, through Jeremiah, prophesied about a new covenant; one that is better. The law will not have to be taught any more as it will be in everyone's heart. Also, no one will have to say to the other, 'Know the Lord', as everyone will know the Lord (Jeremiah 31:31–34).

Living the gospel is different from proclaiming the gospel. In a country like India, which is multi-cultural, multi-religious and multi-linguistic, much has been done to proclaim the gospel; but there has been opposition from many religious groups accusing Christians of religious conversion. However, there are untold stories of Christian men and women who spent their lives in the service of the sick, the destitute and the downtrodden. They have not proclaimed the gospel but have lived the gospel by which many have seen Christ in them and have accepted Christ as Lord.

A few years back I visited a government office in Jaipur to submit a request regarding the church. Recognising that I was a Christian minister, the senior administrative officer welcomed me to his room and with great humility listened to my problem. He then told me that the principal of the school where he had studied was a Catholic priest and had influenced him tremendously. He showed me a Bible which he kept on his table and said, 'I am not a Christian but I read this every day and try to be like Jesus.'

† O Lord, help us, the followers of the new covenant, to live the gospel in the areas that you have placed us, so that those who see us may see you. Amen

For further thought

- How many people have influenced you through the way they lived their life? How many have you influenced through yours?

Tuesday 17 April
New way of worship

Read Hebrews 9:1–14

… how much more will the blood of Christ, who through the eternal Spirit offered himself without blemish to God, purify our conscience from dead works to worship the living God!

(verse 14)

The Tabernacle was a portable tent in which the Israelites worshipped before the Temple was built. The ark, a rectangular wooden box containing the covenant (stone tablets with God's laws given to Moses), was kept in the Holy of Holies. Only the high priest was allowed to enter here during worship after having offered blood for himself and the people. They believed that sinful man could not approach a holy God without first cleansing himself of sin and this cleansing was done by rituals and sacrifices. However, we read that all these external regulations failed to clear the conscience of the worshipper.

In the new covenant, according to Hebrews, the blood of Jesus redeems us from sin. We are free from all guilt and therefore we can come with confidence before the Holy and living God for worship. Not that we are holy or are worthy to stand before God, but we depend on God's free mercy and grace through Christ.

If we genuinely confess our shortcomings both individually and as a community and depend on the Holy Spirit to guide our thoughts, words and actions, we can have a clear conscience. This good conscience will help us to worship in spirit and truth and lead us to a life which will be like a sweet-smelling sacrifice, holy and acceptable to God.

† O Holy God, we come with confidence before your throne of grace because of the blood of Christ. Help us to find joy and meaning in our corporate worship services. Amen

For further thought

• How is the worship life of your church today? Does the language of Hebrews relate to your experience of worship, or not?

Wednesday 18 April
New promise

April

Read Hebrews 9:15–28

For this reason he is the mediator of a new covenant, so that those who are called may receive the promised eternal inheritance, because a death has occurred that redeems them from the transgressions under the first covenant.

(verse 15)

From time immemorial, human beings have pondered life after death. Different religions visualise this differently even though they affirm the continuation of life. While Vedic Hindu philosophy talks about rebirth, Christian traditions acknowledge a new life with God which is eternal. As a minister I have visited several terminally ill patients. Some of them are radiant and expectant while others are gloomy and scared when they contemplate their future. Also I have noticed that those without hope based on faith are in panic and become miserable after they lose a dear one.

What is this hope? The new covenant gives us the hope of a life with God that goes beyond death. The hope of eternal life comes from knowing the living God and Jesus Christ (John 17:3). This hope comes from believing the Son of God (John 3:16) and by loving and obeying Jesus (John 14:23).

Having lived a life for Christ, Paul during his last days confidently says, 'I have fought the good fight, I have finished the race.' He also looks forward to the crown of righteousness that the Lord, the righteous judge, would reward him on that day (2 Timothy 4:6–8).

Ultimately the hope of eternal life is a gift from God, and we are not to judge who will or will not be part of it. Let us with fear and trembling lead holy lives controlled by the Holy Spirit so that we can be confident of being with our God and our fellow believers on the other shore.

† O eternal and living God, we thank you for the hope of eternal life. Help us to live a life worthy of your calling. Help us love and serve your creation in the spaces you have allotted, until our last breath. Amen

For further thought

• What do God's love and hope look like in a hospice ward?

Hebrews – Abraham Mathew

Thursday 19 April
New offering: commitment

Read Hebrews 10:1–18

When he said … 'You have neither desired nor taken pleasure in sacrifices and offerings and burnt-offerings and sin-offerings' (these are offered according to the law), then he added, 'See, I have come to do your will.' He abolishes the first in order to establish the second.

(verses 8–10)

Gadhimai festival was a sacrificial ceremony held every five years in a temple in Nepal. It is said that in 2009 about 500,000 animals were sacrificed there by devotees in order to stop evil and receive prosperity. However, due to the protests of animal rights activists and other religious sects, this festival has been banned since 2015, thus avoiding unnecessary bloodshed of animals.

Offerings and sacrifices were believed to please God and obtain forgiveness and blessings from God according to the Jewish Law. Year after year people offered sacrifices but there was no change in their hearts. They continued in their sinful ways.

Christ, however, through the new covenant talks of a better offering, the offering of oneself, the giving up of one's will in exchange for God's will. Christ has shown us through his life how he was obedient to God even in death. Paul compares his life to a drink offering being poured out for others. The lives of many men and women of God also show us that a life lived according to God's purposes is the most excellent offering.

There are numerous decisions that we take in our life, such as the course we study, the profession we choose, the life partner we select, the place we live, work etc. Do we make these choices based on the profit we can make and the advantages they afford us? Do we make some decisions to please our family and friends? Or do we take a moment to ask 'what is God's will?' by which our life can become an offering?

† O Lord, help us to offer ourselves and our will as you did. No matter how painful it may seem, help us to realise that your ways are always best. Amen

For further thought

• What has motivated some of your major life decisions recently?

Friday 20 April
New fellowship

Read Hebrews 10:19–25

And let us consider how to provoke one another to love and good deeds, not neglecting to meet together, as is the habit of some, but encouraging one another, and all the more as you see the Day approaching.

(verses 24–25)

I grew up in a village in Kerala in South India. It is believed that St Thomas, the disciple of Jesus, came to India in AD 52 and established the first church in Kerala. For centuries since, a liturgical form of worship has been followed in most traditional churches. One of the rules set by my strictly Orthodox grandfather for our family was that on Sunday morning we had to attend the morning worship at our local church. We became so accustomed to this routine that even after I left home for my higher studies, on Sunday morning I had to attend worship service somewhere. My friends who grew up in more liberal settings said they had no such urge. Old habits die hard. As an adult the drive for me was more than just a habit; it was a need to worship.

In the new covenant, after setting our relationship right with God and with ourselves, we are to work on our relationship with others. It is easy for a believer to remain isolated and say, 'my spirituality includes only me and my God.' Although our relationship with God may be personal, it can become practical only in a community. The fellowship that is formed by meeting together is meant to encourage each other, provoke each other to love and do good deeds – not just for each other but, more importantly, for those outside the church.

Let us all begin by encouraging our family, especially our children, to develop and practise these spiritual habits so that as they grow, they will not depart from them.

† O Lord, help us to make our churches and fellowships a place where everyone feels accepted and loved. Open our eyes and ears so that we can sense each other's need and pain. Amen

For further thought

- How many in your church are you familiar with? Befriend a new person this Sunday and share a word of encouragement.

Saturday 21 April
New response: endurance

Read Hebrews 10:26–39

But recall those earlier days when, after you had been enlightened, you endured a hard struggle with sufferings, sometimes being publicly exposed to abuse and persecution … For you need endurance, so that when you have done the will of God, you may receive what was promised.

(parts of verses 32, 33 and 36)

Though Indian Christianity traces its origins from the first century itself with the arrival of St Thomas, the Christian population in India remains at 2.3 per cent and Christians often face some kind of hostility due to their distinctive faith. A student in seminary from Orissa recently told me of his conversion experience. Being the only one who had accepted Christ in his family, he had to face the wrath of the elders in the family. He is studying to become a missionary as he wants to share Christ's love with his people. I have noticed in him a zeal for worship and learning which many of his counterparts from traditional Christian backgrounds lack. In 2008, Kandhamal, Orissa was in the news for the persecution of Christians by Hindu extremists. Many nuns, missionaries and believers were burnt alive, raped and tortured for their faith. But their passion has only increased.

Persecution has always been a part of Christianity ever since its inception. The new covenant and values taught by Jesus are often at loggerheads with the worldly values, and so for a true Christian it is difficult to conform to the ways of the world. Though the early Church was persecuted, it was resilient and grew in leaps and bounds. Today we can see that the church has become complacent and hence inert in many places where Christianity once thrived. However, in places where Christianity had been suppressed for centuries there is a spurt in growth. It is the testing of our faith that produces endurance and much fruit.

† O Lord, who suffered undeserved pain and suffering, help us to endure when we are mocked or persecuted. Give us faith and zeal to live and die for you. Amen

For further thought
• Pray for Christians in places of persecution.

Hebrews
3 Faith and works

Notes by **Alesana Fosi Pala'amo**

 Alesana Fosi Pala'amo is a lecturer in Practical Theology at Malua Theological College in Samoa. A minister of the Congregational Christian Church of Samoa, his research interests include Christian ministry, youth and social ministries, pastoral theology, worship and pastoral counselling. Alesana is completing his PhD research in pastoral counselling through Massey University, New Zealand. Alesana and his wife Lemau have three sons, Norman, Alex and Jayden. Alesana has used the NRSVA for these notes.

Sunday 22 April
Champions of faith

Read Hebrews 11:1–16

Now faith is the assurance of things hoped for, the conviction of things not seen. Indeed, by faith our ancestors received approval.

(verses 1–2)

The authorship of the letter to the Hebrews is unclear – many say the apostle Paul, some say Luke or Barnabas – but regardless of who the author is, the letter shares important messages. It includes some important lessons taught through the Old and New Testaments.

The biblical characters from today's reading I consider as 'champions of faith'. They all show traits worthy of any champion – the passion, skills and dedication to become the best one can amongst equals. Abel gave the best sacrifice he could, Enoch had his life taken, literally, by God, and Noah prepared the ark although ridiculed by his peers. They are seen as champions through land (Abel's sacrifice), through air (Enoch's ascension) and upon waters (Noah's ark). Abraham, 'father' of all champions, obeyed and allowed God to lead him and his family towards the promised inheritance.

These 'champions of faith' teach us how we can become champions of our time. We need passion in the faith we live. We need the skills – to read our Bible, reflect and pray – to grow as Christians. We must dedicate our time, energy and love to serving Christ. Doing so makes us 'champions of faith' who hope and believe in all things not seen.

† Lord God, empower us with the gift of faith to trust you with our lives and become 'champions of faith'. Amene

Monday 23 April
Faith gives life

Read Hebrews 11:17–31

He considered the fact that God is able even to raise someone from the dead – and figuratively speaking, he did receive him back.

(verse 19)

Today's reading includes the story of Abraham's faith in God that saved his son Isaac, and the faith and actions of Moses' parents that saved his life. Both stories highlight the intervention of parents to save their children. This reminds me of another parent and son story. When I was around five years old, my father and I went fishing off a wharf in Ohope Whakatane in New Zealand. Dawn was just breaking and we were alone on the wharf. I remember my father instructed me to stay in the car out of the rain, while he fished ten metres away. The next memory I have was being in the sea and sinking, while looking up at the sky disappearing away. I then felt a hand trying to grab me, which finally got hold of my long ponytail floating above my head – it was my father's hand. He stopped me from sinking, but then we both struggled to stay afloat in the rough sea because of the winter jumper my father had on. Eventually we found safety on a concrete pillar under the wharf. A man heard our screams for help and pulled us up out of harm's way. Later my father told me that I said I jumped into the sea to help him catch some fish.

These stories show how faith in God moves people to intervene and give life to others. Having faith in God reminds us to trust that God can overcome all difficult situations and give us the strength and ability to pull through. Faith in God gives life.

† Lord, help us to trust you when we are faced with life's challenges, in knowing that our faith in you gives us life. Amene

For further thought

• Whom do you have faith in to get by? Yourself, others or God? Our faith in God helps us and each other through our struggles.

Faith enables us to run the good race

Read Hebrews 11:32–12:2

Therefore, since we are surrounded by so great a cloud of witnesses, let us also lay aside every weight and the sin that clings so closely, and let us run with perseverance the race that is set before us.

(verse 1)

When one prepares for a race, important considerations are required. The type of race must be addressed – whether on land, sea or through the air. The duration and tools needed for the race must also be considered. A successful outcome from the race depends upon how well-prepared the person is who runs the race. The metaphor of running a 'race' can be applied to the year-long journey for many Samoans. During the first week of each year, the Congregational Christian Church of Samoa conducts daily worship services called *Lotu Talosaga* (prayer services). The aim of these devotions is to praise God for the year that has passed, and seek his guidance for the new year ahead. Speakers from the congregations are invited to share their testimonies of thanksgiving for the new year, and offer inspiring messages of encouragement. These speakers include deacons, lay-preachers, youth and the elderly. This practice serves as preparation for the 'race' ahead – the year-long journey for the parish and also personal individual journeys through many challenges and triumphs.

Our reading today names several biblical characters that add to the list of 'champions of faith' discussed earlier this week. Such people ran the good 'race' in their own contexts, because of their faith in God. We too can learn from them and prepare ourselves for the race of life we run daily. Our faith in God equips us with the tools necessary for good to overcome evil, so that we too can run the 'good race' just like those mentioned in today's passage who faithfully served God.

† Lord, may our faith in you help us to run the good race in our daily lives, to serve and praise you always. Amene

For further thought

• To run any race, you must first stand up and move. Do you sometimes procrastinate before the race even begins? Make a difference, starting today.

Wednesday 25 April
Faith disciplines

Read Hebrews 12:3–13

Now, discipline always seems painful rather than pleasant at the time, but later it yields the peaceful fruit of righteousness to those who have been trained by it.

(verse 11)

For readers in Australia and New Zealand, today is a significant day – Anzac Day. This day commemorates the day that began a military campaign of the Allied forces during the First World War. On 25 April 1915, soldiers of the Australian and New Zealand Army Corps (ANZAC) fighting alongside the Allied forces landed on the beaches at Gallipoli in Turkey in the early hours of the morning. A campaign began to overthrow the Ottoman Empire, an ally of Germany. Troops were evacuated after eight months of battle. Amongst the Allied forces' casualties during the Gallipoli campaign, the fallen Anzacs included 8,709 Australian and 2,721 New Zealand soldiers. Amongst these fallen Anzacs were 33 Samoans. Anzac Day is celebrated annually to remember the fallen men and women from the Australian and New Zealand Army Corps. 'Lest we forget.'

From today's reading, the author of the letter to the Hebrews refers to two key themes: children and discipline. The lesson is that we must become like children, i.e. children of God, and be disciplined as a child is disciplined. The purpose is to correct any crooked paths we may have. Our lives as God's children require us to live according to God's ways. Soldiers like the fallen Anzacs lived disciplined lives for their love of their countries and beliefs in their just causes. Likewise, as soldiers for Christ and children of God, we too must be disciplined in the war that we fight daily for what we believe in – our faith in our Risen Lord. Faith disciplines us to serve God.

† Gracious God, help us to remember our fallen brothers and sisters. May we honour and serve you, Lord, in our daily battles to live disciplined lives according to your ways. Amene

For further thought

• What non-violent ways can we use to discipline children? How can we serve as role models for them?

Faith in God as our foundation

Read Hebrews 12:14–29

Therefore, since we are receiving a kingdom that cannot be shaken, let us give thanks, by which we offer to God an acceptable worship with reverence and awe ...

(verse 28)

Fa'avae i le Atua Samoa (Samoa is founded on God) is the motto that governs this Pacific nation. The constitution of the Independent Samoa from 1962, together with its motto, demonstrate that God continues to hold a vital role for Samoans. One of the tragic events in Samoa's history that highlighted its national motto was the most destructive tsunami of recent times. In September 2009, an earthquake measuring a magnitude of 8.1 struck Samoa. The tsunami that followed resulted in 143 fatalities with an estimated 5,200 left homeless. It was a time of extreme grief and shock for Samoans, yet it was also a time that God's grace was abundantly displayed. Neighbouring villages rallied together to search for those unaccounted for and retrieve bodies of the dead. Foreign aid and emergency relief networks reacted immediately. Samoans responded this way – to rebuild their lives and help others find hope – since 'Samoa is founded on God'.

It is important for any structure to have a solid foundation, to withstand being 'shaken'. The Samoan family places God as foundation; which aligns with its national motto. The kingdom of God cannot be shaken, so all those who imitate God's kingdom also will not be shaken. By having faith in God as our foundation, all trials and challenges can be overcome. Death itself did not shake our Lord; he rose victoriously to life. Similarly, we too can rise victoriously from all life challenges faced, because our faith in God means that we also cannot be shaken. That is the 'Good News' of having faith in God as our foundation.

† Lord God, thank you for your grace through Jesus Christ that gives us hope in our times of need. Remind us to have you as the foundation to our lives. Amene

For further thought

• Consider what is the foundation of your life and that of your family – is it culture, money or getting ahead at work? Or is it God?

April

Hebrews – Alesana Fosi Pala'amo

Friday 27 April
Faith in reciprocated love

Read Hebrews 13:1–17

Let mutual love continue.

(verse 1)

By reciprocated love, what I mean is the love that is returned to the one who gives love. Such love is the situation when someone is loved back by the person to whom love is directed. Love is good even though it may be one-directional at times, but love is at its greatest when it is reciprocated. The idea of reciprocated love drawn from today's reading is similar to shared love or 'mutual love' as found in the text. Reciprocated love occurs for living creatures that have the ability to experience emotions. Therefore, this type of love is only possible for human beings and some domesticated animals. Reciprocated love excludes the love given to items that cannot love you back. For example, the love for your car, house, tablet, laptop, smartphone – a love for these material belongings that make our lives comfortable is one-directional, because these items do not have the ability to love you back.

Jesus simplifies how we must love – 'You shall love the Lord your God with all your heart, and with all your soul, and with all your mind'; 'You shall love your neighbour as yourself' (Matthew 22:37 and 39). Faith in reciprocated love involves reciprocating God's love back to God. It also involves the concept of 'paying forward' the love shown to us, extending that love to our neighbour. When someone does good to you, reciprocate that love either directly to the giver, otherwise extend that love to someone else. Expressing love in this way – to love God and to love your neighbour – ensures that mutual love continues throughout the generations.

† Lord God, may we always show the love that Jesus taught of loving you our God, and loving our neighbour. Amene

For further thought

- 'Pay forward' the good deed you have received, and one day someone will pay it forward to you. Such practice demonstrates sharing God's love.

Saturday 28 April
Faith in God's blessings

Read Hebrews 13:18–25

Now may the God of peace, who brought back from the dead our Lord Jesus, the great shepherd of the sheep, by the blood of the eternal covenant make you complete in everything good … through Jesus Christ, to whom be the glory for ever and ever. Amen

(verse 20 and part of verse 21)

Fa'amanuia le Atua (God bless) is commonly heard as a blessing sought for events that Samoans are involved in. For whatever the occasion – a birthday celebration, a journey about to begin, or for any family, village or parish gathering – the belief is that seeking the blessing from God leads to a successful event. Such words are voiced from parents to their children, elders and *matai* (title-holders) to village members, and church ministers to parishioners. To hear these words tells those who carry out various tasks that what they are about to undertake is supported by others and especially by God. In addition to seeking God's blessing at the start of an event, thanksgiving is also given to God at its conclusion together with asking for God's continuous blessings.

There is no greater blessing that one can ask for other than the blessing of God's grace – an understanding that although we are sinners and continue to fault God, our faith in the Risen Christ ensures that our wrongful paths have been made straight. The author of the letter to the Hebrews has come to the end of the epistle and reminds us all of the grace of God through Jesus Christ – a fitting end to a document that has taught key biblical messages about God and his love for humankind. To be blessed by God teaches us that in faith we believe in the sacrifice that Jesus has made for all sinners, through his death and resurrection to eternal life. God bless – *fa'amanuia le Atua!*

† Our Loving Father, we thank you for your Grace in our Lord Jesus Christ. Help us to always seek your blessings in all that we do. Amene

For further thought
• What type of blessing do you seek in your context? It is great to know that someone prays for the success of what we do.

Going viral: communication in the Bible
1 Face-to-face with God

Notes by **Delroy Hall**

Delroy Hall is a bishop in the Church of God of Prophecy, UK, and currently sits on the Bible Doctrine and Polity Committee at the church's international offices in Cleveland, Tennessee, USA. He is an academic and a trained counsellor with over 20 years' experience in various institutions. Delroy enjoys teaching and training, which he says energises him. In 2015 he completed his first sprint triathlon, and he completed an Olympic triathlon in 2016. He is married to Paulette and is the proud father of twin young women. Delroy has used the NIVUK for these notes.

Sunday 29 April
The intimate God

Read Genesis 2:4–9

Then the Lord God formed a man from the dust of the ground and breathed into his nostrils the breath of life, and the man became a living being.

(verse 7)

Once a good friend of mine fainted after a long, strenuous day at her sister's funeral. Over the phone, emergency services asked me if she was breathing. Fortunately she was; if not, I would have performed CPR on her. She was brought to hospital, checked, and discharged. Later, we reflected that performing CPR would have changed our friendship. The possibility of life-saving contact brings about a new closeness and intimacy in any friendship.

There are many ways God could have created humanity. He does not have literal hands, a mouth or lungs, yet he formed us and breathed into us in almost a form of divine CPR. God's actions indicate an intimacy between us and him.

God's intimacy and its importance to us did not begin and end with the creation of Adam. It continues as he wants a close friendship with us. As we come face-to-face with God this week, we are invited to explore this intimacy and friendship in the readings and in all aspects of all our lives.

† Father, help us to understand that you want a close relationship with us. Help us to embrace you, who desires to embrace us. Amen

Monday 30 April
How long?

Read Psalm 13

How long will you hide your face from me?
How long must I wrestle with my thoughts and day after day have
sorrow in my heart?

(verses 1b–2a)

You do not have to read the Psalms for too long before you meet the feelings of loneliness, despair or abandonment. Such feelings are common to being human, especially during times of crisis. Whatever the nature of the predicament, be it the news of terminal illness, death of a loved one, the breakup of a marriage or a love relationship, we will at some point be subjected to such feelings. Your dilemma may not be as severe, but you get the point.

When we go through such times it feels like good days and bad months, but wait a moment. Consider this: Donald Witney, author of *Praying the Scriptures,* states that the Psalms are songs from God to be sung back to him as an act of worship. For weeks or months due to a variety of reasons we get caught up in our personal dramas, especially in times of deep distress, and can often forget to worship God. Maybe it is *God* who is saying 'How long will you hide your face from me?' We often forget that God has emotions, too, and he wants us to spend time with him. Can you grasp the enormity of this idea? The One who created the heaven and earth, formed us from the dust of the earth, breathed into us and made us alive longs to see us face-to-face. How glorious is that?

† Lord, forgive us for forgetting you have feelings too and that you long to see us face-to-face. Help us to grasp how incredible that is. Amen

For further thought
• How does the fact that God has feelings influence your relationship with him?

April

Going viral: communication in the Bible – Delroy Hall

Moses and the elders with God

May

Going viral: communication in the Bible – Delroy Hall

Read Exodus 24:9–18

He said to the elders, 'Wait here for us until we come back to you. Aaron and Hur are with you, and anyone involved in a dispute can go to them.'

(verse 14)

What a brilliant example of waiting in the presence of the Lord to receive something of substance. Moses waited, unhurried, unburdened with pastoral issues and pondered in God's presence until God spoke. Clergy and believers alike are quick to run to commentaries, concordances, the internet, or even flee into books. Now, don't get me wrong: such tools are indispensable in helping us to understand the culture and custom of the day, but in an age of over-busyness and information overload God wants us to wait and be still until he speaks.

Today we, too, must choose mature church people to address such pastoral matters. Just as Moses asked his elders to preside over pastoral matters as he went in the presence of God, we see something similar in Acts 6. An issue arose where the widows were not being well cared for, and this upset some of the Greek church members. There was a sense that the ministers had to deal with this, but no, the apostles were crystal clear. The apostles were called to prayer and ministry of the word. The apostles felt that others of good character and maturity could see to pastoral matters.

Imagine spending 40 days waiting on and with the Lord. Waiting, fighting the urge to get on with stuff, because stuff needs doing; waiting to hear the still, small voice amidst the many voices in our mind and in contrast to our common addiction to competing worldly noises.

† Forgive us, Father, of our addiction to noise, over-activity and information overload. Teach us the blessings of sitting and waiting with you. Amen

For further thought

• Have you ever taken a few days off to sit and think? Try it.

Wednesday 2 May
Face-to-face

Read Numbers 12:1–9

But this is not true of my servant Moses; he is faithful in all my house.
With him I speak face to face, clearly and not in riddles.

(verses 7–8a)

'I speak with him face-to-face.' What an accolade. What rich comments to be said of a human being. In England, if you want to speak to the Queen, the Prime Minister, any high-ranking official or a popular celebrity, it is by invitation and only after much vetting. This scripture, though, has a twist.

Moses is criticised for his choice of a foreign and black bride and his leadership is called into question. God demands a meeting with Miriam, Aaron and Moses. Taking Miriam and Aaron aside he tells them how he speaks through his prophets through dreams and visions, but look what he says about Moses. What a contrast. He does not say that 'Moses speaks with me', but he says, 'This is not true of my servant Moses; he is faithful in all my house. With him I speak face to face …'

Maybe the person we are criticising – questioning their authority, feeling they are not up to scratch, who is offering inadequate leadership in our eyes and is not worth much – is actually the one whom God speaks with face-to-face. We must be always be careful what we say about people, especially those who are called to lead God's people.

Maybe you are like Moses, heavily challenged, criticised, mistreated and having your authority contested. You know you are doing the best you can, but it is still not good enough. God wants to meet you face-to-face. Meet with him.

† Father, in my time of criticism I often want to retaliate, but help me to meet with you face-to-face as a way of coping. Amen

For further thought

• Criticism comes with leadership. Can spending more time with God help you cope?

Elijah ascends

Read 2 Kings 2:1–15

As they were walking along and talking together, suddenly a chariot of fire and horses of fire appeared and separated the two of them, and Elijah went up to heaven in a whirlwind.

(verse 11)

What an awesome account of the man of God: Elijah's encounter with God, the demonstration of the Holy Spirit working in his life and the way in which he went to be with his Maker. That is Elijah; what about me and you?

Now, let me be clear. Elijah had a specific task to do and God was with him, but we serve the same God who wants to meet us face-to-face and do great things in our lives. Are we willing to pay the cost of that intimacy with God?

One preacher grew a congregation of many thousands after years of faithful ministry. Oftentimes he would say to the congregation and to the other thousands who watched his broadcasts, 'You might see the glory, but you don't know the story.'

It is highly unlikely that most of us will see our creator via chariots and horses of fire and a whirlwind, but we can end our journey of faith and ministry well. How can we do so?

A brief look at Elijah's life indicates a life of total commitment and obedience to God. He was faithful in exercising obedience, which triggered the response of God being faithful to his word. If you want to ascend like Elijah in a metaphorical sense, you must be prepared to risk all and witness how God will respond to your obedience.

† Father and friend, you were faithful in Elijah's life and you want to be faithful in our lives. Help us learn the lesson of obedience. Amen

For further thought

• Meditating on God's word and living his truths are vital ingredients for seeing him and finishing well. Do we have the right mix?

Fire in the bones

Read Jeremiah 20:7–12

> *But if I say, 'I will not mention his word*
> *or speak any more in his name,'*
> *his word is in my heart like a fire,*
> *a fire shut up in my bones.*
> *I am weary of holding it in;*
> *indeed, I cannot.*

(verse 9)

What despair and anguish confront us in our reading. Jeremiah is deceived, derided, mocked, ridiculed and violently treated: graphic words of reproach that let us know how difficult life and ministry were for him. Unsurprisingly, he buckles under the relentless and vicious onslaught. Hear his words, 'I will not mention his word or speak any more in his name.' Yet these are not Jeremiah's final words. As we continue reading the story we must ask, what continued to propel Jeremiah in proclaiming the message of God under such torrid circumstances? The motivation factor is partly captured by these 26 profound words: 'His word is in my heart like a fire, a fire shut up in my bones. I am weary of holding it in; indeed, I cannot.'

The book of Jeremiah uses vivid imagery to convey to us something about God, and more importantly provokes us in thinking, how did the words get into Jeremiah's heart? Not his head or his mind. He must have spent much uninterrupted and undisturbed time with God. It is the only way.

In these few words Jeremiah sounds like the psalmist, especially in Psalm 119 where he talks of despair and anguish, but vows never to stray from God's word.

Through the words of his life Jeremiah is teaching us that it is impossible to proclaim the message and pay the cost if the word of God is not in our hearts. We simply will not experience God's fire in our lives.

† Many Christians hover between cold and tepid in their walk of faith. Father, may we allow your words to dwell in our hearts with life and fire. Amen

For further thought

• In certain parts of the world religious freedoms have been eroded. God's word must be etched in our hearts in readiness for the times ahead.

May

Going viral: communication in the Bible – Delroy Hall

Transfigured

Read Matthew 17:1–12

This is my Son, whom I love; with him I am well pleased. Listen to him!

(part of verse 5)

In our Bible readings this week a hidden theme has threaded its way between the lines, and if we have hurried our devotions we will miss it. That hidden theme is unhurried time. We can seldom see or do anything significant when rushing about.

I recall one day deciding to walk the three miles from my home into the city centre. I saw many sights: beautiful gardens and a small sub-power station, just to name a couple of things. They had not suddenly appeared. They had always been there, but I was, more often than not, travelling in a car.

Here, Jesus takes his disciples up a mountain. You cannot rush going up a mountain, and there, away from the noise of daily life and other conflicting distractions they have a divine encounter of seeing Jesus, Moses and Elijah. Three for the price of one! What an out-of-this-world in-the-world experience.

The story is descriptive and Peter, with his usual impulsive self, exclaims, 'If you wish, I will put up three shelters: one for you, one for Moses and one for Elijah,' but God speaks a timely and humbling word. The disciples hear his voice and are afraid. Jesus ministers to them and asks them not to share this vision with anyone.

We can have deep experiences in and with God, but it is not in order to boast or brag to anyone, but rather to deepen our walk with and understanding of God.

† Lord, take us deeper into you. Help us to see you face-to-face. As we read your words remind us always, as God, you have not changed. We have, so turn us again. Amen

For further thought

• God wants to transform us. As we spend time with God we must become open to God's ways of working. Are you ready?

Going viral: communication in the Bible
2 Messengers of God

Notes by **Paul Nicholson SJ**

 Paul Nicholson is a Roman Catholic priest belonging to the Society of Jesus, a religious order popularly known as the Jesuits. He currently works in London as Socius (assistant) to the Jesuit Provincial. He is the editor of *The Way*, a journal of Christian spirituality, and author of *Growing into Silence* (2011) and *An Advent Pilgrimage* (2013). Since being ordained in 1988 he has worked principally in ministries of spirituality and of social justice, and was novice-master between 2008 and 2014. Paul has used the NRSVA for these notes.

Sunday 6 May
Two places to discover God

Read Psalm 19:1–10

The heavens are telling the glory of God; and the firmament proclaims his handiwork.

(verse 1)

Ignatius of Loyola, the founder of the religious order to which I belong, lived for the last 16 years of his life in central Rome. His days were occupied with directing the work of a group of men who had soon dispersed throughout the world, dictating letters and receiving visitors. Yet at night he loved to spend time on a small balcony outside his office, marvelling at the night sky (easier, I imagine, in those days before street lights) and recognising, in the moon and stars, the creative work of God. It is this same impulse that touches the writer of the psalm we pray with today. Many Christians find it easy to discover God in the natural world around them.

In addition to the starry sky, Psalm 19 points to another place to encounter God's message. Scripture presents the teaching of God in the Law, and the psalmist is convinced that studying these words can be every bit as life-giving as refreshing yourself by gazing at the night sky, or relishing a country walk. Early Christian writers spoke of two 'books' in which God was made known: nature and scripture. Each complements the other. Where do you go to hear God's message? Who are God's messengers to you?

† O God, speaking to us in the words of the Bible and the glory of creation, give us eyes to see and ears to hear. Amen

Bringing good news

> ### Read Isaiah 52:7–10
>
> *How beautiful upon the mountains*
> *are the feet of the messenger who announces peace,*
> *who brings good news,*
> *who announces salvation.*
>
> *(part of verse 7)*

Last year my parents celebrated their diamond wedding anniversary. In the UK, it is possible to mark this event with a message of congratulations from the Queen. My brother, sister and I had decided to organise this, but it's not entirely straightforward. I got hold of a copy of their wedding certificate, we made the application, made sure that we'd be in when it arrived – and all without my parents knowing. We were both relieved and grateful when the courier turned up, bright and early on the morning of their anniversary, to deliver the card conveying Her Majesty's best wishes. Framed, this now occupies pride of place on the wall of their living room.

The scripture today invites us to focus not so much on the message as on the messenger. Most often, the word of God comes to us through other people. Some, including preachers in church, will be very conscious that it's God's word that they are seeking to put across. Others will help us understand what it is that God wants to say to us simply by a casual word, or even by their silent example. These 'messengers' could be wholly unaware of having passed on a message from God, but they may nevertheless have been used by God to put across whatever it is that God wants to say.

Maybe today there is someone who will bring you the good news of the gospel. How will you recognise them, and how will you welcome them?

† Lord, help me to recognise those who bring your word to me, to welcome them and to be grateful for the gift that they bring. Amen

For further thought

• Can you recall any of the times and places when God has used you as a messenger, bringing the good news to those around you?

Tuesday 8 May
Meditate in order to appropriate

Read Psalm 119:1–16

I delight in the way of your decrees as much as in all riches.
I will meditate on your precepts, and fix my eyes on your ways.

(verses 14–15)

As I write these words, a meeting of representative Jesuits from throughout the world is taking place in Rome. These meetings only happen about once a decade, and recent ones have all produced documents to adapt and guide Jesuit lives and works to better meet contemporary needs. This time around, the question is being raised insistently: how can such documents best be appropriated? How do we move from paper and ink to a powerful force capable of transforming every aspect of our lives and ministries?

Such concerns are not foreign to the psalmist. The Law, the Jewish Torah, offers people the word of God, the teaching that God wishes to offer them. How does this become an active force in the lives of those who will read it, from one generation to the next? 'Meditation' is the main answer that the psalmist offers. A deliberate pondering of what is written, carried out in a prayerful setting, while asking to be enlightened by God.

Notably, what accompanies this meditation is delight. It is a privilege to be brought the word of God, not a burden. Even if I first find myself acknowledging ways in which I fall short of the Law's demands, ultimately it will reveal to me a God whose love and faithfulness far outshine my own fitful response. Once I have experienced that, I will undoubtedly want to pass the experience on to those whom I meet.

† Lord, come to meet me as I ponder your Law. Help me to see how I can best apply it to my own life today. Amen

For further thought

• If somebody asked you to demonstrate some of the effects that God's message has in your own life, how would you respond?

Why parables?

Read Matthew 13:10–17

Blessed are your eyes, for they see, and your ears, for they hear. Truly I tell you, many prophets and righteous people longed to see what you see, but did not see it, and to hear what you hear, but did not hear it.

(verses 16–17)

'The medium is the message.' These words of Marshall McLuhan are an invitation to consider the form in which God chooses to transmit the good news. It is clear from the gospel that Jesus had one preferred way of doing this: by telling parables. A parable in its original form is not a story in which each element has a single fixed meaning. It is, rather, meant to be provocative, inviting the hearer to wrestle with its meaning. In telling a parable, Jesus doesn't hope for the response, 'Ah yes, now I understand, it's all clear now!', so much as 'What on earth was all that about?' as you go away turning his words over and over in your mind and heart.

To make the content of a parable your own in this way, though, requires time and effort. Then, as now, many of those who heard these stories were unable, or unwilling, to grapple with them in the way that they demanded. It is clear from the gospels that Jesus recognises this, but considers that it is worth the risk to put his message across in this way. Even when the disciples question him, suggesting that he might do better to speak more plainly, he is not to be deterred.

Only, perhaps, in struggling to see what a parable means will you come to that moment of insight that the story is meant to lead you to. Then, but only then, you come to know the truth of Jesus' own reflection on this whole process. 'Blessed are your ears, for they hear.'

† Help me, Lord, to engage with the words of your stories, so that I may more fully come to know their meanings in my own life today. Amen

For further thought

• Which of Jesus' parables is your favourite? What makes you choose that one in particular?

Thursday 10 May (Ascension Day)
Look around, not up

Read Acts 1:1–11

Suddenly two men in white robes stood by them. They said, 'Men of Galilee, why do you stand looking up towards heaven? This Jesus, who has been taken up from you into heaven, will come in the same way as you saw him go into heaven.'

(part of verses 10–11)

You have probably had the experience of seeing a loved one off on a journey, and watching until they turn the corner at the end of the road, or their bus or train disappears into the distance. It is natural, then, to feel a moment of emptiness. When will you see them again? What do you do now? That is the moment at which we catch the disciples at the end of this account of the ascension of Jesus.

It is at this moment that the two mysterious men in white appear, traditionally identified as angels, messengers from God. These are very no-nonsense angels! Their message is simple and direct. Stop gazing into the sky, and get on with it. There's work to be done, while you wait for Jesus to come back (as he undoubtedly will).

Karl Marx attacked Christianity in part because he thought that it prevented people from tackling the social problems that were all around them, encouraging them instead to gaze passively into the sky waiting for a saviour to come and rescue them. His critique had some point to it. Those who hear God's message are meant to respond by looking around them and acting as Christ would do – to reach out to the needy people that they encounter. We are people invited to look around, not up.

† Lord, keep my gaze on the people you send my way, so that I may use your power to meet them in their need, as I wait for you to come again. Amen

For further thought
• Take time to gaze around you today, just as Jesus might do. What do you notice, and how might you respond to what you see?

How do you come to know Jesus?

Read John 14:15–24

Judas (not Iscariot) said to him, 'Lord, how is it that you will reveal yourself to us, and not to the world?' Jesus answered him, 'Those who love me will keep my word, and my Father will love them, and we will come to them and make our home with them.'

(verses 22–23)

It is possible to study scripture objectively, dispassionately, in the same way as you might study Roman history or French literature. There are doctorates to be gained in outlining the social structures of Galilee in the time of Christ, or establishing the most accurate text of a Greek manuscript. Such study can be of great value to believers, helping them come to a deeper understanding and appreciation of the context of Jesus' life and ministry. But Jesus did not come principally to provide material for doctoral studies!

This passage speaks, rather, of a message that can only be adequately understood by those who commit their lives to it, who allow it to shape them and their relationships, to transform the ways in which they relate to the world around them. Only in this way can its promise, that God will make his home with them, be realised. But to those who will commit themselves in this way, the promise is assured.

Here, then, is a choice and a challenge. By all means study the scripture as an ancient text, with all the academic and analytic tools that scholarship makes available. But will you at the same time commit your life to it, allowing it to guide and mould you? For only in this way will its deepest meanings be revealed.

† Lord, help me to live your message more fully day by day; so that by living it, I may come to know the message, and you the messenger, more deeply. Amen

For further thought

• Can you think of something that you have come to know about God through your experience of trying to live as a disciple of Jesus?

Knowing through arguing

Read Acts 1:12–14

They returned to Jerusalem from the mount called Olivet, which is near Jerusalem, a sabbath day's journey away. When they had entered the city, they went to the room upstairs where they were staying ... constantly devoting themselves to prayer.

(part of verses 12–14)

Chaim Potok's novel *The Chosen* presents a vivid picture of life in a *yeshiva*, a Jewish school of scripture study. Far from being a place of academic calm and silence, the school is full of noise and argument as the students vigorously debate the meaning of the texts, and come to grips with them through vocal prayer and repetition. This is the way, it's suggested, that the message of God can best be understood and made one's own.

After the ascension, Luke tells us in Acts, the disciples return to Jerusalem and gather in prayer, waiting for the promised coming of the Spirit. Traditional views present a circle of venerable men and women, with Mary the mother of Jesus at their centre, peacefully contemplative as they wait. Maybe, though, the reality was more like a *yeshiva*. Fierce debates about what to do now. Shouted recollections of things that Jesus had said, and arguments about what he had meant. Urgent prayer for guidance, with growing confidence in the power of the message they had been entrusted with.

Luke reminds us later that 'the whole group of those who believed were of one heart and soul' (Acts 4:32). This fundamental unity gives freedom to explore the deeper meaning of Christ's message, and how it is to be applied to the world. So Paul can disagree with Peter, and Barnabas with Paul, and we can see more clearly because of their debates. If fellowship and study are important for coming to grips with God's message – and they are – they thrive on vigorous exchange and exploration of contrasting views.

† Help me hear your message in words of those with whom I agree, and of those with whom I disagree. Speak your words in unfamiliar ways and places, that I may discover a greater God. Amen

For further thought

• Read a familiar Bible passage today in a translation other than the one you usually use. What might you learn from these less familiar words?

May

Going viral: communication in the Bible – Paul Nicholson SJ

Going viral: communication in the Bible
3 Tuning in

Notes by **Catherine Williams**

 Catherine Williams is an Anglican priest working in discernment and selection for the Ministry Division of the Archbishops' Council in the Church of England. Her role is to facilitate the processes by which new clergy are selected to train for the ordained ministry. Catherine lives in the English town of Tewkesbury and works in London. She is married to Paul, also a priest, and they have two adult children. Catherine is also an experienced spiritual director. In her spare time she enjoys singing, theatre, cinema and reading and writing poetry. Catherine has used the NRSVA for these notes.

Sunday 13 May
Renewing the team

Read Acts 1:15–26

Then they prayed and said, 'Lord, you know everyone's heart. Show us which one of these two you have chosen to take the place in this ministry and apostleship from which Judas turned aside to go to his own place.'

(verses 24–25)

This week we continue our exploration of the ways that God and his people communicate with each other, and especially some of the mystery, challenges, and sticking points that are indicated in scripture and continue to be experienced today. Our readings lead us into the great festival of Pentecost and the outpouring of God's Holy Spirit on all who have faith in Jesus.

We begin today with the disciples after the ascension waiting for what's to come next. Turning to the scriptures Peter discerns that if this emerging community is to be an integral part of the renewal of Israel then they need to restore their core leadership to 12, after the betrayal and death of Judas. Just as Jesus chose the original 12, so his followers pray to the Lord to guide their decision-making. Lots are drawn. Matthias is chosen.

How often do we remember to turn to God when we have important decisions to make that affect the Christian community? Do we believe that God will lead us through prayer, a mature use of scripture and the wide consultation of the people of God? Do we trust that God will make his ways clear in the Church today?

† Lord God, teach your Church to listen for your guidance. Send your Holy Spirit to lead us into all truth. Amen

Monday 14 May
Teach me

Read Psalm 119:25–40

Teach me, O Lord, the way of your statutes, and I will observe it to the end.
Give me understanding, that I may keep your law and observe it with my whole heart.

(verses 33–34)

Have you ever had a time when you've hit rock bottom and felt that you could go no lower? It may have happened through bereavement or chronic illness, or through committing acts that you knew to be very wrong, and you were ashamed and horrified by your behaviour. The psalmist articulates just such an experience in the passage today. It's like lying in the dust – returning to the earth from which we were formed. The sadness is so great that it feels like we are in danger of dissolving away and ceasing to exist. We are terrified that we will be humiliated. Whilst we might want to hide away from everyone and especially from God, our faith teaches us that this is the time to turn back to our Creator and trust in his love for us. It is through fuller engagement with God that new life comes and new beginnings are possible.

This psalm shows us powerfully how to ask God to lead and guide us into new life. The psalmist asks God to teach, lead, help, give and confirm. Our response to the possibility of a new beginning is to motivate ourselves to learn more of God's ways and to grow in understanding of God's promises. These will come to fulfillment when, with humility, we apply ourselves to God's ways and turn our hearts again to follow him. Whole-hearted engagement with God, turning again to his word, both in scripture and in Jesus, especially when we are in a very demoralised state, is the way to resurrection and new life.

† Lord, you are the source of hope and life. Help me to keep learning and growing in faith. Be my constant teacher, and continually guide me in your ways. Amen

For further thought

• In what areas of faith do you need to widen your understanding? Ask God to help you grow and develop in faithfulness and love.

Going viral: communication in the Bible – Catherine Williams

Sharing the load

May

Going viral: communication in the Bible – Catherine Williams

Read Numbers 11:4–29

The Lord came down in the cloud and spoke to him [Moses], and took some of the spirit that was on him and put it on the seventy elders; and when the spirit rested upon them, they prophesied.

(part of verse 25)

God has rescued the Israelites from slavery and provided daily food that can be turned into interesting and nutritious meals. However, they continue to grumble and complain to each other and to Moses. They have selective memories – longing for the succulent food of Egypt but forgetting their harsh enslaved conditions under Pharaoh. Moses is exhausted trying to lead such a tetchy crowd and he complains to God. He no longer wants to lead and mother these people. He is run ragged trying to satisfy their longings. He cries out to God in his frustration and misery.

God hears and comes up with a plan that makes all the difference. God divides the spirit that rests on Moses so that the 70 elders can share the joys and burdens of prophetic leadership. Moses is delighted and relieved that others are joining in the task of stepping up to lead, and he looks forward to a time when all God's people will receive the spirit and prophesy. God hears the cries of the Israelites too and provides an abundance of quails to satisfy their longing for meat.

How often do we fail to appreciate God's provision and long for something more? Do we remember a time before we followed Jesus and think it was all easier then? Do we complain and grumble to others but forget to tell God when we are struggling? And if we're a church leader do we take upon ourselves too much responsibility for others? Shared leadership ensures that no one gets overburdened and all God's people are nurtured and enabled to flourish.

† Lord God, thank you for your many gifts, and especially for the gift of the Holy Spirit who enables me to witness to Christ and lead others in faith. Amen

For further thought

• How is leadership organised in your church? What more could be done to enable leaders to work collaboratively? How might you make a difference?

Wednesday 16 May
Signs of commitment

Read Proverbs 3:1–10

Do not let loyalty and faithfulness forsake you;
bind them round your neck,
write them on the tablet of your heart.

(verse 3)

On the third finger of my left hand I have a small gold ring. My husband has a matching one and we've been wearing them for 30 years. Round my neck I have a gold cross, and most days I wear a white piece of plastic in the collar of my shirt. If I were to lose one of these tokens I would be very upset, not because they are expensive or valuable in monetary terms, but because what they signify – my marriage, Christian discipleship and priesthood – are beyond price. The promises, commitment and vows made to God have deep roots from which flow out love, faithfulness and loyalty to others – family, friends and strangers.

The writer of the book of Proverbs urges God's followers to hold fast to God's commandments forever. Following instructions in Deuteronomy, many Jews to this day wear phylacteries containing scriptures on their forehead and left arm during prayer. These symbolise that God's Law is written on their hearts. Sometimes it is helpful to have an outward symbol to remind us of, and communicate to others, our inner commitment. These small things indicate a deeper and permanent truth about where our faithfulness and loyalty lie and whose ways we are following. The writer of Proverbs reminds us that God must come first – in our loving, giving and decision-making, and with this primary commitment life is assured. A South African pastor taught me this saying many years ago: 'It's our job to be faithful, and God's job to provide.' When we are faithful we discover God's overwhelming provision.

† Lord God, may my heart be engraved with loyalty and faithfulness to you. May all those I meet see your ways of truth and love reflected in my words and actions. Amen

For further thought

• 'It's our job to be faithful, and God's job to provide.' In what ways does this saying ring true in your experience of faith?

May

Going viral: communication in the Bible – Catherine Williams

Thursday 17 May
God: yesterday, today and forever

Read Psalm 77

> I will call to mind the deeds of the Lord;
> I will remember your wonders of old.
> I will meditate on all your work,
> and muse on your mighty deeds.

(verses 11–12)

There may come a time in our Christian journey when God seems very distant or appears to have abandoned us. Despite our faith, difficulties arise, and we can be ambushed by life events, injustices or destructive thoughts and actions. Being a follower of Christ does not protect us from all the world might throw at us, or from our own inner negativity and doubts. Many mature Christians can point to such periods in their lives, sometimes called a 'dark night of the soul', and to the growth and renewed faith that can come from working harder to hear God, crying louder for help, and being truly honest about negative, angry or ambivalent feelings that have arisen.

Through his lamenting the psalmist shares with us such a time from his own life, and offers guidance for dealing with his sense of abandonment. It feels to him as though all God's promises have ceased, and God has forgotten how to be gracious and loving. Faithfulness in such adversity is retained by recalling God's mighty acts and works of goodness and grace from the past, and making them live again in the present. He remembers that God is a God of mercy, faithfulness and hope who loves and saves his people. God is constant and his future acts will mirror his past engagement. Christians have an advantage over the psalmist. We can also recall God's greatest act of all time – the giving of himself in Jesus for the salvation of the cosmos. We can trust that however dark and chaotic life becomes, God will break through.

† Thank you Lord, for your constant love and mercy throughout history. Help me to share news of your goodness and grace, especially with those who are struggling with faith. Amen

For further thought

• Read regularly God's mighty acts in scripture so that you have a solid supply to draw on when believing becomes tough and God seems distant.

Friday 18 May
Beyond conversion

Read 1 Corinthians 2:1–13

We speak God's wisdom, secret and hidden, which God decreed before the ages for our glory.

(verse 7)

How did you come to faith? Do you remember? Perhaps you were born into a Christian family and learned to love the Lord Jesus as a child. Perhaps you were taught the stories of Jesus at school and chose to follow him then. Or maybe someone told you about Jesus when you were an adult, and carefully led you into the kingdom. You may have had a dramatic conversion experience and met the Lord in a dream or vision, like Paul. Writing to the Corinthian Church, Paul was at pains to stress that by the power of the Spirit he delivered the message of Jesus Christ crucified as plainly as he could. It is the power of God working through the incredible act of Christ's death and resurrection that brings about conversion, not human wisdom or persuasion. It reminds us that as ambassadors of Christ we need to communicate the basic Christian story and allow the Holy Spirit to work through our simple words and actions, transforming hearts and minds.

However, faith doesn't end with conversion and to come to the full stature of Christ and a mature faith, Christians need to explore and engage with the deep mystery of God. There is always more to learn of God. However much we seek we will never, in this life, know all there is to know of God. But because we have received the Holy Spirit we can begin to grasp some of God's hidden wisdom. It's important that we continue to learn, grapple with scripture, discuss with others and explore our faith with openness and humility.

† Lord, thank you for those who have shared their faith with me. Help me to tell the good news of Jesus as simply as I can, trusting in the power of your Spirit. Amen

For further thought

• The Christian community is divided on a number of issues. Choose one and explore it fully, investigating all sides. What do you learn?

Going viral: communication in the Bible – Catherine Williams

May

139

Getting ready to celebrate

Read Psalm 51:1–12

> *Create in me a clean heart, O God, and put a new and right spirit within me ...*
> *Restore to me the joy of your salvation, and sustain in me a willing spirit.*
>
> *(verses 10, 12)*

As we come to the end of this week so we turn our attention to tomorrow's great festival of Pentecost, when we celebrate again the pouring out of the Holy Spirit onto all who follow Jesus. Psalm 51 is often used at times of corporate repentance such as Ash Wednesday and during Lent. It helps us to prepare for celebrations by reminding us of our need to confess our sins, repent and be washed so that we can receive afresh God's power and joy within us. The psalmist asks to be purged and scrubbed clean deep within so that even his bones can jump for joy.

The good news is that God's grace is sufficiently vast to forgive and renew us over and over again, however far we fall. The psalmist asks for a clean heart and a new and right spirit. These are the words that priests say as they ritually wash their hands before presiding at the Eucharist. It reminds them that it is by the grace of God that they handle holy things, and it is Jesus who is the host at the table – welcoming everyone who comes. Through the shedding of his blood salvation is open to all and a fresh start is truly possible.

We started this week with the disciples renewing their number so that they were fit and ready to receive God's power. It's good to spend time today preparing ourselves so that tomorrow we too can celebrate the gift of the Holy Spirit given to all those who confess Jesus Christ as Lord.

† O God, help me confess today so that I am washed clean and ready to celebrate Pentecost tomorrow with all the saints, past, present and yet to come. Amen

For further thought

• Wear something red, yellow or orange tomorrow to celebrate the fire of God's love shown through the giving of the Holy Spirit.

Going viral: communication in the Bible
4 Going viral

Notes by **Tim Yau**

Tim Yau is a Pioneer Missioner who works for the Anglican Diocese of Norwich. His role is to establish a worshipping community in the new housing development of Round House Park, Cringleford, and also act as a Mission Enabler encouraging Fresh Expressions of Church across the region: 'not trying to get people to go to church, but trying to get the church to go to the people.' To his children's delight, he is a Star Wars geek and still dreams of becoming a superhero. Tim has used the NIVUK for these notes.

Sunday 20 May (Pentecost)
Spirit speak

Read Acts 2:1–13

When they heard this sound, a crowd came together in bewilderment, because each one heard their own language being spoken.

(verse 6)

I was flying to an international conference, and was told on arrival I'd be picked up by a local driver. Entering the airport lobby I was confronted with a confusion of handwritten signs being brandished at me and a myriad of voices vying for my attention, none of which I recognised or understood. As I waited, all that activity and sound just became background noise. Unable to be distracted by the incomprehensible conversations and public-address announcements, my mind switched off. As the hours went by I started to daydream about what I'd do if the driver didn't turn up. I felt a long way from home. Suddenly, a voice broke through my mental fog, asking me in broken English, 'Are you Tim?' Hearing and understanding those three simple words meant I was known, and was saved from a hungry night alone, sleeping on a cold airport floor.

That voice was important to me that day. How much more significant is it that at Pentecost, God's Spirit spoke to the people of the nations in their own language, not just for ease of communication, but to declare that they too were known by God, and included so that they could hear the message of true salvation and the wonders of God?

† Holy Spirit, equip us to speak your words of wonder and salvation to the nations in our neighbourhoods. Amen

Monday 21 May
Spirit sermon

Read Acts 2:14–21

Then Peter stood up with the Eleven, raised his voice and addressed the crowd: 'Fellow Jews and all of you who live in Jerusalem, let me explain this to you; listen carefully to what I say.'

(verse 14)

Where were you celebrating on the eve of the millennium in 1999? Can you place yourself on 9/11 when Al-Qaeda attacked the New York World Trade Center? Most of us would be able to pinpoint our whereabouts on such universally memorable and world-changing days. However, some important occasions go by unnoticed and it's not until much later that the significance of them is fully recognised. For example, it was in March 1989 that an English computer scientist, Tim Berners-Lee, invented the World Wide Web, which ushered in the Digital Age and became the primary way for billions of people to communicate across the internet.

Pentecost was the ushering in of a new Holy Spirit Age; it was memorable, world-changing and unprecedented. It ultimately decentralised the way God communicated, interacted and inhabited the world. From the Temple in Jerusalem to the temple of the human heart. From one High Priest to the priesthood of all believers. From the Jewish people to the people, tribes and tongues all over the world. God was doing a new thing, but not everyone understood.

Enter the apostle Peter, an uneducated fisherman from a sleepy backwater in Galilee. He stands before the erudite urbanites of Jerusalem and the multicultural, multilingual pilgrims from across the Roman Empire and preaches. By the empowering of the Spirit, Peter recalls the promises in scripture and is enabled to speak with such clarity, persuasiveness and authority that 3,000 believe. We may not feel qualified, and probably won't have to preach to thousands, but the Spirit wants to inspire and equips us to speak out too.

† Holy Spirit, use us to boldly proclaim the transforming message of Christ, not relying on our own ability, position or qualifications, but on the power of God to speak through us. Amen

For further thought

- How does God want to use your personal experience of him to communicate his message?

Tuesday 22 May
Spirit song

Read Psalm 98

> *Sing to the Lord a new song,*
> *for he has done marvellous things …*

(verse 1a)

In my youth I had a sparkly red guitar. I'd dream of playing to arenas of admiring fans, but I only ever achieved the deafening squeal of feedback. So goes my adolescent love affair with being an indie-rock star, all pomp and posturing and no skills or songs.

Sometimes we want to be the centre of attention, to be loved, worshipped and adored. When we were babies we cried and we were attended to, we smiled, giggled and burped and we were fussed over. Our every action was scrutinised and graciously dealt with. Thankfully most of us grew out of this and learned to think of others, but there is that residual narcissistic inner 'rock star baby' that lingers. That song is about the self.

At other times in life our attention is focused on another, whether it's the passionate confusion of unrequited love or the selfless, overstretched, exhausted parent who frantically tries to soothe and serve their child. Occasionally, when we are emotionally drawn into a one-sided relationship, we lose ourselves. That song is about the other person.

The psalmist offers us another option. Not a song about you or them, but a new song to God. Not a one-sided solo, but a melody that echoes back God's salvation love and creates harmonies with the whole of creation. Our new song joins with all the heavenly hymns throughout history and resonates with the original song of love that spoke the universe into being. Our new song is no longer self-important or self-deprecating, but subjects ourselves to God's sovereignty and consequently all the blessings of that station.

† Holy Spirit, sing a new song in us, that we may sing a new song to God, so that the world can hear the song of salvation and join the song of heaven. Amen

For further thought

• If we sing what we believe and believe what we sing, what are we communicating? What are the 'marvellous things' we should be singing about?

May

Going viral: communication in the Bible – Tim Yau

Spirit signs

Read Acts 2:37–47

Everyone was filled with awe at the many wonders and signs performed by the apostles.

(verse 43)

One summer I holidayed in the Wolfgansee Valley, part of the Austrian Alps. From my chalet in St Gilgen I was surrounded by peaks higher than any found in Britain. Mount Schafberg dominated the view at 5,850 feet high, and so I decided to climb it. The mountain was the classic squat triangular shape. However, once I reached the crown I realised that on the other side the slope fell away into a vertical cliff, creating breathtaking views of distant vistas unexplored. Here I noticed two main reactions from fellow tourists: some boldly advanced to the edge, hunkered down and lingered, awestruck; others gingerly approached and then beat a hasty retreat in fear.

After Pentecost the fellowship of believers was beginning to grow, not just by persuasive preaching, or compelling teaching, but by the miraculous acts of the apostles. Our reading says that 'everyone was filled with awe', which seems positive; however, I imagine it also divided people. Interestingly the Greek word *phobos*, used for 'awe', is often also translated as fear: that which strikes terror and makes people want to flee.

We know that not everyone believed and followed this new emerging faith. For some the miraculous signs gave the apostles divine authentication, for others the supernatural wonders caused apprehension, confusion or scepticism. When I first began to follow Jesus I was desperate to experience a miracle. I thought I'd be able to point any cynics to the extraordinary occurrence and prove God's existence. Some amazing things did happen, but sadly they didn't make everyone believe. My miracle was not everybody's miracle moment.

† Holy Spirit, we pray for wonders, not for our own benefit but as signs that God is present and active. We ask for miracles so that the world would know and follow the miracle-maker. Amen

For further thought

• What miracles does your community long for? Do you have the faith for it? If signs and wonders happened would there be more faith or fear?

Spirit season

Read Joel 2:23–32

> '*And afterwards, I will pour out my Spirit on all people.*
> *Your sons and daughters will prophesy,*
> *your old men will dream dreams,*
> *your young men will see visions.*'

(verse 28)

I came to faith in the Pentecostal Church, and although it wasn't perfect, the one thing that it did excel at was its expectation that the Spirit would pour out on all people. The culture of anticipation would manifest in various ways, some more extreme and ecstatic than others. The attitude was that God would do what God wanted to do, and we therefore shouldn't constrain how the Spirit would speak through us and to us.

Joel's prophecy comes during a time of extremes, wavering between misery and hope. Most scholars place it during the period of the Jewish return from exile, when the Judean community endeavoured to make sense of their feelings of God's absence during a succession of calamities. We join the prophecy at a joyous point where God responds to the people's repentance, frees the land and promises an era of restoration and prosperity. Then comes this prophecy, which is picked up by Peter in Acts 2, an assurance that 'before the coming of the great and dreadful day of the Lord' (verse 31), all within God's covenant community will receive the Spirit, regardless of age, gender or status. This meant that the Spirit would no longer be given to a select few for specific tasks, but inaugurate a new season fulfilling the hope of Moses who said, 'I wish that all the Lord's people were prophets and that the Lord would put his Spirit on them!' (Numbers 11:29).

Today prophecy is rarely about foretelling the future, but commonly about forthright speech, calling God's people back to right living, faith sharing and sacrificial service.

† Holy Spirit, we pray that you will grow in us an expectation that you will use us for prophecies, dreams and visions. Give us courage to speak out and faith when you seem silent. Amen

For further thought

• What would prophecy, dreams and visions look like in your community? If God seems silent, what might be interfering with you hearing God's prophetic voice?

May

Going viral: communication in the Bible – Tim Yau

Friday 25 May
Spirit sending

Read John 20:19–23

Again Jesus said, 'Peace be with you! As the Father has sent me, I am sending you.' And with that he breathed on them and said, 'Receive the Holy Spirit.'

(verses 21–22)

There's an old camp song I used to sing in the Scouts: 'Everywhere we go/ People always ask us/ Who we are/ Where we come from/ So we tell them/ We're from … / And if they cannot hear us/ We shout a little louder.' The chant started off as a whisper and got progressively louder until it was shouted at full volume, coming to an abrupt end by replacing the final line with, 'Well then you must be deaf.'

I think this song would have been apt for the early apostles as they travelled by foot on their long and arduous missionary journeys. As they walked and discussed the emerging faith an early catechism must have begun to form in their minds. The reading today starts to map out some of those questions. Who are we, where are we going, what are we going to do and how are we to do it?

The 'who' question is easy to answer; we are the people who follow Jesus, the one who was crucified, died and entombed, but lives forever. For the 'where' and 'what' we have the Great Commission: 'go and make disciples of all nations, baptising them in the name of the Father and of the Son and of the Holy Spirit, and teaching them to obey everything I have commanded you' (Matthew 28:19–20). For the 'how' Jesus spells it out in what I call the Greater Commission (verses 21–22). Being sent, like Jesus was sent, empowered by the Holy Spirit, and with all the sacrificial implications that go with that sent-ness.

† Holy Spirit, send us out in your strength, not our own. Guide us to go and make disciples of all nations, and help us to embody Christ in our thoughts, words and actions. Amen

For further thought

- If sent-ness is about incarnation – embodying a Christ-like life for the transformation of others – what does your sent-ness look like and how is it expressed?

Spirit symbolism

Read Revelation 22:1–5

Then the angel showed me the river of the water of life, as clear as crystal, flowing from the throne of God and of the Lamb down the middle of the great street of the city.

(verses 1–2a)

In my 20s I went through a relationship break-up. To get some perspective on it I went to visit a friend in London, but even there I struggled to shake off my grief and couldn't pull out of my despair, so we decided to go for a walk. We went silently side-by-side for hours, punctuated with angry outbursts, followed by tears. We lumbered on until we came across a river running fast and free across the tarmac. With our curiosity provoked we followed the flow until we found its source, a burst water pipe jetting high into the air. The long cathartic walk in the humid summer night had physically drained me, so without a second thought I stripped off and leapt through the spray. Suddenly we began to laugh; the invigorating waters, the physical exercise and my friend's prayerful Spirit-led attentiveness had cleared my emotional fog and that fortuitous fountain was the symbol of the beginning of my healing.

The reading today paints a picture of restoration, well-being and abundance. God descends with the New Jerusalem to be with humanity on a new earth, picking up on the prophetic writings of Ezekiel 47:1–12 and Zechariah 14:8, but ultimately drawing on the imagery in Genesis 2. The earth is made like new again, Eden is restored with God's glory not confined within a temple, but at the very centre of a garden city. Flowing from the throne of the Father and the Son comes 'the river of the water of life', a potent symbol of the Holy Spirit, forever refreshing and renewing the divine urban paradise.

† Do not cast me from your presence or take your Holy Spirit from me. Restore to me the joy of your salvation and grant me a willing spirit, to sustain me (Psalm 51:11–12).

For further thought

- In scripture water is one of the symbols of the Holy Spirit. What does this communicate to you and what hope does this offer others?

May

Going viral: communication in the Bible – Tim Yau

Readings in Mark (2)
1 On the road

Notes by **Michiko Ete-Lima**

Michiko serves alongside her husband, Peletisala Lima, for the Congregational Christian Church of Samoa in Fairfield, Australia. She is passionate about working with women of the parish, as well as the young people, and watching them grow spiritually in God's Word and ways. She loves visiting different eateries and then burning off the calories at the local gym. She also enjoys watching a good movie. She enjoys her quiet times and learning more about Jesus Christ daily. Michiko has used the NRSVA for these notes.

Sunday 27 May
Death and new life

Read Mark 6:14–29

King Herod heard of it, for Jesus' name had become known. Some were saying, 'John the baptiser has been raised from the dead; and for this reason these powers are at work in him.'

(verse 14)

Who is Jesus to you?

This week you are invited to consider this question, and many others, as we continue our readings in the Gospel set for this lectionary year, the Gospel of Mark.

Today's reading begins with Mark relaying the emotions of Herod as he listens to the different interpretations of who people say Jesus is. The one interpretation that is of great significance to Herod is that Jesus is the reincarnation of John the Baptist. This interpretation causes Herod to replay in his mind the actions that took place when he ordered the beheading of John the Baptist.

Herod is distraught, and his replaying of the John the Baptist situation could have been avoided had Herod accepted Jesus Christ for who he really is. Herod would have come to the realisation that accepting Jesus into his home would mean a new life for him, and one that has a hopeful future and not one that replays a person's past mistakes. How can you begin a new life in your reading of Mark this week, rather than replaying past mistakes?

† Dear Lord, open our eyes so that we may accept you for who you are; for you have given us life and life abundantly. Amen

Readings in Mark (2) – Michiko Ete-Lima

Monday 28 May
Unexpected guests

Read Mark 6:30–44

Taking the five loaves and the two fish, he looked up to heaven, and blessed and broke the loaves, and gave them to his disciples to set before the people; and he divided the two fish among them all.

(verse 41)

At every major Samoan event, food will always play a pivotal role. Providing a feast is an indication that those who are responsible for the event are generous and capable. When anyone asks about an event they would normally want to know about the kind of food that would be served and of course if there would be enough for all. The success of any major event would be based upon the quantity of food!

In this story, we see that Jesus and his disciples are responsible for the event taking place and we, too, can imagine the horror of the disciples as they see the numbers. For them, there is the obvious fear that they are unable to provide for all those who have come. It's almost like a family who have a wedding and can see that the people they invited have brought over more people than expected. Panic! How can they provide for all the guests present?

The worry presented by the disciples shows that they themselves are not too sure about what Jesus can do. They didn't know that Jesus could feed a multitude from just a few food items. It is in the realisation and the full knowledge that Jesus truly is our provider that we let go of our worries and doubts.

† Dear Lord, let us not focus on what we do not have but be reassured of what we have in you alone. Amen

For further thought

• What are the customs of hospitality in your own culture? How are these the same or different from the customs in your church community?

Readings in Mark (2) – Michiko Ete-Lima

Food for the fearful

Read Psalm 111

He has gained renown by his wonderful deeds;
the Lord is gracious and merciful.
He provides food for those who fear him;
he is ever mindful of his covenant.

(verses 4–5)

As a lover of movies, I look forward to trailers to decide the next movie that I will see. Trailers will highlight the exciting parts of the movie and will naturally present what they know will attract the potential viewers.

This psalm is very much a trailer for the works of Jesus as presented by the Gospel writers. It highlights the great works of Jesus. In our reading yesterday, verse 5 was enacted in the feeding of the multitude: 'He provides food for those who fear him.' Further, the 'wonderful deeds' in verse 4 and the 'power of his works' in verse 6 correspond to the many miracles and healings performed by Jesus. Verse 9 then relates the ultimate act whereby Jesus Christ is 'sent' to be the redemption for all.

Psalm 111 is a beautiful recognition of how great and wonderful our God is. It even provides a preview of how God's greatness and love are performed graciously by Jesus Christ, our redeemer.

† Dear Lord, thank you for sending your Son Jesus Christ who loves us unconditionally and faithfully. Thank you that his love is personified in great and wonderful deeds. Amen

For further thought

• What do you think it means that the 'fear of the Lord is the beginning of wisdom' (verse 10)?

Reflection and action

Read Mark 6:45–56

Immediately he [Jesus] made his disciples get into the boat and go on ahead to the other side, to Bethsaida, while he dismissed the crowd. After saying farewell to them, he went up on the mountain to pray.

(verses 45–46)

I enjoy getting up early in the morning to have my quiet time with the Lord. I read God's word and then pray a prayer of thanksgiving for blessing us with a new day, and pray for renewal of strength for the duties and tasks of the day to come. My prayer time rejuvenates me and I feel that I can handle the responsibilities and tasks that need to be performed throughout that day.

In today's passage, Jesus has taken time out to pray. Jesus has just finished feeding the multitude and then he purposely makes his disciples leave so that he can have his time alone to pray. After his time of prayer, Jesus walks on water and then heals the sick. These are deeds and feats that would require physical and spiritual strength. It is no wonder that Jesus took time out to pray. Jesus knew the power of prayer and the need for prayer in order to successfully perform the related miracles.

When I read this passage I am keenly reminded of how important prayer is. If the Son of God needed to take time out to pray, how much more do we need to?

† Dear Lord, help us realise that only with a strengthened relationship with you in our prayers are we able to successfully perform our given tasks and responsibilities. Amen

For further thought
• How much time would it add to your morning or evening routine to set aside a restful moment with God?

May

Readings in Mark (2) – Michiko Ete-Lima

Thursday 31 May
Open heart procedure

Read Mark 7:1–23

He [Jesus] said to them, 'Then do you also fail to understand? Do you not see that whatever goes into a person from outside cannot defile, since it enters, not the heart but the stomach, and goes out into the sewer?'

(part of verses 18–19)

In many places around the world, it is common to be given a bowl of water to wash one's hands before one starts the meal. It is all for the sake of hygiene and so one can easily relate to the beginning of today's passage. The Jewish custom related in this story is readily seen in many other cultures.

What is unique in today's passage is how Jesus almost qualifies what a person eats. Jesus clearly states that all food is clean (verse 19). Jesus then goes on to say that it is not so much the food that we eat that will 'defile' a person, but rather it is what we say. So rather than the popular idiom, 'we are what we eat', this verse is rather saying, 'we are what we speak.'

It connotes a clear relationship between the words that we speak and what it is that we have in our hearts. So when we speak evil, hatred and dissension, we are merely projecting what is in our hearts. When we speak of life, goodness and kindness, again we are conveying our hearts. This passage really highlights the importance of our words. The words we speak will show to all the heart we have inside.

† Dear Lord, renew our hearts and minds daily, so that we may speak words of compassion, goodness and kindness. Let our words be a true reflection of our hearts that are based on your love and mercy. Amen

For further thought
• In biblical Hebrew there is no word for 'mind', and the word for 'heart' often fulfills this function.

Friday 1 June
Bold outsider

Read Mark 7:24–37

But she answered him, 'Sir, even the dogs under the table eat the children's crumbs.' Then he said to her, 'For saying that, you may go – the demon has left your daughter.' So she went home, found the child lying on the bed, and the demon gone.

(verses 28–30)

In the story of the Syrophoenician woman, Jesus recognises the woman's faith and then releases the woman's daughter from the bondages of the demon. Jesus is clearly stronger than any evil force that might tie a person down. The forces may come to us in different forms. For some it may be the addiction to alcohol, for others it is the addiction to drugs. Still for others there is the force of gluttony.

This story reminds us that no matter what the powerful forces are in our lives, our faith in Jesus Christ and our true acceptance of what Jesus can do will release us from these strongholds. We need to have faith like the Syrophonecian woman to overcome whatever might hold us back in our lives.

Both the Syrophoenician woman and the friends of the deaf and mute man are insistent that Jesus act on their behalf. Jesus listens, reaches out and heals. What difference does their insistence make?

† Dear Lord, give us faith in you so that we may overcome and remain strong in our lives and be healed of any sickness. Blessed be your name, Jesus Christ. Amen

For further thought
• What do the Syrophoenician woman's boldness, and Jesus' response, suggest about what Jesus desires for our relationship with him?

June

Readings in Mark (2) – Michiko Ete-Lima

Saturday 2 June
Second sight

Read Mark 8:22–26

Then Jesus laid his hands on his eyes again; and he looked intently and his sight was restored, and he saw everything clearly.

(verse 25)

As a person who is far-sighted I can readily relate to this passage – in particular when the man said that he 'can see people but they look like trees walking'. I can see people at a distance but their faces are always a blur. Often I have been known to wave frantically to someone, thinking it was someone else. I now try to avoid waving at people when I am not wearing my glasses.

When reading this passage, I am intrigued by the fact that Jesus takes this man out of the village and heals him. Then once he is healed, Jesus says to him to go straight home and not into the village. It is as if Jesus does not want spectators to this particular miracle.

I wonder if when we spend quality time with Jesus alone our spiritual eyes are attuned and opened. When we deliberately take ourselves out and make time to spend alone with Jesus, our eyes will truly see the great miracles and the blessings that Jesus performs in our lives.

† Dear Lord Jesus Christ, help us to see you more clearly. Open our eyes to see the wonders of the miracles that you perform. Amen

For further thought
• What is blocking the sight of your 'spiritual eyes' at the moment? Can you ask for healing to see more clearly?

Readings in Mark (2)
2 On the holy mountain

Notes by **Paul Faller**

Paul Faller taught in Catholic primary and secondary schools before becoming National Coordinator of Religious Education at the Catholic Institute of Education in Johannesburg. He works to promote meditation in schools, distance learning in religious education, and research into a new curriculum. He holds a Masters in Theology from St Augustine College in Johannesburg and a Masters in Religious Education from the Australian Catholic University. Born in Cape Town, he is married with a 14-year-old son. Paul has used the NIVUK for these notes.

Sunday 3 June
Starting the journey

Read Mark 8:27–9:1

Then he called the crowd to him along with his disciples and said: 'Whoever wants to be my disciple must deny themselves and take up their cross and follow me. For whoever wants to save their life will lose it, but whoever loses their life for me and for the gospel will save it.'

(verses 34–35)

Who is Jesus of Nazareth? This is the crucial question raised in the passage, and all this week in Mark. Whatever the prevailing popular opinion about him was – and by this time in his life people had begun to take notice of his challenging words and actions – Jesus puts the question squarely: 'But who do YOU say I am?'

There's clearly a difference between knowing someone and knowing about them. I can read a biography of, say, Martin Luther King and answer any number of factual questions about him. But I cannot claim to know him on that account. I need at least to walk and talk with him. For you and me today, the question Jesus poses entails a journey, an encounter with and a dwelling within his spirit.

And what will the nature of this journey be? After Peter's rebuke of Jesus, and Jesus' rebuke of Peter in turn, Jesus sets out the way, instructing all within hearing what the title Messiah, Christ or Anointed One really means. In response to Peter, Jesus calls himself Son of Man, or, as Chet Myers puts it, the Human One (in *Binding the Strong Man: A Political Reading of Mark's Story of Jesus*, Orbis Books), indicating that the journey is not just for Jesus, but for any and every human being wishing to be part of the Body of Christ.

† Most merciful Redeemer, Friend and Brother, may we know you more clearly, love you more dearly, and follow you more nearly, day by day. (Richard of Chichester)

Monday 4 June
Encouragement on the way

Read Mark 9:2–13

His clothes became dazzling white, whiter than anyone in the world could bleach them. And there appeared before them Elijah and Moses, who were talking with Jesus. Peter said to Jesus, 'Rabbi, it is good for us to be here.'

(part of verses 3–5)

What is it about being on the mountain? It is a place of solitude, far from the bustle of the marketplace, where horizons are expanded beyond the everyday and great clarity of vision is enjoyed.

To learn about the way of Jesus would seem very discouraging, ending as it does, to all appearances, in the cross. And so surely it was for Peter, James and John and the other disciples. If this is so, who would want to follow? Is this really the end of the road? And so after the revelation of the way of the cross, the three chosen disciples experience the revelation of its fulfillment.

What about the two figures talking with Jesus? Jesus is the fulfillment of God's revelation that began with the creation of the world. Moses, the bringer of the Law (*Torah*), Elijah, the prophet (*Nebi'im*) who challenged the people to be faithful to the Law, and Jesus, the Wisdom of God (*Kethubim*) which reveals the result of being true to the Law, sum up the whole of scripture (*Tanak*). The voice from the cloud, the vehicle of God's glory, confirms what Jesus had said earlier concerning the way he would walk.

What did Jesus himself experience here? And what will our experience be at the appointed time? Jesus was bathed in a light that transformed his whole being as he was 'taken up' into the fullness of the kingdom. It was for him an encouragement. He was sent back to his mission after a mountain epiphany, as had been the experience of Moses (Exodus 33:18) and Elijah (1 Kings 19:11).

† For the Son of God became man so that we might become God.

– Athanasius, fourth-century bishop of Alexandria

For further thought

• Jesus reveals God, but also what it means to be fully human.

Tuesday 5 June
Causing to stumble

Read Mark 9:42–49

If your hand causes you to stumble, cut it off. It is better for you to enter life maimed than with two hands to go into hell, where the fire never goes out.

(verse 43)

In Africa, when a hunter wants to catch a monkey, he takes a jar with an opening slightly larger than a monkey's hand and places in it some food to attract the monkey. The monkey reaches its hand into the jar and grabs the food, making a fist with its paw. Now, the monkey cannot get its hand out of the jar unless it drops the food. The neck of the jar is simply not wide enough. Of course, the monkey could drop the food and easily get its hand out, but it won't. Despite having at its command the means to escape, it does not – it holds his hand grasping the food until a hunter throws a net over it, capturing it.

Jesus might well have told such a parable had he lived in a different milieu to drive home the truth that to find life, we must be prepared to die to something. Only those who are prepared to leave their possessions behind will survive the sinking ship. Anything that gets in the way of our entering the kingdom of God has to be let go of.

Hands are for doing: we should cut out any action that diminishes God's reign. Feet are for walking: we should go where the Spirit leads and not walk into the trap like the monkey. And eyes are for looking, but we should not be fascinated by the careless freedom of the fool.

† Christ has no body now but yours. Yours are the eyes through which he looks. Yours are the feet with which he walks. Yours are the hands through which he blesses all the world.

– Teresa of Avila

For further thought

• When stressing a point, Jesus often uses hyperbolic or exaggerated language. Is he really asking us to maim ourselves? No, but the kingdom is worth any sacrifice.

June

Readings in Mark (2) – Paul Faller

The way children travel

Read Mark 10:13–16

'Truly I tell you, anyone who will not receive the kingdom of God like a little child will never enter it.' And he took the children in his arms, placed his hands on them and blessed them.

(verses 15–16)

Jesus brings the least of the least in his society – the children – into the centre of the community, rescuing them from the margins. He hugs them, showing affection; he lays his hands on them, giving them a certain standing; and he blesses them, making them happy despite their status. He does this for two reasons. Firstly, this is another instance of the gospel paradox: the first shall be last and the last, first. Jesus affirms the little ones for it is to them that the kingdom belongs.

The second reason is this: St John of the Cross describes the soul as 'an unopened parcel and only God knows what He has put in it'. In childhood the parcel is almost transparent, but in the adult the unopened parcel is now covered over with many layers of wrapping and string tied with hard knots. The many layers of wrapping in the adult soul are there for security, but the transparency that children experience allows them to see. This is why Jesus says, 'In truth I tell you, anyone who does not welcome the kingdom of God like a little child will never enter it.'

And so the theme of our readings continues. What must we leave behind if we are to enter the kingdom? In this instance it is the typical attitude of the adult. In contrast, we need to reawaken the qualities that are characteristic of childhood. Children are open, receptive, grateful and full of wonder at life. Indeed, because of where they are on the social scale, they intuitively know that all things come to them as gifts.

† I praise you, Father, Lord of heaven and earth, because you have hidden these things from the wise and learned, and revealed them to little children.

– Matthew 11:25

For further thought

• What are we doing today in our homes and churches to prevent children from approaching Jesus? And what attitudes within us prevent us from entering the kingdom?

Thursday 7 June
The cost of the journey

Read Mark 10:17–30

Jesus looked at him and loved him. 'One thing you lack,' he said. 'Go, sell everything you have and give to the poor, and you will have treasure in heaven. Then come, follow me.'

(verse 21)

In yesterday's passage, Jesus emphasised the need to receive the kingdom like a child, being open, receptive and content to be dependent on others. This may sound easy and comforting, but there is a paradox here. There is great effort involved in becoming like a child and receiving the kingdom. However, Jesus assures them that all things are possible with God. Here again is good reason not to rely on one's own status and strength of character, as it seems the rich young man did, but to let go of what gets in the way, making space for what is really worthwhile.

While effort is required, there is reward to look forward to as Jesus promises. In leaving one's soul in trust to God, one receives a hundredfold in this life and inherits eternal life into the bargain. Who, indeed, is more generous! The rich young man was being encouraged to give his riches to the poor, or, in other words, to invest them in God's bank which pays dividends way beyond one's dreams.

There is another side to riches, whether legally gained or otherwise. In his response to the rich man, Jesus puts justice before piety, teaching the need to distribute wealth across society more fairly rather than simply staying on the right side of the law – keeping the commandments – in one's economic dealings. Jesus' critique at the same time debunks the prosperity gospel – the teaching that wealth indicates a blessing from God, and poverty a curse – that is spreading in various countries among the greedy and gullible.

† It is only through the poor we can offer anything to God, who also has need of the poor in order to ask anything of us.

– Francis of Assisi

For further thought

• To be in the kingdom of God means to be a child of God, and as a child of God the kingdom is one's inheritance.

Turning the world upside down

Read Mark 10:31–45

'Whoever wants to become great among you must be your servant, and whoever wants to be first must be slave of all. For even the Son of Man did not come to be served, but to serve, and to give his life as a ransom for many.'

(verses 43–45)

Jesus and his followers are on the road to Jerusalem, the place of God's peace. It is a road strewn with difficulties, even persecution, but a road that leads to fullness of life. This is the road, too, for his followers today.

It is understandable that the disciples – and we, perhaps – are bewildered and follow with faint hearts, and they try to motivate their perseverance on the way by asking for a particular reward. Having witnessed the power of Jesus in so many instances, they are not shy to treat him almost like the genie of the lamp. 'Will you give us whatever we ask for?' While it was not in Jesus' power to grant this particular request, they would have done well to recall the saying from Isaiah (64:4), later elaborated by Paul: 'What no eye has seen, what no ear has heard, and what no human mind has conceived – the things God has prepared for those who love him' (1 Corinthians 2:9).

There is deep irony in the situation at the end of Jesus' earthly road that the two who 'sat at his right and left in glory' at the coming of the kingdom were the two thieves on the cross. As in so many instances that we have met in these readings, there is an inversion of what we – and they – would expect.

And there is a further irony in the last phrase of this passage. Jesus 'gives his life as a ransom for many'. But the freedom his death brings inverts the way of slavery or servanthood into the way of liberation.

† God, grant me the serenity to accept the things I cannot change, courage to change the things I can, and wisdom to know the difference.

– Reinhold Niebuhr

For further thought

• Freedom grows from the decision to open our hearts and minds to God's will, and to acknowledge our dependence on God as a child would.

Saturday 9 June
Reaching our destination

Read Psalm 110

> *The Lord says to my lord:*
> *'Sit at my right hand*
> *until I make your enemies*
> *a footstool for your feet.'*

(verse 1)

Most commentators read this psalm as one used in the Temple for the investiture of the king as the vice-regent of God. Sitting at the right hand of God indicates this, as it is a place of honour. The psalm, while difficult in part to understand, is nevertheless important, as it foreshadows God's Messiah, Jesus, whose victory over his enemies is assured.

But Jesus' victory on the 'day of battle' is not brought about by 'crushing the rulers of the whole earth'. Again, we witness a paradox: victory is gained when the King is crushed by these rulers – the social, political and religious leaders of the land. The cross absorbs the venom of evil and renders it powerless.

The psalm also affirms the union of throne and altar in the kingdom of God when the oracle pronounces the Messiah as priest of the order of Melchizedek. Melchizedek, priest-king of Salem, as narrated in Genesis 14, in bringing bread and wine, also foreshadows the gifts that Jesus gives to his disciples the night before he dies.

Yesterday we reflected on the request of James and John to sit either side of Jesus in his glory – a request Jesus was not able to grant. Yet, just as this psalm foreshadows Jesus enthroned, James and John could take comfort from an earlier promise that Jesus had made: 'Truly I tell you, at the renewal of all things, when the Son of Man sits on his glorious throne, you who have followed me will also sit on twelve thrones, judging the twelve tribes of Israel' (Matthew 19:28).

† At the end of our journey may we hear your words: 'Well done, good and faithful servant! You have been faithful with a few things; I will put you in charge of many things. Come and share your master's happiness!'

– Matthew 25:23

For further thought

• Where shall we sit on the day of victory? Let us be humble and hope to hear the words: 'Friend, move up to a better place' (Luke 14:10).

Readings in Mark (2) – Paul Faller

Readings in Mark (2)
3 In the holy city

Notes by **Raj Patta**

Raj Patta is ordained in the Andhra Evangelical Lutheran Church, a South Indian church of approximately 1.5 million members. Until 2014 he was the National General Secretary of the Student Christian Movement in India and he previously worked for the National Council of Churches in India in their advocacy work for Dalit Christian rights. He is from Andhra Pradesh, India, and is married to Shiny. They have two sons. Raj blogs at www.thepattas.blogspot.com and is passionate about reading the Bible from the margins of society. Raj has used the NRSVA for these notes.

Sunday 10 June
Hosanna – save us!

Read Mark 11:1–11

> 'Hosanna! Blessed is the one who comes in the name of the Lord! Blessed is the coming kingdom of our ancestor David! Hosanna in the highest heaven!'
>
> *(part of verses 9–10)*

Jesus' political march in the streets of Jerusalem was well-supported by the people, the citizens of that nation who were shouting, 'Hosanna to the son of David, blessed is the one who comes in the name of the Lord! Hosanna in the highest heaven!' In contrast to the empire slogans of 'hail Caesar', the co-citizens of Jesus were shouting, 'Hosanna, son of David.' This was the genuine yearning of the citizenry as they were looking for 'freedom' from these oppressive political regimes. Save us from what? Or save us from whom? The shouts could have been 'Save us from Rome' or 'Save us from Caesars', which depicts the peoples' anti-empire cries and aspirations to save them from the rule of oppression.

Today and all this week, the call is to commit our faith communities to join with Jesus on his march against empire, shouting 'Hosanna! God save us from these oppressive regimes of our times!' Jesus' alternative to the Roman Empire, which he inaugurated in the kingdom of God, should be our public faith, narrative and our aspiration.

† God of liberation, help us join with Jesus in the mission of liberation today, and every day. Amen

Monday 11 June
Clean hands and pure hearts

Read Psalm 24

Who shall ascend the hill of the Lord? And who shall stand in his holy place?
Those who have clean hands and pure hearts, who do not lift up their souls to what is false, and do not swear deceitfully.

(verses 3–4)

Psalm 24 is considered to be an entry song into the Temple, and this psalm sings of the sovereignty of God over all that is in the earth. For me, however, reading this psalm in the context of an Indian caste system which is run on notions of purity and pollution, it becomes spiritually and theologically difficult. Dominant caste groups discriminate against people born outside of that system by denying them entry to the holy rooms of the temples. Is it possible to find words of life in Psalm 24 for India today, and for us all?

The psalmist mentions four requirements for those who seek entry to the holy place: those who have clean hands, those who are pure at heart, those who resist falsehood and those who do not make deceitful promises can enter. These characteristics contradict the characteristics of temple entry based on descent, occupation, colour, caste and class, for God invites all people irrespective of their identities and ethnicities. God's place is for all people in all places, for 'the earth is the Lord's and all that is in it', and no barrier or hurdle may deny the entry into God's presence.

The challenge for us is to resist all barriers and divisions that hinder people coming into God's presence. Our churches and worshipping places should be inclusive, welcoming and hospitable to all, with a preferential option for those outside of our memberships and church buildings.

† God of all, the earth is yours and all that is in it. May all people find welcome in you. Amen

For further thought

- How can we as faith communities become just, inclusive and hospitable? Make a theological audit of your church based on the qualifications in Psalm 24.

Tuesday 12 June
Overturning empire

Read Mark 11:15–19

He [Jesus] was teaching and saying, 'Is it not written, "My house shall be called a house of prayer for all the nations?" But you have made it a den of robbers.'

(verse 17)

In the context of Roman colonisation, the Temple in Jerusalem became a centre for money exchange, selling, buying and other commercial activities. Jesus resisted the empire tooth and nail, and to express his public protest against empire he drove out all those engaging in commercial activities, overturned the tables of money-exchangers and 'would not allow anyone to carry anything through the temple' (verse 16). The last point may reflect Jesus' concern to protect the holiness of the Law of God rather than the law of empire.

In the context of Palestinian struggle for justice and liberation, the Boycott, Divestment and Sanctions (BDS) campaign against occupation and on goods from such territories is an act which resonates with the acts of Jesus, for both express their resistance against empire. When the powerful oppress others, Jesus' actions and voice come alive, for he shouts: 'My house shall be called a house of prayer for all the nations … But you have made it a den of robbers.' Jesus drives away the occupiers, the robbers and the settlers who have taken faith, spirituality and religiousness captive. He attempts to liberate the vulnerable and protect their spaces, lands and rights to live.

The call for us is to join with Jesus in resisting and driving away the forces of occupation and join in liberating vulnerable people, wherever they are found around us.

† God of liberation, may our zeal for you burn brightly enough to overturn all who oppose you and your rule of justice and peace. Amen

For further thought

• How can we as faith communities join in movements to show our commitment to Jesus' movement against empire?

Wednesday 13 June
Discipleship and citizenship

Read Mark 12:13–17

Jesus said to them, 'Give to the emperor the things that are the emperor's, and to God the things that are God's.' And they were utterly amazed at him.

(verse 17)

Those in the corridors of power were leaving no stone unturned in their effort to provoke Jesus, frame him on sedition charges and arrest him. His protest against all the forces of the empire was dangerous. 'Is it lawful to pay taxes to the emperor or not?' came the question; 'Give to the emperor the things that are the emperor's and to God the things that are God's' was Jesus' reply. It was one of his best theological articulations about empires and faith in God. By this reply, Jesus distinguishes between emperor and God, for in his context of the Roman Empire, emperors were ascribed divinity and divine was understood in terms of emperorships. Jesus publicly breaks that forced norm. He challenges the society to give boldly the things that are God's and not to compromise in that giving because of the oppressive regimes of empire.

Historically the state ascribed the divine powers to itself, and made citizens subject to it. The state and those in power have always spoken in the categories of faith, and controlled the communities in the name of God and faith. Today, the challenge for us is to be and become 'faithful citizens'; as citizens we should be faithful to our God, and as faith communities be responsible citizens questioning the normativity of power and oppression. In other words our citizenship should complement our discipleship, and our discipleship should correspond to our citizenship.

† God, guide us so that our discipleship is reflected in our citizenship, and our citizenship is rooted in our discipleship. Amen

For further thought

• How can speaking in defence of freedom of religion be an aspect of Christian discipleship?

Readings in Mark (2) – Raj Patta

Spirituality of scripture

Read Mark 12:18–27

Jesus said to them, 'Is not this the reason you are wrong, that you know neither the scriptures nor the power of God?'

(verse 24)

After the turn of the Pharisees to try to trap Jesus, now it's the turn of the Sadducees. The Romans' colonial project worked on the principle of 'divide and rule', and therefore encouraged the theological rivalry between the Pharisees and Sadducees. Now it is on the doctrine of resurrection that the Sadducees want to put Jesus in a fix and want to score a point over the Pharisees by quoting the scriptures. Jesus is presented with an ethical case study on marriage and resurrection. In turn, Jesus confronts his questioners by exposing their ignorance of the scriptures and of the power of God.

This incident brings to the fore how scriptures have been used, misused and even abused in practice. In support of racism scripture is (mis)used, in support of patriarchy scripture is (mis) used, in support of heterosexuality as the only acceptable sexuality scripture is (mis)used, in support of prosperity and money-making as blessings scripture has been (mis)used. In the case of caste systems, Hindu scriptures are invoked. Jesus exposes our ignorance, and our misuse and abuse of scriptures, for it is the 'Spirit of the letter' that is of faith relevance today. The Word became flesh in Jesus Christ, and we are called to interpret the signs of our times from such a perspective, for the power of God in scripture is revealed by that principle.

† Gracious God, may the power of your Spirit lead and convict us to seek justice and liberation from our reading and rereading of your scriptures. Amen

For further thought

• How is 'rereading' the Bible different from 'reading' it? How is it the same?

Friday 15 June
Loving God, loving neighbour

Read Mark 12:28–34

When Jesus saw that he answered wisely, he said to him, 'You are not far from the kingdom of God.'

(part of verse 34)

In the Roman Empire, love for the emperor and the unquestioning submission to the empire were demanded. Therefore, Jesus openly refuted and contested one's submission and devotion to the empire by emphasising love of God and neighbour in his answer to the scribe. These commandments must never be eclipsed by the love for emperor and empire. In this way, Jesus displays open resistance to such commandments. Love of God and neighbour has a clearly subversive anti-colonial spirituality.

When the enquiring scribe in this text echoes these commandments and further extends them by discounting the ritual practices of the Temple in burnt offerings and sacrifices, Jesus recognises that this scribe is nearer to the kingdom of God. The reign of God contrasts with the rule of the empire, for in the former, love of God and neighbour take centre stage and become foundational. The kingdom of God is found in acts of love, and comes closer in all such practices and performances.

Let us therefore resist and defeat all forces of empire in our times, and allow ourselves to stay nearer to the kingdom of God by loving God and by loving our neighbour unconditionally!

† God of love, let us dedicate ourselves to stand firm, committed to love you and our neighbour today and every day, and make your rule a reality for our times. Amen

For further thought

• Do you think nations have a duty of love to other nations, or only individuals to other individuals?

Saturday 16 June
Hypocrisy and condemnation

June

Readings in Mark (2) – Raj Patta

Read Mark 12:35–44

'Truly I tell you, this poor widow has put in more than all those who are contributing to the treasury.'

(verse 43)

Jesus' final public theological engagement both condemns and commends. He condemns the hypocrisy of the unjust scribes, who in their lust for power exploit the vulnerable. On the other hand he commends the poor widow for her generosity in comparison to the rich, who give lavishly at the Temple.

Jesus publicly condemns the hypocrisy of the religious authorities; they have been deceiving the colonised communities and devouring widows in the name of God. They 'for the sake of appearance say long prayers', for they wanted to project themselves as pious and saintly, putting up an external pseudo-spirituality. Jesus not only exposes their pseudo-spirituality, but also prophesies 'great condemnation' as their reward in the presence of God.

At the treasury of the Temple, Jesus commends the poor widow, for she by contrast loved God in her poverty and gave generously. Jesus is not concerned about the amount of giving, but rather observes givers' intentions and their love for God. The wealthy put in large sums as offerings from their unaudited and unaccounted sums of money that they had plundered from the poor. Jesus wasn't concerned with who was the highest giver to the treasury of the Temple.

Our calling is to give up hypocrisy, pseudo-spirituality and external displays of faith and instead encourage a spirituality that allows us to give our full and best to God.

† Loving God, drive away our hypocrisy in our lives, and help us be humble and generous in our giving. Amen

For further thought

• Whom would Jesus single out today as examples of hypocrisy and greed?

A place to stay
1 Wandering

Notes by **Deseta Davis**

Deseta Davis is currently an assistant pastor of a Pentecostal church. Her main vocation is as a prison chaplain helping to bring hope to those who are incarcerated. Having obtained an MA in theological studies, she previously worked as a tutor in Black Theology, bringing the study of theology to a range of people who had not considered such study. Deseta is married to Charles; they have two grown-up children and a granddaughter. Deseta has used the NRSVA for these notes.

Sunday 17 June
Nowhere

Read Luke 9:57–62

And Jesus said to him, 'Foxes have holes, and birds of the air have nests; but the Son of Man has nowhere to lay his head.'

(verse 58)

Homelessness is a worldwide problem. Today, as in first-century Palestine, people are forced to wander around finding a place to sleep wherever they can.

Jesus told the young man who wanted to follow him that even the unclean scavenger animals such as foxes and birds had somewhere to live. In comparison, Jesus himself had nowhere to lay his head.

Today, many sleep in doorways and shelter where they can. Sometimes their only covering is a cardboard box. Others wander from place to place, village to village or country to country seeking refuge.

Jesus identifies with each and every one. He knows what it's like to be rejected. He knows how it feels to be hungry. He knows the degradation of sleeping where he could find a boat or a friend's bed. He knows what it is like to wander around depending on people's generosity. He had nothing to call his own, nothing that belonged to him.

Many people wanted to follow Jesus but some turned back when they found he had nothing physical to offer. This week we discuss the pain of wandering around, depending on others and just hoping and praying for a change in situation.

† Homelessness may happen because of war, displacement or even family break-ups. Pray for those who are homeless in your area.

Monday 18 June
There but for the grace of God!

Read Genesis 4:8–16

Cain said to his brother Abel, 'Let us go out to the field.' And when they were in the field, Cain rose up against his brother Abel and killed him. ... And the Lord put a mark on Cain, so that no one who came upon him would kill him.

(verses 8, 15)

Cain was punished for committing one of the worst crimes known to the human race at the time. He killed his brother. It was the first recorded murder and he killed his own flesh and blood. Part of his punishment was that he would be a restless wanderer on the earth. Cain felt that his punishment was too harsh and God, in his mercy, put a mark upon him to stop anyone taking revenge for the crime that he had already committed.

Crimes like this are a lot more common today. In some situations we may have become desensitised to some of the crimes and accept them as a fact of life, yet we still expect the perpetrator to be punished. Some people say, 'lock them up and throw away the key – they take too much of the taxpayers' money.'

Yet what did God do to Cain? He made him a wanderer with nowhere to settle, destined to find a space and bed down where he could. Yet God, although expecting Cain to take his punishment, put a mark on him – isn't that an act of grace?

As much as we expect people to be punished for their wrongdoing, we need to have some aspects of grace. Many perpetrators of crime come out of prison and end up wandering around with nowhere to live. They continue to be punished. However, like God, we need to have empathy and treat those who have fallen out of the way with grace and mercy.

† Gracious God, many prisoners and victims are suffering because of crime. Please help prisoners to see the errors of their ways and make right where they can and give the victims the grace to forgive. Amen

For further thought

- Is there anything you can do to help people in your area transitioning from life in prison to life in society?

Theirs today, ours tomorrow

Read Genesis 7:1–16

And Noah with his sons and his wife and his sons' wives went into the ark to escape the waters of the flood. … And those that entered, male and female of all flesh, went in as God had commanded him; and the Lord shut him in.

(verses 7, 16)

On entering the ark, Noah and family were obliged to give up their home and all their worldly goods and sail away – not knowing where they were going or what lay ahead.

Many people cannot escape the ravages of nature. In some areas the sun burns the land, leaving no water to grow the crop and people die from starvation. Yet there are other areas where there is so much rain the crops drown and people then die from the floods as well as lack of food. How do they escape?

The weather causes many people to flee their homes, seeking a place where there is food and water. They walk for miles and become refugees in other lands. The land they have reached could be a land of protection. Yet in some lands, rather than refuge or asylum, people find hostility and hatred.

God made a way for Noah. God shut the door of the ark, shut his creatures in for protection and helped them to escape. Like God, those in affluent lands must be careful to show love and protection to asylum seekers and refugees. The weather is very unpredictable; *any* land could be swallowed up in floods. In the past few years, the UK has had many floods, and as I write I hear that parts of the USA are also flooding. We expect help when we are suffering the ravages of the weather as we move around trying to find alternative accommodation. The question is, will we help others who are suffering today? Remember that what is theirs today, may be ours tomorrow.

† Loving God who controls the winds and the waves, please help those who are displaced due to weather patterns. May they find a place of peace and refuge. Amen

For further thought

- What is your national government doing to prevent global warming?

June

A place to stay – Deseta Davis

Somewhere over the rainbow

Read Genesis 12:1–9

Now the Lord said to Abram, 'Go from your country and your kindred and your father's house to the land that I will show you.'

(verse 1)

Leaving home can be an exciting time if you know where you are going and have put things in place. Yet it can also be a very daunting prospect depending on the circumstances.

During my college course, I wrote a poem about a migrant family, leaving their home due to a drought. It started with:

> I had a nice home back there, somewhere.

It wasn't the best poem but I always remember the first line – 'back there, somewhere'.

The lives of migrants were the same then as now: people walking for miles to evade war and drought, leaving home, risking their lives, not necessarily knowing where they are going but hoping and praying they will find a better place somewhere.

Somewhere, over the rainbow… Many people are looking somewhere over the rainbow where there are no sounds of bombs. Somewhere they will get some food and live a little better than where they have left behind.

Abraham leaves his home with all his possessions for a land 'somewhere'. Not knowing where he was going or what it would look like when he reached there, but hoping to find that land of milk and honey. Today people are trying to find the Promised Land only to realise that they are strangers in an unfriendly world.

† Pray for those who are searching that they may find that land over the rainbow where they can be free.

For further thought

• Put yourself in the place of a migrant family seeking a new land. Write a poem, song or story about your journey.

Women in poverty

Read Ruth 1:1–5

The name of the man was Elimelech and the name of his wife Naomi, and the names of his two sons were Mahlon and Chilion; they were Ephrathites from Bethlehem in Judah. They went into the country of Moab and remained there.

(verse 2)

Moab was one of the nations that oppressed Israel during the time of the Judges, and there was constant hostility between the two nations. Friendly relations with the Moabites were discouraged. Yet due to a famine in Judah, Elimelek, Naomi and their family moved to Moab and lived what seem peaceable lives. Their sons even married Moabite women, which was strictly forbidden by Jewish Law.

The time came when all three women lost their husbands to death. Suddenly they were all widows. There was nothing worse than being a widow in ancient Israel. You were poor, taken advantage of and ignored, especially if you had no sons. Women had no rights as property was passed down from father to son – this left women in financial ruin. Women belonged to men, whether to a father or husband.

Today there still remain gender disparities in poverty. Women tend to be disproportionately poor. According to the United Nations, in many countries, women continue to be economically dependent on their spouses. In developing countries, statutory and customary laws continue to restrict women's access to land and other assets, and women's control over household economic resources is limited.

Naomi leaves Bethlehem to escape the famine, yet she ends up in a bigger famine than she started with. She now has no husband or sons and is left with two other women with no access to land or food. Left with nothing, her only answer was to go back to Bethlehem (which she heard now had food) and try her luck.

† Gracious God, help us to remember those in poverty, especially the women who have no access to land or other assets. May we help in any way possible. Amen

For further thought

• If you do not already do so, how about contributing to a charity that helps to alleviate poverty?

June

A place to stay – Deseta Davis

Friday 22 June
Love thy neighbour

Read Ruth 1:6–18

But Ruth said, 'Do not press me to leave you or to turn back from following you! Where you go, I will go; where you lodge, I will lodge; your people shall be my people, and your God my God. Where you die, I will die – there will I be buried.'

(part of verses 16–17)

We continue from yesterday where we heard that Naomi, Ruth and Orpah had just lost their husbands. Naomi hears there is food in Judah and encourages her daughters-in-law to go back to their home. She had lost every source of security and comfort and was returning to Bethlehem to a life of loneliness and despair. She had nothing left to give them except a life of poverty and pain. As a widow, Ruth would have been better staying in Moab as there were few suitors in Judah and there was no guarantee she would be accepted.

Ancient Israel believed the Ammonite or Moabite could never enter into the assembly of God (Deuteronomy 23:3). Ruth as a Moabite had no right to worship the God of Israel, yet her heartfelt words in verses 16–17 have resonated down the ages.

'Your people shall be my people, and your God my God.' Ruth worshipped the God of the Israelites and was accepted. She eventually married Boaz and became the grandmother of King David and ancestor of Jesus Christ.

God does not work according to race, gender or nationality. Ruth is one of the few women included in the genealogy of Jesus in Matthew's Gospel. No matter their background, people enter countries with differing skills and abilities. Given a chance they may become someone great in the history of the country. As God accepted Ruth, the Moabite, may we follow his example and accept those that may be 'different' from us and treat them with respect.

† Loving God, as you make us all one in you, may we be open to diversity and make people feel at home in our presence no matter their background. Amen

For further thought

• In recent years, especially in Africa and the Middle East, the world has seen the largest numbers of displaced persons ever in recorded history. How do Ruth's words apply to current situations?

Whom do you identify with?

Read Luke 10:1–11

'Go on your way. See, I am sending you out like lambs into the midst of wolves. Carry no purse, no bag, no sandals.'

(part of verses 3–4)

Sending his disciples out, Jesus told them to bring no money, traveller's bag or sandals. These were basic travelling items in first-century Palestine. As they were travelling to different cities, how could they travel without them? Just as Jesus lived among the people; without money, the disciples were expected to identify with the poor. Without a bag, they could bring no food and therefore identify with those that were hungry. People who were in mourning in those days did not wear sandals; the disciples were to identify with them also. They were to live among the people and accept their hospitality. Whoever was kind enough to give them a place to stay, they would stay with until they travelled to the next town. Thus they were identifying with Jesus.

In his Sermon on the Mount in Luke 6, Jesus pronounced a blessing on all these categories of people: those that are poor, those who mourn and weep, those who are hungry and those that are hated for the cause of the gospel. Without their basic travelling items, the disciples would no doubt know how it feels to be poor, hungry and in mourning and would be able to minister to these people in a much more empathetic way. Jesus goes on to pronounce sorrow or distress on those that are rich, the well-fed, those that laugh and those who are popular and spoken well of.

God is saying the same today. As disciples we are to identify with the poor, hungry and mourners. It is upon these lives that God evokes blessings.

† Dear God, help us to remember that discipleship is about sacrifice. May we identify with those that are on the margins of society so we are able to minister in a much more empathetic way. Amen

For further thought

• Write down ways in which you could identify with those on the fringes of your local community.

June

A place to stay – Deseta Davis

A place to stay
2 Settling

Notes by **Helen Van Koevering**

After living in southern Africa for 28 years, Helen, raised in England, has recently moved to West Virginia, USA, with her US-citizen husband, a bishop in the Episcopal Church. Helen is also ordained in the Anglican/Episcopal Church. She had previously served as a parish priest and as Director of Ministry for the rapidly growing Anglican Diocese of Niassa in northern Mozambique, during a decade of extensive and transformative church growth that doubled the size of the church. She now finds herself settling into a different view of God at work in a new context not of her roots nor of her formation. Helen has used the NRSVA for these notes.

Sunday 24 June
Hopes for a homecoming

June

Read Zephaniah 3:14–20

I will deal with all your oppressors at that time. ...
At that time I will bring you home, at the time when I gather you ...

(parts of verses 19–20)

What does 'home' mean to you? In rural Mozambique, the family unit often lives as one mutually supportive household that includes three or four generations. In developed countries, families tend to live apart – sometimes just a street or block away, but sometimes even a continent away. Some say that home is where you were born or where your roots are. Some infer you can always return to this place, because 'home is where the heart is'.

Migration affects more than those who are doing the leaving. You have been part of 'home' for others wherever you have lived life and connected with others, and your leaving changes their home. Good farewells allow for grieving and healing. New circles of friendship and support take time to develop, possibly cushioned by communities connected by social media. Imagine moving on without those means of connecting, as do so many refugees who flee danger, forced to leave everything and risk life in seeking a new home.

Can God be the place of belonging at the heart of all our human homeward yearning?

† Lord, our Creator and Provider, hold all those unable to feel 'at home' today, whatever the circumstance. May you meet them in their homeward journey. Amen

Monday 25 June
Naomi arrives home

Read Ruth 1:19–22

So Naomi returned [from Moab] together with Ruth the Moabite, her daughter-in-law ... They came to Bethlehem at the beginning of the barley harvest.

(verse 22)

For many years, Naomi, with her husband and two sons, had lived in a strange land. They had left their homeland in time of famine and integrated themselves in Moab society where their sons had even married Moabite women. As a widow and on the death of her sons (how do we name a mother who has lost her children?), Naomi hears of better harvests back home in Judah and sets out to return. No longer a wife nor a mother, she releases her daughters-in-law to start her life again not as Naomi, but as Mara; as bitterness.

In this story, we learn with Naomi that what was thought to be going backwards (see verses 8, 10 and 15) was in fact moving forward. In Ruth's determination to remain with her mother-in-law, 'the two women went on'. In that moving forward, they were going to be redefined in a new place. Ruth's faithful love was to find redefinition in marriage to their kinsman-redeemer, Boaz, and Naomi was to find herself known again as joyfully belonging and included in her community. This remembered identity and inclusion returned love, security and a future not only for her own self but for those throughout time and space. Naomi's grandson, Obed, was to be the grandfather of King David in the family line of Jesus.

† Loving Lord, let me move forward and find newness and identity in you. You hold this world, the past and future, in your hand; may I learn to live the future into my present always. Amen

For further thought

• Take some time to consider the meaning of 'moving forward' and 'arriving home' for you in whatever circumstances you find yourself today.

June

A place to stay – Helen Van Koevering

Paul settles in Rome

Read Acts 28:11–16, 30

'There [in Puteoli, en route to Rome] we found believers and were invited to stay with them for seven days ... The believers from there, when they heard of us, came as far as the Forum of Appius and Three Taverns to meet us ... He [Paul] lived there for two whole years at his own expense and welcomed all who came to see him.'

(parts of verses 14, 15, 30)

The church was receiving a returning missionary family to live and work with them. Marcia brought a chicken dish and a bright bunch of flowers; Kathy had tucked some freshly baked cookies into the basket of 'welcome' goodies that another had put together and John had stocked the fridge. It was also John who came round the next day and took the family shopping. Kent dropped in a couple of days later to offer a tour of the new town. Maybe it was the invitation to do a series of talks about the life that the family had left behind that showed the deepest hospitality and welcome to these strangers in a strange land, and they became guests. Leading a small mission trip back to the old home of the missionaries was the tilting moment, when the guests became the hosts.

Settling involves a process of homecoming. Strangers become guests, and then hosts, and join the onward flow. What is learned is that newcomers are all at some point in this process, and having connections and bridge-making friends provides the movement and makes all the difference. Going through the process opens up awareness of others in the process. Recognising one another as hosts and guests is hospitality. Practise hospitality.

† Lord Jesus, you are the host and the guest at our table and in our companionship on the road. May we learn from you, and live hospitably amongst and with all. Amen

For further thought

• People you meet today may be struggling with strangeness, loneliness, pain and misunderstanding which only God knows. Be hospitable and pray for them.

June

A place to stay – Helen Van Koevering

Seek the welfare of the city

Read Jeremiah 29:1–9

'But seek the welfare of the city where I have sent you into exile, and pray to the Lord on its behalf, for in its welfare you will find your welfare.'

(verse 7)

Moving to an urban setting brings a myriad of new experiences to learn, new cultural cues to acquire, and choices to make – akin to a move to any underdeveloped rural village overseas. Whether moving to the city or countryside, it's deskilling and challenging, destabilising and tiring, and brings excitement, renewal and new opportunities. Recognising commonalities brings potential to the transition.

Annual floods in rural Mozambique hit communities near the rivers Shire and Zambezi and lasted the whole of the rainy season. Resultant food insecurity, sickness and loss of property left those communities vulnerable to hunger, crime, corruption, unstable government and future hardship. Poverty limited the ability of communities to help one another and increased vulnerability and dependence on outside help. Our churches encouraged the mobilisation of communities for their own development and ongoing well-being, and poverty didn't hide the effect of human effort and the desire to respond to communal crisis.

Unexpected spring weather conditions brought flash floods to West Virginian communities, too. Houses were washed away and some lost their lives. Professional 'first responders' as well as folk from the drier end of the street pitched in, providing lodging, food, clothing and transport.

Glimpsing common signs of human agency and God's presence, and seeing a weaving-together of a vision for a future and a common good, we discover clues for prayerful involvement. Praying specifically for peace and prosperity for our neighbours has the power to integrate communities – wherever we find ourselves.

† Lord, teach us to pray for the common good, and for peace and prosperity to be seen in our neighbourhoods, whether cities or villages. May your kingdom come, Lord! Amen

For further thought

• How can you be a part of the change you want to see in your community?

June

A place to stay – Helen Van Koevering

Thursday 28 June
Be subject to the authorities

Read Romans 13:1–10

Owe no one anything, except to love one another; for the one who loves another has fulfilled the law.

(verse 8)

For most of my adult life, I lived in a country struggling to develop and recover from decades of conflict – Mozambique. Although we earned local salaries and lived more simply than we had in our childhoods in the developed world, our neighbours' agrarian lives were much more vulnerable, dependent on the rainfall and surrounded by rumours of renewed conflict and authorities that used corruption to benefit from their power. We were always the outsiders, *mazungus*, except in our immediate *bairro*, churches and marketplaces. Women were always more vulnerable and children's health was always a concern. I learned that personal power (privilege?) could be used to empower others.

It isn't difficult to see the meaning of power in a privileged life when life is lived in the midst of great contrasts. It is harder to see when, even as a stranger settling in a new land, you are no longer the minority but part of the majority race, language and culture. After all the immigration formalities were finally completed, the authorities welcomed me. I continue to be welcomed daily when people hear my accent! Many, many others live as we do, many much better. It takes longer to discover what separates a society between 'us' and 'them', the 'ins' and the 'outs'. From being in the midst of the majority, I am learning that power should be stewarded with others.

In Romans, Paul speaks of loving one another as a debt to the law, the divine authority wherever we find ourselves. Power and love for others, whether they be the privileged or the marginalised, leave us subject to one another. Can we be committed to living a different way, given inner authority to love?

† Trinitarian God, in the power of your love, love is shared with all of us and all creation. Let us be known as those submitted to you in love with all our hearts, souls and strength. Amen

For further thought

• How do you understand your power and privilege, and our call to respond with love in our world?

Friday 29 June
Sharing land and water

Read Genesis 26:12–33

He [Isaac] moved from there and dug another well, and they did not quarrel over it; so he called it Rehoboth, saying, 'Now the Lord has made room for us, and we shall be fruitful in the land.'

(verse 22)

Land and water are both as vital to agrarian and nomadic life as to modern urban life, but it is the urban dwellers who forget most easily as needs are met at the turn of a tap. History and geographical boundaries have been determined by land and water, and they are our concern into the future. Land and water are vital to the story of all creation, integral to the inspiration of art, poetry and music, and as influential to our inner lives as they are necessary to our survival.

Land and water: God's gifts. Though we know that quarrelling over land and water is inevitable, in our reading today we see the presence of a well as a space-creating gift for security, peace, blessing and flourishing. God's gifts: we so easily call his gifts 'ours' and change the meaning of gift to fighting, curse and destruction. Not only that, but our systems create and hold high those who have the power of land and water whilst the majority dwell on the margins unremembered and disempowered by our meaning of poverty.

Technological advance has bridged much of what land and water divided in recent history. Knowing face-to-face how others live out their need and desire for land and water, for daily bread and flourishing, has benefited all. Once you've lived and befriended those on the margins, wherever you settle on the other side of the bridge, life connects together differently. Land and water come together.

† Lord of land and water, may we all hear and see the room and the flourishing you intend for all. Amen

For further thought

• Take some time to learn about a particular country or situation in the world, such as the plight of refugees, and consider your response.

June

A place to stay – Helen Van Koevering

Saturday 30 June
Offering the first fruits

Read Deuteronomy 26:1–15

You shall set it [the basket of first fruits] down before the Lord your God and bow down before the Lord your God. Then you, together with the Levites and the aliens who reside among you, shall celebrate with all the bounty that the Lord your God has given to you and to your house.

(verses 10–11)

The ultimate harvest festival, offering of the first fruits and celebration of God's goodness and God's homecoming is the Thanksgiving holiday in the US. As I write, I look forward to celebrating Thanksgiving for the first time in my entire marriage with my husband's family, and our children will come home to be together with their grandmother, aunts, uncles and siblings – and parents! I love the opportunity for a big feast, and will aim to cook all the traditional dishes – turkey, pumpkin and apple pies, sweet potato – everything! It will be great fun and we all look forward to it.

Not that I haven't celebrated Thanksgiving before, but it has been overseas, where the resources are different and less. Friends gather and find new ways to celebrate Thanksgiving, the giving of thanks to God for all the good things of the last year. Even with families far away, the focus has always been the same – thankfulness.

One brief step connects this thankfulness to Eucharist and the remembrance of the greatest gift always being given. How good it is that *this* thanks–giving is not just once a year! Eucharist invites us to be frequently interrupted by thanks, calling us to newness of life in our gratitude each time. When all of life's rites of passage – the moments of baptisms, weddings, funerals – are marked by such thanks, we practise joyful celebration in our responses to life.

This year, we shall practise joyful celebration of family togetherness and sharing because we can. Moving here has made it possible to be included in celebrations together, the ones specific to a place and a family. It is good.

† With joy, we celebrate your love and life given for us. With thanks, we know our blessing. Lord, we ask that you teach us to pass on that blessing and gratitude. Thank you, Lord! Amen

For further thought

• Refocus your life by writing down some significant thing for which to be thankful every day this week. Keep going for a month. Share your list with a friend. Enjoy!

A place to stay – Helen Van Koevering

A place to stay
3 Welcoming

Notes by **Pete Wheeler**

Pete Wheeler is currently Curate for the Aylesbury Deanery and St Mary's Church, having spent the previous 20 years working as a musician composing, producing and licensing music for film and TV. He trained at St Mellitus College and is married to Ali, a graphic designer. They have two teenagers. Together they have led a Fresh Expression's church, and they speak regularly on ministry for those in their 20s and 30s. As well as music, Pete's hobbies involve not enough golf, some geeky board games, lapsang souchong tea, keeping chickens and the Theology of Wine. Pete has used the NIVUK for these notes.

Sunday 1 July
We were all foreigners once

Read Leviticus 19:33–34

When a foreigner resides among you in your land, do not ill-treat them. The foreigner residing among you must be treated as your native-born. Love them as yourself, for you were foreigners in Egypt. I am the Lord your God.

(verses 33–34)

My friend took his wife along to a church service at which he was the visiting speaker. By the end of the service, no one had spoken to his wife, until, as the lights were being switched off, someone noticed her sitting, waiting.

'Are you OK?' she was asked.

'Yes, I'm just waiting for my husband,' she gently replied.

'Oh!' came the response. 'If I'd known you were his wife, I would have spoken to you earlier!'

Why are we sometimes so slow to welcome or even see the strangers in our midst? Perhaps it is out of apathy or embarrassment. I suspect it might also be a forgetfulness that all we have is given to us by God. At the heart of this teaching is remembering that God not only loved us first, but came looking for us in Eden the moment we went astray (Genesis 3:9). In Jesus we are found, his best cloak wrapped around our shoulders (Luke 15:22).

This week, let's dip our toes into a theology of welcome … for we were all foreigners once.

† Loving Father God, as you have welcomed us, open our hearts to teach us what it means to truly welcome others. Amen

Monday 2 July
Bringing down the walls

Read Ephesians 2:12–22

Now in Christ Jesus you who once were far away have been brought near by the blood of Christ. For he himself is our peace, who has made the two groups one and has destroyed the barrier, the dividing wall of hostility.

(verses 13–14)

Contrary to the values we ourselves were brought up with, my wife and I have tried to encourage our children to (safely) engage with strangers – to be courteous and kind, not keeping their distance.

God does not keep his distance. Even when we were still far off, he ran out to meet us (Luke 15:20). When we fail to welcome others into our own spheres of life, keeping our distance, we build up a 'wall' (verse 14) between us.

These walls get higher when our identities 'in Christ' become second to any cultural, social, tribal, national (or any other) identity that we adopt. Last year I visited Rwanda, where, in 1994, many Christians let their tribal identities outgrow their identities in Christ, leading to genocide. Martin Luther King also spoke of the 'dividing wall of hostility' that is constructed where racism exists.

The Ephesians would have recognised Paul's reference to the walls of the Temple's inner courts, which divided Jews from Gentiles. Paul reminds the Gentiles how they used to be – far away, without hope and without God. Now, Paul describes not just a new person, but a new humanity – united through the faith, love and grace of Jesus Christ!

Make no mistake – this is not a bridge that spans the division. Dividing walls must be completely brought down sooner or later. This is a new unity and equality before God, and therefore with each other.

Now you, too, belong. Your status is no longer refugee, or stranger. You are resident.

† Thank you, Jesus, that you chose to use your own body to bring down the wall of division and hostility. Give me the confidence to welcome those you long to reach. Amen

For further thought

• Listen carefully for the language of wall-building and division – breeding discord and disunity. Learn to recognise it, then pray and act against it.

Abraham and the three strangers

A place to stay – Pete Wheeler

Read Genesis 18:1–8

The Lord appeared to Abraham … while he was sitting at the entrance to his tent in the heat of the day. Abraham looked up and saw three men standing nearby. When he saw them, he hurried from the entrance of his tent to meet them and bowed low to the ground.

(verses 1–2)

Whenever we are at a wedding together, it has become a little tradition that my friend Nicki invites (and eventually has to pester) me to dance with her. Nicki loves to dance, and when she dances I suspect that she 'feels God's pleasure' – in other words, it's a physical expression of the delight with which she lives in relationship with Jesus. She really feels alive when she dances!

We see this dance of delight echoed in the intertwining, mutually glorifying and pre-existent Trinitarian relationship between Father, Son and the Holy Spirit. A bit like a barn dance (a bastion of Englishness and church halls everywhere), into which I have reluctantly been drawn many a time, God welcomes us into this life-breathing relationship – a choreographic adventure! We may not always be able to see the big picture of the part we play (especially when we get it wrong), but we know that, were you to see it from a balcony above, together it is indeed good (and sometimes fun too!).

Abraham hurries to welcome the strangers in – adventure awaits! The artist Andrei Rublev captures just a little glimpse of this idea in his famous fifteenth-century icon, *The Trinity*. It depicts Abraham's three visitors curiously seated around a table, leaving an enticing space that seemingly draws in the viewer. It beckons us to join in their conversation, their meal, their mutual relationship of love and delight – their 'dance'. This is the heart of the Triune God – a relationship that welcomes us in to partake in and enjoy the adventure of life.

† Father, Son and Spirit, thank you for inviting and welcoming me into your wonderful life-giving relationship. Teach me a new dance and take me on an adventure that leads deeper into you. Amen

For further thought

• Want to go just a little deeper in thinking about the Trinity? Michael Reeves' book *The Good God* is brilliant and very easy to read.

From welcome to hospitality ...

Read Ruth 2:1–14

At this, she bowed down with her face to the ground. She asked him, 'Why have I found such favour in your eyes that you notice me – a foreigner?' Boaz replied, 'I've been told all about what you have done for your mother-in-law ... May you be richly rewarded by the Lord, the God of Israel, under whose wings you have come to take refuge.'

(verses 10–12)

Whilst Israel's law demanded certain things for the protection of widows, Naomi was not only widowed, but a foreigner in Moab too. Ruth relieves Naomi of her foreign status, choosing to become the foreigner herself by returning to Bethlehem with her mother-in-law.

Ruth has already gone beyond what Naomi expected of her. But now, Ruth receives similar treatment from Boaz. So, what we notice in this part of the story is how Boaz's response to Ruth echoes Ruth's response to Naomi, going far beyond that which the law expected of him! Like Ruth before him, He acts patiently and wisely, gradually drawing Ruth into his family's protection, to restore Ruth's honour in this foreign society.

It used to be fashionable in the UK for comedians to tell mother-in-law jokes, but I consider myself blessed to have a mother-in-law who has always exceeded my every expectation! She has been a constant provider of security for me and my family. Nevertheless, for many, our family relationships can be some of the most difficult we will ever experience. In the West our culture has lost something of what it means to welcome and care for our extended family.

This passage challenges us to ask ourselves, 'Is it enough to do just enough?' It urges us to think beyond the minimum that might be expected of us. This is when welcome becomes hospitality. The hospitality of God not only welcomes us, but provides for us – lovingkindness, security under his 'wings of refuge', reconciliation, restoration, peace and comfort. This is the God who beckons us in while we are still foreigners.

† You went beyond what I deserved, through the sacrifice of your Son, to restore my honour and bring me home. Help me to go beyond what others expect, to show your love for all. Amen

For further thought

• In what ways might you go beyond the welcome expected of you? I have always found food to be a great starting point for hospitality!

Welcoming Jesus

Read Luke 10:38–42

As Jesus and his disciples went on their way, he came to a village where a woman named Martha opened her home to him. She had a sister called Mary, who sat at the Lord's feet listening to what he said.

(verses 38–39)

At the heart of God's desire to reconcile us to him is a welcoming nature.

My friends, Dan and Benedict, were welcomed into a shop selling old furniture. Despite not having any need for any furniture, an old table happened to catch Dan's eye. Loving a bargain, Dan set about checking it out, while Benedict began chatting to the shop owner. After thorough examination, Dan decided what he was going to offer the owner for the table, and, bolstering himself for the negotiation, marched confidently back to the desk.

He was surprised to discover both Benedict and the owner praying quietly together. Having spent the last ten minutes listening to the shop owner's own spiritual journey, Benedict had asked him if he would now like to renew his faith and resolve to get to know Jesus better.

To truly welcome others into our space, lives and worlds, means being prepared to listen, give them time and learn from them. To 'sit at the feet' of someone means exactly this – to intently listen and learn from their experiences. Whom have you made time to sit at the feet of? Sometimes we learn most from those whom we might least expect.

God desires that our *doing* comes primarily out of our *being* – our actions are to be a response to our new status – being 'in Christ'. Martha's *doing* has taken precedence over her *being*. She often gets a hard time in this story, but I want to finish by noting that it's into her own home that she welcomes Jesus first!

† Holy Spirit, come and fill me anew, that I might be someone who lives in, and responds to, your welcome. Grow in me the skills I need to listen intently to the experiences of others. Amen

For further thought

• Make time today to undertake some new learning. Commit to reading a book, listening to a podcast series or even to 'sit at someone's feet'.

A place to stay – Pete Wheeler

July

Friday 6 July
Welcome. Mentor. Transform. Repeat.

Read Acts 18:1–3

Paul went to see [Aquila and Priscilla] and because he was a tentmaker as they were, he stayed and worked with them.

(part of verses 2–3)

You remember that table I told you about yesterday, the table that my two friends Dan and Benedict went on to buy? It turned out to be an old 'campaign table' – the sort maps would have been laid out on. It looked a mess, but Dan has an eye for things that can be transformed – and not just tables. Dan and his wife Alex live out their faith by continually welcoming people into their lives, and investing in them.

Likewise, Paul, having been welcomed in by Priscilla and Aquila, spent quality time with them making tents. Paul was committed to discipling people through working *with* them in this way, notably Timothy. When we welcome others into our lives we open ourselves to the potential of transformation, through their story and their wisdom. This requires the humility of knowing we are not the finished article, but a tent-in-progress.

Why is this important, that we have these types of relationships? Well … look what happens next, from verse 26 onwards! Priscilla and Aquila empower Apollos for ministry. They see in Apollos a potential and hope. In turn, Priscilla and Aquila invest in Apollos' life, taking him into their home, feeding him and providing for his physical needs so that he can concentrate on the ministry he is called to. They mentor him, they encourage him and they release him to do his work.

This is 'tent-making' – the transformational work of the Holy Spirit. Or to put it another way, have you seen any campaign tables recently that would appreciate some time and attention?

† Teach me, Lord, that to welcome the stranger is to offer myself to you in the hospitality and generosity of your love. Help me to invest wisdom and skills wisely in others. Amen

For further thought

• What has led you to know Jesus more personally – great sermons and talks or the time that you've been generously given and shown by others?

Who are you in the room?

A place to stay – Pete Wheeler

July

Read 1 Corinthians 16:5–11

When Timothy comes, see to it that he has nothing to fear while he is with you, for he is carrying on the work of the Lord, just as I am. No one, then, should treat him with contempt. Send him on his way in peace ...

(part of verses 10–11)

You may have noticed that Christians sometimes talk about being 'sent out'. Christians love to gather and worship together, but equally important is a corporate sense of being sent out into the world. When we feel truly welcomed, comforted and secure in our new Christ-identities we stop building walls and lose our fear of setting foot out in the world again.

Paul desires that, through receiving a proper welcome, Timothy should have 'nothing to fear' in order that he might carry on the 'work of the Lord' (verse 10). To truly welcome others then is to both prefer them, and enable their flourishing – sometimes at the expense of our own time, strength or standing. Yet in doing so, our reflection might be that it was us that truly flourished as a result.

How can you help the person you are welcoming into your country, church or home-space feel welcome and at home? How can you allow them to be and become all that God intends for them to be? When you are at a church meeting, or a party, or at work, who are you in the room, that allows others around you to flourish? This is what it means to embrace and express the welcoming and hospitable heart of God.

As we come to the end of another week of Bible notes, I invite you to engage with these deeply challenging questions, in order that we might allow the Holy Spirit to continue the renewing and transforming of our minds and our mindsets. For we were all strangers once!

† Lord, renew and transform my mindset, that I might open my heart and home, enabling others to flourish through my welcome and hospitality. Amen

For further thought

• There's a big difference between existing and flourishing. Whom can you enable to flourish today? It will likely take some sacrifice on your part ...

The creative Spirit
1 ... forming and dancing

Notes by **Jane Gonzalez**

Jane Gonzalez is a Roman Catholic laywoman. She is in the second year of a Professional Doctorate in Pastoral Theology looking at collaborative ministry. She has a keen interest in studying scripture, is a visiting preacher at a local Anglican church and occasionally pops up on local radio reviewing the Sunday papers. Other interests include singing, gardening and sewing. Now that she is retired she hopes to visit all the English cathedrals and walk the Camino de Santiago. Jane has used the NIVUK for these notes.

Sunday 8 July
Bodies of God

Read Genesis 2:15–23

The Lord God said, 'It is not good for the man to be alone. I will make a helper suitable for him.' But for Adam no suitable helper was found ... Then the Lord God made a woman from the rib he had taken out of the man, and he brought her to the man.

(verses 18, 20b, 22)

This week's readings give us an opportunity to reflect on the creative power of God and God's activity in the world. Human beings are his helpers. God gives human beings privileges denied to his other creatures: imagination, the ability to create beautiful things, intelligence and self-awareness. This privileged partnership with the Creator carries responsibilities – to care for creation and mirror God's generosity in right relationships with all.

One of the most difficult relationships to get right is that between men and women. This second account of the creation of humankind has, at times, added to the problems. It has been used to promote the subordination of women to men; in much the same way, the passage about having dominion over the rest of creation has been interpreted to condone exploitation of the earth and its resources (Genesis 1:28). But the language should rather be seen as identifying the affinity and partnership between the sexes. The animals, formed from the dust (as was man), are not suitable to share in the task of caring for God's creation. Woman, intimately connected to and related to man, is the perfect and equal partner for this enterprise.

† Creator God, I thank you for the glories of your creation. Help me to respect and reverence all those with whom I share this earthly home. Amen

Monday 9 July
Mirror, mirror on the wall

The creative Spirit – Jane Gonzalez

Read Psalm 139:7–18

For you created my inmost being; you knit me together in my mother's womb.
I praise you because I am fearfully and wonderfully made; your works are wonderful,
I know that full well.

(verses 13–14)

July

When my mother was expecting my birth we lived for a while with my aunt and uncle. My cousin, Gerald, was then a schoolboy some 13 or 14 years of age. My mother told me, when I grew up, that Gerald learned to knit so that he could make something for the little cousin who was on the way. He produced a pair of bootees. I don't think they were 'wonderfully made' but they were, in her eyes, one of the best gifts she ever received.

There is something very special about home-made gifts, however well- or imperfectly produced they are. It is charming and humbling to be presented with something that has cost not mere money, but the maker's time, care and effort. And it can be very satisfying to make something original to give. Nowadays, as well, there is a growing interest in home-produced arts and crafts and plenty of people taking up the chance to learn new skills and unleash their creative side.

Our reading for today conjures up a marvellous image of life being shaped and formed perfectly by the Creator God. Each human person, even if they may not appear so on the outside, is unique, a work of art. To the eye that does not see clearly, there may be some dropped stitches, a piece of pattern gone awry, but that is to miss the glory of God reflected in each and every one of his children. Can we learn to see others as beautiful creations of God? Even more so, can we see ourselves in this way?

† Father, I thank you for the life you have given me. Help me to give glory to you by living it to the full. Amen

For further thought

• Look in the mirror each day this week and say to yourself, 'I am God's work of art.' Be thankful and mean it!

Blood, sweat and tears

Read Exodus 35:20–35

He has filled him with the Spirit of God, with wisdom, with understanding, with knowledge and with all kinds of skills – to make artistic designs for work in gold, silver and bronze, to cut and set stones, to work in wood and to engage in all kinds of artistic crafts.

(verses 31–33)

There is an old saying: 'Genius is one per cent inspiration and ninety-nine per cent perspiration.' Artists of all persuasions may have their 'muse' – something or somebody that ignites the spark that triggers the creation of a painting or sculpture or poem. But the production of the finished piece involves many hours of hard work, often involving a lot of revision and recrafting. Much perspiration is shed!

We may sometimes gasp at the price of a piece of original art or craft until we recognise the hours of patient and painstaking labour that go into each unique and individual piece. Mass-produced items may enable us to furnish our homes or adorn ourselves but they rarely have the character that individually crafted things have.

As Christians we recognise that the ultimate muse in any artistic or creative enterprise is the Holy Spirit. Creativity is not merely the ability to produce an attractive piece of artwork; authentic pieces of art, as opposed to mere copying or reproduction, delve deeper. They tell us something about the human condition – and this is surely because the Spirit works to bring the gifts of wisdom and discernment into the artist's endeavour, alongside the manual skills necessary. The artist can be an agent of truth – even in art that we ourselves may not find attractive or appealing. The Spirit moves in mysterious ways. His constant invitation is to see God at work and God's revelation in the most unlikely places. Have we the courage to push the boundaries of our faith? To think outside the box?

† Father, you have gifted me in so many ways. However humble or modest my gifts, may I use them always in your service. Amen

For further thought

- Spend some time meditating on your favourite painting or piece of art. How is the Spirit speaking to you through this?

Wednesday 11 July
Give me joy in my heart

Read Proverbs 8:22–36

Then I was constantly at his side. I was filled with delight day after day, rejoicing always in his presence, rejoicing in his whole world and delighting in the human race.

(verses 30–31)

Not long ago, I bought a new computer and discovered that there is a program which allows you to paint. You can choose a canvas, oils or watercolours, and different brushes, crayons and pens. Although I enjoy painting and drawing, I am not a particularly proficient artist. Doodling is more my style. However, I have enjoyed and found relaxing messing about with colours and effects in this program.

Recently, also, there has been an upsurge in the sale of colouring books for adults. Purists might mock this new 'painting-by-numbers' approach but colouring books and paint programs allow us to satisfy the creative urge within us. Most of all they are fun.

Fun is not a word that we use much when we speak of God. The word does not have the gravitas of 'joy'. Maybe, however, we should dare to think it when we consider the creation. Our passage today articulates the sheer delight in the act of making that God shares with his creature, Wisdom. God and his helper have such great fun, designing, imagining and bringing forth the beautiful universe we inhabit.

If God can delight in his world, and Wisdom can rejoice in every aspect of it, then we should too. There is much wrong with our world. The temptation to see it in terms of gloom and doom, however, should not blind us to the inherent and intrinsic qualities of the creation that God called good. Call it fun, call it joy – the important thing is to celebrate it, as our Creator does.

† Father, give me a heart full of joy and delight as I gaze on the wonders of your creation. Amen

For further thought

• Spend some time reflecting on Psalm 8: 'When I see the heavens, the work of your hands …' How can you celebrate creation in the future?

Thursday 12 July
The Lord of the dance

Read 1 Chronicles 15:25–28

So all Israel brought up the ark of the covenant of the Lord with shouts, with the sounding of rams' horns and trumpets, and of cymbals, and the playing of lyres and harps.

(verse 28)

When I was a teenager and into my early 20s, my great passion was hockey. I played for my school, the county team and for my university. I was very proud to be part of some winning teams – I still recall the buzz that came with scoring a goal and the pleasure in winning matches. We were restrained in our reactions compared to today's footballers, tennis players and athletes. There were handshakes rather than hugs. Nowadays, in sharp contrast, winning goals or shots are celebrated with high fives, somersaults and cartwheels, to name but a few expressions of delight. It may not be everyone's cup of tea but I like the more overt way today's sportsmen and women have of articulating their joy.

Human beings are physical beings, and it is natural to react to our experiences physically. Cultures differ, and some are more demonstrative than others, but often in times of great sorrow or joy our emotions find expression in gesture. We hug, clap our hands, punch the air …

Our passage recalls the sheer elation felt by the people of Israel as they bring the ark of the covenant to its new dwelling place. It was an occasion for celebration and for rejoicing: music, chants, dancing. We are told – subsequent to these verses – that David danced in exultation. This was seen as entirely appropriate – dance was a means by which God was praised and honoured by the Ancient Israelites. Dancing was not regarded as undignified, but rather an expression of humility and total surrender to the Lord.

† Father, I offer myself to your service – body, soul and spirit. Take me and use me as you see fit. Amen

For further thought

- 'Let them praise his name with dancing' (Psalm 149:3). Reflect on this psalm and, if you dare, dance during your prayer time.

Friday 13 July
Image and icon

Read Psalm 135

The idols of the nations are silver and gold, made by human hands. They have mouths, but cannot speak, eyes, but cannot see ... Those who make them will be like them, and so will all who trust in them.

(verses 15, 16, 18)

'Image' and 'icon': these are words frequently used today. A new apartment development in my home town advertised itself as 'Image'. The billboards showed the ideal young couple in the ideal home. The subtext was that this is a way of life to which all should aspire. 'Icon' has been hijacked from the religious sphere. It is used in terms such as: fashion icon, literary icon, pop-culture icon – reflecting the latest trends or popular way of thinking. The problem with images, as the Bible often reminds us, is that they tend to end up being worshipped. Images become idols and icons cease to point towards a greater reality.

Idolatry of any kind does not give us life. Rather it stifles. The drive towards a perfect lifestyle, figure or relationship can become more important to us than loving God and showing generosity and neighbourliness towards our fellow human beings. The pursuit of material pleasure and the accumulation of worldly goods can deaden our response to the other's needs as we relentlessly pursue the dream society presents to us.

Our passage invites us to choose between the life-giving worship of God who sets us free and the idols that enslave us. Perhaps the most pernicious and seductive idol is that of security. We accumulate money or status so that we feel safe. We worry about our future instead of imagining and creating a better present for all. Have we the courage to identify the idols in our own lives and start to really place our trust in the grace and providence of God?

† Father, take away my fears and worries. Help me to remember that you walk with me always. Amen

For further thought

- Do you have a garden or a window box? Consider planting seeds or bulbs to remind you of the lilies of the field and the care God takes of you (Matthew 6).

The creative Spirit – Jane Gonzalez

July

Saturday 14 July
The body beautiful

Read 1 Corinthians 6:9–20

Do you not know that your bodies are temples of the Holy Spirit, who is in you, whom you have received from God? You are not your own …

(verse 19)

Some years ago, I ran a confirmation class for younger parishioners. During one of the sessions, a teenage girl asked me, 'Why does the Church disapprove of relationships?' The teaching of the Church on sexuality and sexual morality is so much at odds with the attitudes and example of modern society that it often seems disapproving and out of touch, particularly to young people. The young woman and I had a discussion on the subject and I think I was able to help her see why the Church says what it does.

It can be difficult to sail against the wind in these matters. Like the Christians of Corinth, we live in a society that has a very different approach to love, marriage and sex. Like the Christians of Corinth, we need to try to tell the world that seemingly old-fashioned ideas like chastity and continence still have relevance today. The physical body we inhabit is graced and blessed because it is God's creation – the place the Spirit dwells – and so due reverence and respect must be paid to it. Our bodies are for pleasure, meant to be enjoyed, but not for heedless gratification. A physical relationship is holy when each partner respects the other's body.

I think it is important also to understand our passage in a wider sense than merely the sexual. There are many ways to abuse the flesh: drink, drugs, over- or under-eating and cosmetic surgery undertaken for frivolous reasons all can harm the body when done to excess. There are many ways of harming ourselves. All physical excess of this kind must be avoided if we are to honour the Spirit.

† Father, you love me as I am and in your eyes I am beautiful. Give me the grace to see others as you see me and treat them with respect and reverence. Amen

For further thought

- If you did not meet the challenge set on Monday of this week, try again: look in the mirror and praise God for his work of art.

The creative Spirit
2 … speaking, singing and playing

Notes by **John Birch**

John Birch is a Methodist Local Preacher in South Wales who writes prayers, worship resources and Bible studies for his website (www.faithandworship.com) and is amazed at where in the world his resources are used and how God has blessed lives through them. John has four published books, including *The Act of Prayer*, and in his spare time plays guitar, sings, tends his allotment patch and walks the beautiful Welsh coastline. John has used the NIVUK for these notes.

Sunday 15 July
Heart and soul

Read Psalm 33

Praise the Lord with the harp;
make music to him on the ten-stringed lyre.
Sing to him a new song;
play skilfully, and shout for joy.

(verses 2–3)

I cannot recall a time when I didn't sing. I was a boy soprano in our local church choir and can still remember the nervousness of that first solo at the tender age of nine, and the relief felt when I got a thumbs up from the organist!

Since those days I have led many times of worship, accompanied not by ten-stringed lyres but a six-stringed guitar. A few of the new songs we sang in the 1970s are still around, and deserve to be, being well-written and expressing timeless truths about God, but others have been quietly forgotten, being replaced by more contemporary songs that speak to a new generation.

That's the wonderful thing about worship. The psalmist didn't insist that all hymns and songs should be accompanied by harp and lyre – the guitar and organ of his day. Those hymns we love to sing still have their place, but new songs that speak into the world in which we now live, and touch the hearts of today's worshippers are vital. Also crucial is our encouragement of all those willing to stand up and worship God with whatever is their chosen instrument of praise!

† Thank you, Lord, for the God-given talents of those who compose the hymns and songs of worship we love to sing. Continue to inspire them through your creative Spirit, for the glory of your name. Amen

Monday 16 July
Medicine music

Read 1 Samuel 16:14–23

'Let our lord command his servants here to search for someone who can play the lyre. He will play when the evil spirit from God comes on you, and you will feel better.'

(verse 16)

This passage seems straightforward but for one thing. We are told the Spirit of the Lord had departed from Saul, only to be replaced by an evil spirit *from* the Lord that would periodically torment him. It begs the question, 'Why would God fill this spiritual gap in Saul's life with an evil spirit?'

It was widely believed in Old Testament times that God would, if the need arose, use evil spirits, but the word translated 'evil' has other meanings, and could simply refer to the natural human spirit which in some people can be violent, ill-tempered or harmful.

Saul was certainly troubled, and his servants prescribed music therapy to help relieve his distress. David is chosen, and we read that when Saul was afflicted it was David's playing of the lyre that brought peace and calm to his soul.

I love music, and on a stressful day it is the soothing sounds of classical music that bring a little calm and peace back into *my* life, and I actually begin most days by picking up the guitar and singing. It works for me!

Listening to and playing music are known to reduce levels of the stress hormone, cortisol, and may have a positive effect on our immune systems. Recent research has also found that music can be more effective than some prescription drugs in reducing anxiety before surgery.

The final verse says it all – when David played his lyre, Saul would find relief.

† Thank you, Lord, for the restorative power of music, bringing calm and peace into lives that can so often be troubled and filled with stress. Amen

For further thought

• Think how you might use music to lift your own spirit on days when you are feeling low – perhaps by singing, playing or just listening.

Tuesday 17 July
Setting tongues free

Read Luke 1:57–80

'Immediately his mouth was opened and his tongue set free, and he began to speak, praising God. All the neighbours were filled with awe, and throughout the hill country of Judea people were talking about all these things.'

(verses 64–65)

Within this reading is one of the most famous songs to be found in scripture, and one that has been used by generations as part of Christian worship – the 'Benedictus' or Zechariah's song.

Let's consider its origin. Zechariah was born into the priesthood as a direct descendant of Aaron. He was married to Elizabeth and their story had all the makings of a tragedy; the fact that they were elderly and childless was a constant thorn in their daily prayers. Then, out of the blue, there is God's promise of a son!

Zechariah's faith wavers and he is temporarily struck dumb. When the baby is born and a name is asked for, he remembers the angel's instruction to call his son John, and his speech is restored – and greatly blessed! When Zechariah opens his mouth to speak, God's Spirit seemingly pours in and out flow these beautiful words of praise.

Zechariah was not a famous poet prior to this moment, as far as I am aware, just an ordinary man faithfully doing the job he'd been born into. There is a reticence within so many people that prevents them from using God-given gifts that lie dormant within. Whether it is to stand up and lead a time of prayer, consider a call to preach, or simply to put pen to paper and write – sometimes all God wants us to do is open our mouths or pick up that pen, and he'll do the rest, through the Spirit!

† Creative God, thank you for the beauty of words, and the blessing that they can bring into our lives. Inspire us, we pray, to put into words the worship that is on our hearts, that other lives might be blessed. Amen

For further thought

• Try keeping a prayer diary for a week, and practise putting into written words the thoughts that are in your heart.

When the music fades

Read Psalm 137

> '... our tormentors demanded songs of joy; they said, "Sing us one of the songs of Zion!"
> How can we sing the songs of the Lord while in a foreign land?'
>
> *(part of verses 3–4)*

There are times within our lives when hymns and songs of praise are difficult to sing – maybe because of personal tragedy, disappointment, anger, illness or a faith that's weak. The psalmist writes of a time in exile where the predominant emotions were sadness at being so far from home and hatred of the oppressor. How difficult to sing the songs that brought back so many memories of happier days.

I know from experience occasions when I have gone through the motions of singing familiar hymns, only to reach the last line without even considering the words I have been singing. I imagine that others have also been in that place, where worship begins to lose some of its meaning.

One of the best-loved worship songs by Matt Redmond, 'When the music fades …', was written about a period of spiritual stagnation in his own church. The decision was made to get rid of the band and sound system for a season, strip everything away and simply come to God with voices, unaccompanied by music. It was a difficult but ultimately fulfilling experience. Gradually the music was reintroduced, and the song reflects Redman's personal journey through that time to what is the heart of worship.

The style of hymns, anthems, chants or songs we use in worship is less important than what those words say to us as we sing them, and how they reflect our faith in the God to whom they are sung.

† Lord, bring us back to the heart of worship, which is our soul's response to the love that has been shown to us, wherever we happen to be in our spiritual journey. Amen

For further thought

• Consider the familiarity of many of the songs and hymns you sing. Look again at the words in your own time, read them slowly and let them speak afresh to you.

Thursday 19 July
Giving, receiving and growing

The creative Spirit – John Birch

Read 1 Corinthians 14:26–32

What then shall we say, brothers and sisters? When you come together, each of you has a hymn, or a word of instruction, a revelation, a tongue or an interpretation. Everything must be done so that the church may be built up.

(verse 26)

For those of us brought up within a tradition of a structured pattern of worship, with the comfort of knowing what's happening next, Paul's description of worship in Corinth sounds a little chaotic!

I was brought up an Anglican, but now find myself preaching in a Methodist Circuit. I'm not tied to a set liturgy, but anyone who's been to a few of my services knows that they follow a similar pattern, which is one that I feel comfortable with. Old habits die hard, I guess!

Others are more creative in the way they plan a service, using drama, visuals, congregational involvement and always looking at new ways of 'doing' worship. I happen to believe that having a variety of approaches is healthy because it can offer a positive challenge to our comfort zone. However, I have to admit that revelations, prophecy, spiritual tongues and interpretation are sadly not a regular part of my worshipping experience, as they were in Corinth.

What does come across from Paul's description of the early Church is that everyone came feeling they were welcomed as contributors, not merely participants. They came not only to receive, but to give. For this reason, Paul emphasises that this sharing of spiritual gifts was not about one person's love of hearing their own voice, but about building up the body of believers through teaching, prophecy, song, and however God might wish to speak to and through those gathered together for worship.

† May we never become too 'comfortable' with our worship, Lord, but instead allow you to develop the spiritual gifts that lie dormant within believers, that your Church might grow in faith and confidence. Amen

For further thought

• Do you take the opportunities that might already be there to become involved in the worship within your own church – by reading a lesson, or leading prayers?

Inspired

Read Luke 1:39–56

And Mary said:

> *'My soul glorifies the Lord and my spirit rejoices in God my Saviour,*
> *for he has been mindful of the humble state of his servant.*
> *From now on all generations will call me blessed.'*

(verses 46–48)

Earlier in the week we considered Zechariah's 'Benedictus', a familiar element in the worship of many Christians, and that description certainly fits Mary's song which we know as the 'Magnificat'.

Beautiful as the words are, it also gives us an insight into Mary's upbringing. If you were a boy, then your formal education would start at the age of five. By the time you were ten you would be learning the Jewish Law, and your formal education would be complete when you were 18. But if you were a girl then your education would come mainly from your mother and other women in the community.

I mention this because Mary's song is saturated in Old Testament verse, and particularly here from Hannah's song in 1 Samuel 2:1–10. This is the Hannah, who, when her prayer for a child was answered, offered her baby, Samuel, to God with these words: 'For his whole life he shall be given over to the Lord' (1 Samuel 1:28).

So many of the hymns that I loved as a child, and the worship songs I find so meaningful as an adult, are steeped in the Bible's words and truths. As I sing them I am affirming their meaning both to the people who first heard them, and to myself as my heart is lifted in praise and adoration.

God's Word and God's Spirit are working creatively in the hearts of gifted individuals to produce songs and hymns of such beauty and inspiration. Mary was one such individual!

† Thank you, Lord, for all those who introduce the words of scripture to our children with such enthusiasm that it encourages them at the start of their own spiritual journey. Amen

For further thought

• As an exercise, take one of your own favourite passages from the Bible and write a simple prayer as a response to how those words touch your heart and soul.

All that has breath

Read Psalm 150

Let everything that has breath praise the Lord.
Praise the Lord.

(verse 6)

This wonderful poem of praise is one of five (Psalms 146–150) known as the 'Hallelujah Psalms' because they all begin and end with 'Hallelujah!' or 'Praise the Lord!' and this one seems such a fitting conclusion to the whole collection, almost throwing out a challenge to the reader to 'Follow that!'

But we're looking at the creative spirit this week, so let's celebrate the creativity of the writer of this psalm and see how a carefully thought-out pattern can be seen in this outpouring of praise: one which we could use as inspiration for our own writing, be it a diary entry, short prayer, poem, story or even the beginning of a song of praise.

The writer answers the 'Where? Why? How? Who?' of worship without us possibly even realising what he's doing. God is not confined to church or place, and neither should our worship be confined to temple or church, but overflow into our daily lives. We offer praise both for who God is and what God has done for us, and we use the instruments that are available to us, be they wind, string or percussion. And not only instruments, please note, but other gifts such as expressive dance.

Above all of this, worship is an outward expression of our love of God. We are not called to be passive participants in church services, but to live worship-full lives.

As a writer, Psalm 150 challenges me. I hope it inspires you to explore your own creativity.

† Free our hearts to worship you wherever we might be, that we might be blessed, and in turn become a blessing to others in our daily lives. Amen

For further thought

• How might you explore your own creativity within the church fellowship to which you belong?

The creative Spirit – John Birch

July

Colossians
1 The fullness of God

Notes by **Michael Jagessar**

 Michael Jagessar is a minister of the United Reformed Church. He is currently responsible for Global and Intercultural Ministry. More on Michael's biography and writings can be found at www.caribleaper.co.uk. Michael has used the NRSVA for these notes.

Sunday 22 July
Being thankful and bearing fruit

Read Colossians 1:1–8

In our prayers for you we always thank God, the Father of our Lord Jesus Christ, for we have heard of your faith in Christ Jesus and of the love that you have for all the saints.

(verses 3–4)

Whoever wrote Colossians, here is a letter broadcasting a generous love which shouts out: 'Grace abounds, believe!' For the author, what matters is God's compassion through Christ. The meaning of life is to be engaged in that life and love. Christian faithfulness must flow from this. All else are additions.

Subversion is at work from the start of this letter! It may not be evident. Being always thankful, especially for others, runs counter to the conspiracy that insists on trusting only in ourselves and the dominant 'me and mine' ideology of the times. The love is for all the saints, not Caesar.

The other part of the subversion is related to the writer's focus on bearing fruit. Through faith and love, the community has demonstrated much fruit-bearing in striving to live out the gospel. So the writer prays that the community will continue to 'lead lives worthy of the Lord' and 'bear fruit in every good work' (verse 10). This will not be an easy undertaking given the demands of empires, Roman and otherwise, with their claims for allegiance.

For the biblical writers, fruitfulness is integral to faithfulness. Lurking dangers take the form of idolatry and being wrapped up in self (Luther's *incurvatus in se*). This may be the demands of Caesar. The result though is fruitlessness.

† Pray that God's Spirit will bring freshness to your thoughts and words and actions, energising you to take risks in the adventure of walking the way of Jesus.

Sustaining prayers

Read Colossians 1:9–14

For this reason, since the day we heard it, we have not ceased praying for you and asking that you may be filled with the knowledge of God's will.

(part of verse 9)

My whole life has been and continues to be sustained by the prayers of others: those of my now-deceased parents, grandparents, aunts, siblings (Muslims and Hindus), ordinary punters in the pews and a host of others. In my ministry in the Caribbean, in Europe and across the Caribbean Diaspora Church Communities, many continue to pray for my well-being and that of my family. When I served as a moderator of the General Assembly of the United Reformed Church (2012–14), my task felt lighter and manageable with the assurance of steadfast daily prayers.

The prayers for others carry us. So for the young Christian community, the writer prays his agenda: that they 'may be filled with the knowledge of God's will in all spiritual wisdom and understanding' (verse 9). The goal being *that* they 'may lead lives worthy of the Lord, fully pleasing to him' (verse 10), bearing fruit in every good work. The concern here is not about reeling off abstract theological formulations and edicts. It is about a story that transforms.

The writer's prayer, like all those who prayed and continue to pray for me, is as simple as it is steadfast: that we may be rooted deeper into the story of the one who offers full life for all. Being rooted in this story bears good, surprising and filling fruit!

† Pray, conscious that your prayer gives the Spirit a way of breaking into word and song unique in all the universe. Pray, inviting the Spirit of life, love and goodness to move freely in and through your words and actions.

For further thought
• Make a list of people past and present that you should remember and pray for. Consider especially those whom you may have forgotten. You may also wish to remember in your prayer minority Christian communities faced with religious persecution.

Colossians – Michael Jagessar

July

On earth and in heaven

Read Colossians 1:15–20

For in him all the fullness of God was pleased to dwell, and through him God was pleased to reconcile to himself all things, whether on earth or in heaven, by making peace through the blood of his cross.

(verses 19–20)

We are not alone. God in Christ is with us. These verses celebrate this fact of the Jesus way. At the same time do not miss the minor word 'all'. It appears around eight times, underscoring the all-embracing scope of God's economy through Jesus (the Son). It is into the Son's way of fullness of life we have been brought. There is no need to fear anything. We are already part of an assured inheritance. Christ is the heartbeat holding all things together (verse 17). Nothing is excluded.

The writer may have been concerned about the anxiety of the new Christian community. Our contexts may not be as that of Colossae, yet we too have our own anxieties. We too need some assurance that we are not alone, given the overwhelming nature of some of our current challenges. So here is a call to remember the reach of Christ and that the gathered community around the Jesus way is a community of centred-ness. So let us remember our anchor (the one who offers God's fullness) and the gathered community (the Church) in and through which this life is lived out.

And do mind the subversion: if resilience and confidence are part of our inheritance of the economy of the Jesus way, then fruitfulness may mean resisting the dominant economy premised on greed. The inheritance we have through Christ is meant for here and now. In fact, Jesus as 'the image of the invisible God' (verse 15) is a direct chant against Caesar, for all 'thrones', 'dominions', 'rulers' and 'powers' are subject to his rule!

So let us beware of spiritualising the inheritance into another world.

† God-who-accompanies-and-sustains: where our hearts are fearful and worried, grant courage and hope; where anxiety is growing and widening, grant peace and reassurance; and where spirits are daunted and weakened, grant soaring wings and new dreams. Amen

For further thought

• Consider all that needs resisting and be intentional about supporting one or two through both prayer and direct action.

Gospel servant

Read Colossians 1:21–23

'… I, Paul, became a servant of this gospel.'

(part of verse 23)

I can still recall all the speeches from a number of people alongside my ordination vows in 1980. The one that sticks out and still haunts me is 'servant of the gospel'. In retrospect, after years of theological formation I was clueless about the full demands of the gospel of the Jesus way. Yes, I was young, full of passion and wanted to change everything wrong around me. I have lost count, though, of the number of times I have stumbled to catch a glimpse of what it really means to be a servant of this 'good news' of Jesus.

It is exciting though – to be 'a servant of this gospel' of chanting down all that robs life of fullness. Empire then and now casts a long shadow. So it is imperative that the community of faith remain faithful and resolute to the hope of the gospel. No one group has more access than the other to God's love. So restrictions cannot be placed on that love.

Our writer makes it clear: the way of Christ as God's wisdom and word is about a loving relationship which will bear the fruits of love. It is not about a system of obligation, rules and regulations. All of creation has heard the gospel, all of creation recognises the Redeemer. It is only us humans who have a hard time seeing what is before our faces.

† Gracious God, give us this day a calm assurance that your will for us is larger than we dare to imagine. Still our minds and hearts in your love and drape your grace around us. And deepen our trust to long for what can only come in the fullness of time. Amen

For further thought

• Commit yourself to one concrete act, rather than a soundbite or armchair declaration, that will make 'a servant of this gospel' come alive.

Thursday 26 July
God's view – frustratingly expansive

Read Colossians 1:24–29

For this I toil and struggle with all the energy that he powerfully inspires within me.

(verse 29)

Whomever the author of this letter, Paul's ministry is located drawing from the story of God's economy in Christ. To the community, Paul is presented as a kind of reinforcement of what has been said. It seems like the authority of the letter hinges on this.

Through Paul, God's expansive love reaches those (the Gentiles) who were considered beyond such a reach. Here the subversion is God's own doing. It had always been God's plan, but had only come to light recently through Christ (verses 25–26).

One can only imagine the conversion of minds and hearts that had to happen as a result of this radical move on the part of God's grace. Not surprisingly, Paul's ministry was filled with challenges. The ministry, though, is made possible through Christ (not Paul), the energising force. We would do well to remember this. Like Paul and others, we are called to participate in the gospel ministry in its fullness – an offer for all.

God in Christ is not in the business of drawing lines, bringing closures and imposing restrictions. What a challenge for all who share in the ministry of Christ: to diminish so that God's love in Christ may increase and flourish!

† Spirit of God, take our words and release them to speak of you; take our minds and broaden them to reflect your overflowing love; take our hearts and set them alight with your desire for goodness. In the name of the one full of love, Jesus Christ. Amen

For further thought

• Reflect on your church's teachings, position or practice, for instance, on the sacraments, sexuality and marriage: are they faithful representations (or are they misrepresentations) of God who loves abundantly and who through Jesus offers full life for all?

Friday 27 July
Metaphors for the journey

Read Colossians 2:1–7

As you therefore have received Christ Jesus the Lord, continue to live your lives in him, rooted and built up in him and established in the faith, just as you were taught, abounding in thanksgiving.

(verses 6–7)

I have always found metaphors helpful for what they point to, and the ways they disrupt my desire for neat boundaries, releasing me from my narrow-mindedness. People of the way are certainly expected to walk – to be moving. At the same time, they must also be rooted, *not fixed*. Like 'living stones' they must constantly be 'building up' or 'shaping up' into that which reflects the way of God in Christ. In other words, our faith journey is not about arrival: it is about growing and overflowing with thankfulness.

'As you have received Jesus as Lord, continue to live in him.' This sums up not only the whole letter but what we are about. All who claim to be followers of the Jesus way (newer and older ones) need to remember this call to 'receive and continue in'. The simple things of the Christian life provide continual and reliable spiritual fuel for growing.

Receiving Christ is the start of a journey. The challenge is to *live* him. There is more to this journey than knowing our way around the Bible, what our Church and faith teaches and what we have learned from studying theology. We have much work to do to get beyond the studying and our preoccupation with words, to living or walking faith. And lest we get too deadly serious and intense: the living must overflow into thanksgiving.

† God-who-lights-up-life, open our hearts and minds to live out your love. When despair creeps in, kindle in us sparks of hope. When fears restrict our acting, free us to grow deeper in your love. Amen

For further thought

• Reflect on the ways you or your community need to both remind yourselves of your inheritance through Christ. Consider a few new metaphors that would help in both the retelling of this story of grace and living it out today.

Colossians – Michael Jagessar

July

209

What holds us captive?

Colossians – Michael Jagessar

July

Read Colossians 2:8–15

For in him the whole fullness of deity dwells bodily, and you have come to fullness in him, who is the head of every ruler and authority.

(verses 9–10)

If you are to identify one thing that has a grip on you and how you live, what would that be? Mine are all the gadgets that give me instant and continuous connection with those close to me and whatever matters to me. Idolatries are not things of the past. They still have their hold on us. For the community at Colossae it was 'philosophy and empty deceit, according to human tradition' (verse 8) which resulted in a way of living that separated body and mind, with disastrous results.

In countering the allure of such dualism, our writer reminds the community (and us) that God is fully embodied (incarnate) in a Galilean Jew (Jesus) and that we share in the fullness through Christ. A resurrection faith is an embodied faith and an embodied faith has no room for dividing up life and living!

But back to what may have a hold on us and whether we are able and willing to name some of these. Can some of these be, for example, the current global economic system, insular patriotism or an imagined insecurity that feeds our fear of others? Are we held captive by a philosophy of progress that exploits the most vulnerable within and between nations and one that justifies continuing militarisation? And what about our ecclesial authority structures – are we their subservient genuflectors, shackled to inherited traditions?

† May the whole of our lives be embodied testimonies of the way of God, the Divine Lover in Christ – the way of love given for the whole world. Amen

For further thought

• Consider this thought which seems to be central to Colossians: only one power matters and that is God, as we know God in Christ. Do you really believe this? What difference will this make in how you approach this week and beyond?

Fresh from the Word 2019

It may seem early, but *Fresh From the Word* 2019 is now available to order.

Order now:
- from your local IBRA rep*
- in all good Christian bookshops
- direct from IBRA
- from online book retailers

To order direct from IBRA
- website: shop.christianeducation.org.uk
- email: ibra.sales@christianeducation.org.uk
- call: 0121 458 3313
- post: using the order form at the back of this book

Price £9.95 plus postage and packaging.

Fresh From the Word is available in Kindle and ePub formats, available to purchase from online retailers.

Become an IBRA rep
*Do you order multiple copies of *Fresh From the Word* for yourself and your friends or people in your congregation or Bible study group?

When you order three or more copies direct from IBRA you will receive a 10 per cent discount on your order of *Fresh From the Word*. You will also receive a free promotional pack each year to help you share IBRA more easily with family, friends and others at your church.

Would you consider leaving a legacy to IBRA?

What's valuable about a gift in your will to the International Bible Reading Association's International Fund is that every penny goes directly towards enabling hundreds of thousands of people around the world to access the living word of God.

IBRA has a rich history going back over 135 years. It was the vision of Charles Waters to enable people in Britain and overseas to benefit from the Word of God through the experiences and insights of biblical scholars and teachers across the world. The vision was to build up people's lives in their homes and situations wherever they were. His legacy lives on today in you, as a reader, and the IBRA team.

Our work at IBRA is financed by the sales of the books, but from its very start, 100 per cent of donations to the IBRA International Fund go to benefit our local and international readers. To continue this important work, would you consider leaving a legacy in your will?

Find out more

Leaving a gift in your will to a Christian charity is a way of ensuring that this work continues for years to come: to help future generations and reach out to them with hope and the life-changing Word of God – people we may never meet but who are all our brothers and sisters in Christ.

Through such a gift you will help continue the strong and lasting legacy of IBRA for generations to come!

To find out more please contact our Finance Manager on 0121 458 3313, email ibra@christianeducation.org.uk or write to IBRA, 5–6 Imperial Court, 12 Sovereign Road, Birmingham, B30 3FH

- To read more about the history of IBRA go to page 28.
- To find out more about the work of the IBRA International Fund go to pages 369–372.

Colossians
2 Clothed in a new self

Notes by **Terry Lester**

Terry Lester has been a priest in the Diocese of Cape Town for over 35 years. He and Colleen have been married for over 30 years and have three adult children and a granddaughter, Frances. Terry is involved in community educational, heritage and restitution projects where he serves in Constantia as a parish priest, a job he loves and thrives in. Terry has used the NRSVA for these notes.

Sunday 29 July
Growing

Read Colossians 2:16–19

The whole body … grows with a growth that is from God.

(part of verse 19)

There is a citrus tree in the rectory garden which bears both lemons and oranges! At first sight it seems strange having different fruit on the same tree. When they ripen, the oranges are picked while the lemons are used off the tree as needed – either to add zest to your tonic or to squeeze over a crepe or on a piece of grilled fish. Those who farm with citrus graft whatever cultivar they want onto the root stock and grafts take relatively easily. I am not sure how many you can graft, but imagine a root stock grafted with oranges, lemons, mandarins, tangerines, clementines, mineolas, satsumas, limes and grapefruit! Imagine the fragrance of citrus filling the air and the fruit in different shapes and sizes and colours all growing and bearing from one stock!

The early Christian communities consisted of a wide variety of people who were all grafted into the one root stock, which was Christ, and growing with a growth that is from God. Reading Colossians this week we will savour the growth of that fertile tree, enjoying its scent and its taste in our own lives. How will it bear fruit in your life in the coming days? How can you see other Christians around you as fruit from the same tree?

† O Lord our God, your Son invites us to abide in him, as a graft abides in the root stock. Amen

213

Monday 30 July
Self-giving

Read Colossians 2:20–3:4

When Christ who is your life is revealed, then you also will be revealed with him in glory.

(verse 4)

Salvation in Christ, and salvation in everyday life, can both come as a surprise. A lady was waiting in a busy shopping precinct for a bus. She took no notice of the minibus taxis hooting and inviting her to get in. She had resolved to ignore them even though they too were going where the bus would take her.

Directly above her, a few storeys up, a construction worker, attempting to load a bag of cement into a barrow, lost his grip, causing the 40-kilogram bag to drop onto the lip of the barrow, tipping it onto the ledge as it slipped over and off the edge.

A Rastafarian vendor who sold herbs and other natural remedies watched this drama unfold and called to the waiting woman to get out of the way of the falling cement and barrow. She paid no attention, but soon felt his determined hands giving her a jolt backwards out of harm's way. In his desperate lunge he had lost his footing and fell in the place where she had been standing seconds ago. The cement and barrow came crashing down on him, crushing him.

† Lord Jesus, thank you for the gift of life given at such great cost. Amen

For further thought

• Salvation is often from the most unlikely sources. What must I rid myself of so that I can recognise it when it reaches out to me?

Tuesday 31 July
New life

Colossians – Terry Lester

> **Read Colossians 3:5–11**
>
> *[You] have clothed yourselves with the new self, which is being renewed in knowledge according to the image of its creator.*
>
> *(verse 10)*

A new life and a new self! Not only does the woman in our story owe her new life to her dreadlocked saviour, she may also want to think long and hard about how she would want to live her new life. Maybe she would want to live with a greater awareness of those around her – seeing them as potential saviours and rescuers. That may involve having to erase from her consciousness long built-up beliefs about others, how they dress, wear their hair, the kind of jobs they do – a general review of any and the many labels that are used to describe others as unsavoury or irritating and annoying, or to be avoided at all cost.

Maybe she will feel a deep sense of being overwhelmed with gratitude, and live life with a heart brimming with joy for the wonderful gift of life given to her by a total stranger who gave his life so that she could have life – a new life. In a similar way, how can the gift of Jesus' life for us transform our own lives, today?

† Fill my heart with joy overflowing so that it touches others too, Lord. Amen

For further thought

• How much of my time and energy do I spend judging others by their appearance or by the job they do or how they earn a living? How am I helping to give life to others?

Wednesday 1 August
Thankfulness

Read Colossians 3:12–17

And let the peace of Christ rule in your hearts, to which indeed you were called in the one body. And be thankful.

(verse 15)

A few years ago I attended a lecture delivered by the renowned Nigerian writer, Chinua Achebe, to honour the anti-Apartheid activist Steve Bantu Biko. Nelson Mandela was present, because at the time, his wife, Graca Machel, was Chancellor of the University of Cape Town.

When called to speak, Achebe rolled his wheelchair to the podium, took the microphone and began to speak. For about 15 minutes he expressed his thankfulness and gratitude – for those who had arranged his visit, to those present and to Mandela, Ahmed Kathrada and other fighters for justice who were present.

It was eloquent and erudite without sounding trite or gushy. It was poetic and touched my emotions. It came from deep down in his soul and from the core of his being. It was rooted in a continent and a people who had survived colonisation and witnessed the scars and shame left by oppression and greed. Thankfulness shone from his eyes and shaped the words in his mouth, tongue and lips. It was almost tangible and it filled the room and filled us all with a sense of well-being and thankfulness.

† Thank you! Thank you! Thank you, Lord! Thank you! Amen

For further thought

• What are you thankful for today? Feast on thankfulness.

Thursday 2 August
Justice and fairness

Read Colossians 3:18–4:1

Masters, treat your slaves justly and fairly, for you know that you also have a Master in heaven.

(verse 4:1)

In the Cape where I live, 1 December is celebrated as Emancipation Day. The date which was set for emancipation was 1 December 1834, but slaves had to serve an apprenticeship of four years, so were only freed in 1838. The government in the colony ensured that the slave masters got as much back from their investment as possible, squeezing out every last drop of life before ejecting them from their farms and communities.

My ancestors made their way to Genadendal, Valley of Grace, a Moravian settlement in the Overberg district after emancipation. On the evening of 30 November, Emancipation Night, bonfires were lit on the slopes of Table Mountain and spontaneous singing filled the air as the slaves counted down the hours and minutes to the moment of freedom at midnight.

When St Paul wrote these words to the Christians who owned slaves at Colossae, the word 'emancipation' didn't exist in the vocabulary. Instead, he suggested a radical transformation in the way masters related to their slaves who were also fellow believers.

† O just and fair Master, forgive me for the times I have acted unjustly and unfairly. Amen

For further thought

• Slavery continues wherever people are objectified or seen as commodities which satisfy someone's need or greed. What can you do to fight forms of slavery around you?

Speaking tenderly

Read Colossians 4:2–9

Let your speech always be gracious, seasoned with salt, so that you may know how you ought to answer everyone.

(verse 6)

Afrikaans is the third-most spoken language in South Africa. Achmat Davids, a social historian, wrote that Muslim slaves brought to the Cape by the Dutch developed the pidgin Dutch, also called Afrikaans. It was a language of bridge-building, to navigate the space between slave and master. In the 1970s Afrikaans, although widely spoken across races here, was enforced as the language of instruction in black African schools with little regard for the various black African languages spoken by learners. It caused anger and resentment and became the spark which ignited the protests of 1976 and the Soweto uprising.

'Let your speech always be gracious, seasoned with salt' reads our verse today. Language can be a force for good or ill. It can also heal – salt is a healer too – and build communities of diverse cultures and beliefs. This happens through simple gestures like a gracious greeting or kind remark setting a faltering community on a path of hope and to a new life.

† O Lord, shape and form my words so that they are tender and serve as a healing balm. Amen

For further thought

• Where in my community is language a force for bridge-building and how can I get involved in learning from immigrants and newcomers to my area?

Saturday 4 August
Holding together

Read Colossians 4:10–18

… my co-workers for the kingdom of God, and they have been a comfort to me.

(part of verse 11)

A list of people are named in these verses, some whom have accompanied St Paul on his many journeys, while others have been his vocal critics. Some made common cause against him, ganging up and calling themselves 'The Circumcision Party'. When communities are forced to choose sides and state their preference over and against others there is often fallout, which takes years to recover from when one side wins. In the debates, issues are amplified, name-calling becomes commonplace and the caricaturing of the other is an often-used propaganda tool.

Leaders who speak in God's name have a responsibility, though, even in these binary environments to reach across and not let go of the unity which is the action of the Holy Spirit. By referring to people's names, by calling them co-workers and highlighting the comfort they have been to him, St Paul is showing us how to hold together even in contentious situations and with difficult characters.

† We are the Body of Christ, Lord; help us hold together as one even when we disagree. Amen

For further thought

• Where can you look for ties which bind us even as we formulate arguments which threaten to divide us?

Colossians – Terry Lester

August

Laughter – the best medicine

Notes by **Malcolm Carroll**

 Malcolm Carroll is a Baptist minister, in membership at Bloomsbury Central Baptist Church, London. He works for Greenpeace, managing activist networks. His PhD examined organisational issues facing groups which organise peaceful direct action. He practises what he studied and has participated in over 50 direct actions. He believes what he does is proportionate, peaceful and accountable. The courts have disagreed with him on a few occasions. He divides his time between a boat in London and a cottage in mid-Wales, which he shares with his family and other poultry. Malcolm has used the NIVUK for these notes.

Sunday 5 August
Laughter: it makes sense

Read Proverbs 17:22

> *A cheerful heart is good medicine, but a crushed spirit dries up the bones.*

(verse 22)

Laughter is a universal language. Children's play is universal. Laughter and play sometimes serve a serious purpose in helping us to explore, and cope with, reality and relationships.

There is laughter in the Bible. Like everything else, it is to teach us about God, ourselves or both. During this week we'll find words of wit and wisdom from Jesus, Paul, from Old Testament stories and from a donkey.

If the Bible had a joke book it would be Proverbs. (Not that all its jokes are politically correct: 'Better to live on a corner of the roof than share a house with a quarrelsome wife' (Proverbs 21:9). Ouch.) Why the wit? Proverbs belongs to an ancient tradition of teaching – the Wisdom literature. The wit and the wisdom are about sense-making: what does it mean to live and die in this world? Why the bad and the good, enemies and friends?

John's Gospel begins with a nod to the Wisdom tradition, announcing Jesus as the 'Logos' – the Wisdom of God. Jesus is the greatest sense-making act in history. That is where the crushed spirit is transformed into a cheerful heart.

† Let us live with a cheerful heart. Let our worship, prayer and action, and our cheerfulness, be an engagement with reality, not an escape. Amen

Monday 6 August
There is hope, for God has acted

Read Genesis 17:15–22

Abraham fell face down; he laughed and said to himself, 'Will a son be born to a man a hundred years old?'

(part of verse 17)

Not all laughter is open and relaxed; instead you may find yourself laughing in the face of adversity or when challenged by the impossible. Both Abraham and Sarah laughed that, in the context of God's action in human history, their job was to produce another son. The 100-year-old Abraham laughed, as did Sarah. But it came to pass. When the child was born, Sarah remarked, 'God has brought me laughter' (Genesis 21:6).

Roll on a few centuries and there is another unusual pregnancy, this time to a young girl called Mary. Her child was to be born outside of marriage, which at the time was problematic. It is now the most celebrated birth in history. There's lovely footage of Desmond Tutu, surely one of the best people to be stuck in a lift with, telling part of this story with honest mirth: www.youtube.com/watch?v=UHUjnWVsYc0

Mary's reaction contrasts with Abraham's. She embodies cheerfulness, joy, hope, a call to radical action – that far point on the laughter scale where it has become almost pure joy. To begin with, Sarah and Abraham's laughter is at the opposite end where it can slip into scorn. Not all laughter is good. But God works wonders and, as ever, works them within the course of the everyday lives of everyday people.

Today is Hiroshima Day, the seventy-third anniversary of the dropping of the nuclear bomb that destroyed the Japanese city. Hardly a topic for humour, yet, given the 'impossible' challenge of being peacemakers, we can react with scorn, or hope.

† Lord, may my joy be infectious, and my hope irrepressible, for you have acted, your saving love has overcome and will never fade away. Amen

For further thought
• I am a peacemaker. Is there a way in which, this day, I can take a step up in my peacemaking action?

Laughter and adversity

Read Job 42:10b–17

The Lord blessed the latter part of Job's life more than the former part.

(part of verse 12)

'All I needed was a friend, and all you sent me were social workers' – Job (with the usual apologies to all social workers everywhere). The story of Job isn't exactly a barrel of laughs. Misfortune upon misfortune, misery upon misery. There is loss, rejection, the sheer unfairness of life. It's an extreme case, taken to the point almost of absurdity, to address head-on one of the mysteries of human existence: suffering.

There is 'gallows humour' which, I guess, is something of a coping strategy. But though they say 'laughter is the best medicine', there are times when justice is the best medicine. There are also times when medicine is the best medicine. Sometimes, rather than prescribing advice, listening is the best medicine. And yet there is still laughter; the jokes, the play and the gallows humour are all part of our making sense of it all.

Human existence, with its freedoms and responsibilities, incorporates the inevitability of death and the probability of suffering. God allows us to be ourselves and must therefore allow suffering. It's an existence he knows as well as any of us. What we experience, he has experienced and overcome. There is a false cheerfulness which is an escape from reality. There's also a different cheerfulness, a rare one, of those who have looked suffering and adversity in the face, and have overcome.

† Lord, help me to listen to others today, really listen, to what really troubles them, and in those moments to listen also to the Spirit who is the Comforter above all. Amen

For further thought

• To whom, today, are you sending me to be a comforter?

Wednesday 8 August
The whale SUV and the misguided dove

Read Jonah 3

When God saw what they did and how they turned from their evil ways, he relented and did not bring on them the destruction he had threatened.

(verse 10)

We now know that some animals share an important characteristic with us – laughter. It's found in animals as diverse as gorillas and rats; it's a basic communication tool and is used for socialising. However, I'm not aware of any animals that repent, or need to. The book of Jonah introduces us to a few delightful oddities: repentant animals in 3:6–10, a whale that doubles up as a sports-utility vehicle and the dove that's lost its way.

A clue to enjoying this story is in the first few words, when the missionary call comes to Jonah, someone who, in the Hebrew, is called 'Dove, Son of Truth' – two titles that refer to God's people. God's people are happy being missionaries when it means others coming to them, less keen when it means them going to others. 'Come to church' are three words a missionary does not say, for she or he has taken church to others. Jonah stands for us, who go in any direction, jump ship even, do anything but go over there and speak with them, dwell with them. In the Jonah story, everyone else – and everything else – obeys God, everyone except for God's own representative.

Nineveh was big, bad, and foreign and definitely not home to churchy sorts of people. But God has decided they are his kind of people. His compassion is for all, and is so great it wins over them all, repentant animals too.

† Spend a moment reflecting on this: God is a missionary and calls us to be missionaries too.

For further thought
• To which Nineveh is God sending you today?

Thursday 9 August
Found under a fig tree

Read John 1:43–51

'Nazareth! Can anything good come from there?' Nathaniel asked. 'Come and see,' said Philip.

(verse 46)

Jesus didn't finish his messages with LOL, but some of his stories are funny: trumpets announcing the Big Donor making his self-serving deposit, the camel and the eye of a needle and more. Humour, like laughter, is social. Apparently, in every ten minutes of social interaction, we're likely to laugh seven times. Does Jesus laugh with us?

Nathaniel under a fig tree. A religious hint, the fig tree being a symbol of Israel? Or was he asleep instead of working, and his mates sniggered when they heard Jesus' comment? Or was it Jesus' rejoinder to Nathaniel disrespecting Jesus' home town of Nazareth? When a Samaritan village refuses hospitality to Jesus, James and John want divine retribution brought upon it. Jesus gave these two the nickname 'Sons of Thunder'. I reckon the disciples had times when they laughed, Jesus too. Of course he did – he shared our full humanity.

But there may be a sense to his humour which we do not yet know, the laughter of God at the folly of men (women too, but men do folly so much better). In the Old Testament, we read of God laughing at the powerful and at those with grand self-serving schemes. What is it about us humans that makes us think we know it all, can do it all, and do it with such pomp? We must look like children parading around in clothes far too big. G.K. Chesterton suggested that when Jesus went off alone from the disciples it wasn't to hide his sorrow, but his mirth.

† Christianity has the capacity to be the greatest social activity in human experience. Lord, transform my church and my own interaction with others. Amen

For further thought
• There is a positive way in which we can laugh at ourselves, it is part of a special, often forgotten, grace – humility.

The body speaks

Read 1 Corinthians 12:12–27

But God has put the body together, giving greater honour to the parts that lacked it, so that there should be no division in the body, but that its parts should have equal concern for each other.

(part of verses 24–25)

Paul, like Jesus, was well capable of ridicule. And Paul could take ridicule to eye-watering lengths – see Galatians 5:12 (content warning, especially for blokes, contains reference to gore). Here in Corinthians Paul's ridicule shines light on a ridiculous fellowship where different opinions and different agendas cause division. The physical picture is delightfully absurd, pictures of alternative bodies where the foot or the hand rules, where other parts are repositioned or jettisoned.

The ridiculous is followed by the sublime. The next chapter, 1 Corinthians 13, is the famous passage on love, '… these three remain: faith, hope and love. But the greatest of these is love' (13:13). The sublime addresses the same situation as the ridiculous of the previous chapter. And (with the usual apologies to thousands of couples who had the passage read at their weddings) it's not for weddings where lovers are in love. It's for fellowships where followers fall out. It's about mature Christianity, where different opinions and agendas are redeemed by the love of Christ and built into one body.

I've preached around a fair bit and most fellowships are some way from being a perfect body. One is characterised by a domineering foot, another by a self-important belly, another is where the armpits of enthusiasm collide with the posteriors of sobriety.

Paul's answer isn't that one view should prevail: do you want a church that is all armpit or all posterior? It is that, by the miracle of grace, our differences build the one perfect body.

† A church fellowship is an unnatural social gathering, it can only ever work by God's grace. Lord, transform us from followers into fellowship. Amen

For further thought
• Take your sense of humour to church. You'll need it.

Laughter – Malcolm Carroll

August

225

Let us bray

Laughter – Malcolm Carroll

August

Read Numbers 22:21–35

The donkey said to Balaam, 'Am I not your own donkey, which you have always ridden, to this day? Have I been in the habit of doing this to you?'

(part of verse 30)

Theological student disasters. My earliest was when reading publicly from 1 Kings. I came across Jehoshaphat and misread him as Jepheshahot, which got me so nervous that I accidentally shut the Bible and Kings mysteriously disappeared; no amount of flicking though the pages helped me recover it. Another student was undone by technology – the tie-clip microphone. Just before leading worship, you clip it on and then you can forget it's there. He did. He sat down after preaching and prayed out loud, 'God, that was awful.' He had just shared his words with the entire congregation. We entirely shared his sentiment. And then there was a friend I'd better not name, called Alan Thomas, who led prayer, reminding the congregation how God had spoken in diverse ways '… and had even spoken through Balaam's ass'.

This passage is comedic. The donkey sees God's divine messenger; Baalam, God's earthly messenger, doesn't. Balaam's donkey then has words with Baalam (which Baalam doesn't seem to find unusual) and only then does Baalam truly listen. A reminder to theological students and preachers that, since God can speak words of wisdom through a donkey, what extra do we think we add?

Comedy, yes, but as with all Bible stories, it's there because in some way it tells the salvation story. It is sometimes in the smallest of ways, and here, the most absurd, that God intervenes. The story of salvation moves on because a donkey didn't. A donkey features later on in the salvation story too. This time, neither the donkey nor God's messenger will be swayed from their mission.

† Maybe it's because I am so busy doing your work, Lord, that I do not hear what work you want me to do. Help me pause, reflect and have courage to listen to advice. Amen

For further thought

• A feel-good moment: we already are part of the story of salvation.

Who cares?
1 A God who cares

Notes by **Edel McClean**

Edel McClean is a facilitator, trainer, spiritual director and retreat leader living in Bury, just north of Manchester, UK. She is currently employed as a learning and development officer for the Methodist Church in Britain, having previously worked at Loyola Hall, an Ignatian spirituality centre, and Fisherwick Presbyterian Church in Northern Ireland. She has a particular interest in prayer, discernment and in helping people meet with God in all the ups and downs of life. Edel has used the NRSVA for these notes.

Sunday 12 August
God here below

Read Psalm 65:9–13

You visit the earth and water it, you greatly enrich it;
the river of God is full of water; you provide the people with grain,
for so you have prepared it.

(verse 9)

Like most of the globe's farmers today, the people of Ancient Israel had an elemental involvement with the soil. If the earth was not watered, the grain did not grow. If the grain did not grow, the people did not eat. God's enriching of the earth was an intimate way of God enriching God's people. The same deep engagement with the earth and the soil is found in Celtic spirituality, where people recognised God in the rhythm of the seasons and the flow of the weather. For the Israelites and the Celts their belief was not simply in God 'in heaven above', but also in God as near as the rain on our face and the bread in our belly – an intimate God pulsing everywhere we go and in everything we do.

With the move of much of the world's population from rural to urban settings, and with our move away from our agricultural heritage, we risk swapping our experience of an intimate God for an intellectual understanding of God. But God's care for us is not an intellectual theory, but a practical reality. God continues to visit, water and greatly enrich the earth – when we notice, and when we don't. This week I invite you to take notice of this God – a God who cares.

† God of care and compassion, keep my heart and my mind open today to notice the many ways you show your care for me. Amen

Known and seen

Who cares? – Edel McClean

Read Psalm 139:1–6

O Lord, you have searched me and known me.
You know when I sit down and when I rise up; you discern my
thoughts from far away.
You search out my path and my lying down, and are acquainted
with all my ways.

(verses 1–3)

There's a fridge magnet that I once saw in a retreat house: 'Jesus is the secret guest at every table and the secret listener to every conversation.' It's an image that I nickname 'sneaky Jesus' – a Jesus who lurks in the background, watching for the slightest indiscretion, tut-tutting and shaking his head when we disappoint.

At its worst this familiar psalm can be similarly uncomfortable, giving us an image of a sneaky God, an eavesdropping God, waiting to jump out and leap upon us if we put a foot wrong. Such an image might provoke obedience, but is unlikely to encourage growth.

The familiar words of Psalm 139, however, speak of a God who knows us and loves us. Being known by someone who loves us invites us into the freedom to grow, not out of a fear of disappointing, but out of a desire to delight. This is a God who knows every nerve and sinew of us, every longing and fear, every anxiety and triumph. This is a God who knows us as we really are, behind every mask we wear and every smokescreen we create, and who loves us just as we are.

If we could really see ourselves as God sees us, know ourselves as God knows us, we would be overwhelmed. So for today at least, I try to begin to trust that God can both know and love me, and see how such knowledge might change my today.

† God of care and compassion, open me more and more to the knowledge of your all-encompassing love, so that I might live more lovingly in response. Amen

For further thought

• Where in my life might I be attempting to hide from God? What is God's response to my desire to hide?

Tuesday 14 August
Called to co-operate

Read Exodus 6:1–9

'Say therefore to the Israelites, "I am the Lord, and I will free you from the burdens of the Egyptians and deliver you from slavery to them. I will redeem you with an outstretched arm and with mighty acts of judgement."'

(verse 6)

Living in our interconnected, information-sharing world, it's impossible to ignore the suffering of so many across the globe. In recent years our attention has been particularly drawn to the migrant crisis. It's worth remembering that the West receives only a minority of the world's refugees, but those seeking asylum, knocking at the doors of our privileged lives, have focused our attention to the earth's capacity for human misery. In this context it is hard to hear God's assurance that he will free the Israelites from the misery of their captivity without wondering why he seems not to have responded for the previous 430 years!

On the one hand it's easy to reach for truisms, that 'God works in mysterious ways', and that 'ours is not to ask the reason why', but these are of little help to those who are suffering right now. Whether in response to the suffering in our own lives, or to the suffering of our fellow humanity, grappling with such questions is part of integrity in our faith.

It's also worth remembering that God chooses to allow Moses the privilege of responding and co-operating with God's work. And in order to do this, Moses needed to listen. Perhaps God had been flaming in the burning bush for hundreds of years, yearning to free his people, but those passing by had been too preoccupied to notice. Or perhaps I'm just imagining that those fictitious passers-by are a little like me, failing to keep my ears open to God's invitation to co-operate and listen to the cries of God's people.

† God of care and compassion, keep my ears open today to your voice calling me through the voices of my brothers and sisters who suffer. Amen

For further thought

• Where do you think the church needs to co-operate with God in freeing those who live in captivity?

Who cares? – Edel McClean

August

Wednesday 15 August
God's in-crowd

Read Psalm 146

The Lord watches over the strangers; he upholds the orphan and the widow, but the way of the wicked he brings to ruin.

(verse 9)

We don't travel far in our adventure on this earth before dividing the world between the 'insiders' and the 'outsiders'. In my native Northern Ireland I once read a piece of research that found that preschool children were able to identify members of the 'other' community by their shopping bags. Our childhood propensity for dividing girls from boys, the cool kids from the geeks, the 'in' group from the 'out' group strengthens in adulthood to divide 'us' from 'them', liberals from conservatives, segregating genders, races, sexualities, nationalities, sects and religions. We Christians have had our share of such divisions. I heard a joke recently about a Christian rescued from a desert island. Her rescuers asked, 'We're curious – why did you build two churches?' And the Christian responded, 'One to pray in, and one to never set foot in as long as I live.'

Any confident assertion that God is on my side, however, will sooner or later come up against the frustrating truth that God crosses my invented boundaries without apology. As today's passage makes clear, God watches over the strangers precisely because they are not strangers to God. He upholds the orphan and the widow, because to God they are as precious a part of God's 'in-crowd' as everybody else.

† God of care and compassion, open my heart to cross the barriers I have invented to greet my brothers and sisters with love and kindness. Amen

For further thought
• Who are the individuals or groups that I see as strangers that God might be encouraging me to greet as friends?

Thursday 16 August
Curtail the curmudgeon

Read Leviticus 19:15–18

You shall not take vengeance or bear a grudge against any of your people, but you shall love your neighbour as yourself: I am the Lord.

(verse 18)

In my work as a spiritual director I hear, again and again, one of the most heartbreaking aspects of the Church: Christians hurt each other. Not just by accident (though that happens often enough too), but harshly and deliberately. I hear of people in leadership systematically bullied by those they seek to lead. I hear of church members ignored in meetings or pushed out of churches. I hear of those who, because of their gender, or sexuality, or nationality, or colour, or theological outlook, are belittled and undermined. I hear of nasty emails, abusive phone calls, of gossip spread and anxieties encouraged.

The more I hear this, the more I believe that those who behave in this way have not yet begun the hard work of learning to love themselves. The easiest way to hide our own insecurity and sense of inferiority is to go on the attack, creating enough noise and bluster to distract from our own frailty. Those who know themselves to be imperfect and broken, working with God to grow into God's vision for them, are much more likely to be kind to the imperfection and brokenness in others.

At the core of this is the question of identity. The church is a body of sinners loved by God. Things go wrong when we refuse the truth of our own sinfulness, or when we refuse the truth of God's love for us. When I spot the impulse in myself to be curmudgeonly with my neighbour, it's wise to remind myself that I am their sister, a fellow sinner, loved by God.

† God of care and compassion, deepen in me the knowledge of your love for me, in all my imperfection, so that I might better reflect your love for all those I meet. Amen

For further thought

• In your own community, where do you witness Christians hurting each other? How might you bear witness to your own identity as a loved sinner?

Who cares? – Edel McClean

August

Friday 17 August
Divine dizziness

Read Job 38:25–29

'Who has cut a channel for the torrents of rain, and a way for the thunderbolt,
to bring rain on a land where no one lives, on the desert, which is empty of human life,
to satisfy the waste and desolate land, and to make the ground put forth grass?'

(verses 25–27)

I play a game sometimes, imagining what is happening in all the places I have ever visited. I challenge myself to build as many layers of intricacy as possible, before being overcome with a kind of geographical dizziness. I am a geographer by training, and as a student met a prominent theologian who told me that geography and theology are natural companions. A good theologian, like a good geographer, must stand in awe of the intricacy of God's world. I pursued geography because cities, towns and people fascinate me. They are places where God is at work extravagantly, generously and joyfully in obvious ways and secret ways.

Job is being reminded of this fact in today's scripture. We cannot begin to imagine the billions of places and ways that God is at work in this very instant. God is at work in every one of the 7.5 billion people on the face of the earth. It's a thought that is deeply humbling: God is concerned not just with my life, but equally with the lives of my 7,499,999,999 or so brothers and sisters. It is also a thought that is immensely consoling: even with 7.5 billion to keep an eye on, God has infinite time and love for me.

God tells Job that God's love is at work in the world in places Job will never see and can barely imagine. That continues to be true for us, and is both an assurance of faith and a challenge to remember that the world revolves not around us, but around God.

† God of care and compassion, open me to ever-greater wonder at the extravagance and intricacy of your creation, and help me to be both humbled and inspired by remembering my part in it. Amen

For further thought

• What helps you to find a sense of wonder at the work of God? What might you do to deepen that sense of wonder in your life?

232

Saturday 18 August
Enfolded in God's embrace

Read Psalm 131

But I have calmed and quieted my soul, like a weaned child with its mother; my soul is like the weaned child that is with me.

(verse 2)

It's remarkable what advertisers promise will calm us, from candles to shower gels to panpipes. All of these things are based on the erroneous premise that we can find peace by accruing 'stuff'. The urge to acquire, to look to things to give us peace, at best brings disappointment and at worst, selfishness and conflict.

The weaned child of the psalm has a greater and deeper wisdom. A weaned child is likely to be walking, to be off exploring, to have a propensity for tantrums. And yet they also know that, when everything becomes too overwhelming they can retreat back into the arms of their parent, the one who knows them, loves them, shelters them and offers them security.

Most of us behave like toddlers sometimes. There are times when we need to be held by God, but instead we try to wriggle out of his grasp, or exhaust ourselves with other things. Psalm 131 says 'I do not occupy myself with things too great and too marvellous for me' (verse 1). But the truth is we do. What quirk in the human personality means that we can long for something and yet resist allowing ourselves to experience it? We long to sit quietly and at peace with God, and at the same time we avoid quiet, we keep the radio on or we engross ourselves with our mobile phones. And all the while, our parent God watches us, loves us, waits, until we lay aside all the things that distract us and allow ourselves to be enfolded again in God's embrace.

† God of care and compassion, help me to leave aside those things that distract me and draw me again into the calm and quiet of your embrace. Amen

For further thought

• What do I use to distract myself from God's invitation to God's calm and quiet? How might I make more room for God's calm today?

Who cares? – Edel McClean

August

Who cares?
2 When no one cares

Notes by **Stephen Willey**

Stephen Willey is a Methodist Minister who has been involved in mission to the economic world for several years. His work has included offering industrial chaplaincies and establishing a regional anti-trafficking network, which developed to challenge the exploitation of modern-day slavery. Currently Stephen has three churches in Birmingham, England, two of which are in areas of multiple deprivation. Stephen is committed to seeing people's potential fulfilled inside and beyond the church, especially amongst those who are young or vulnerable and living in challenging circumstances. Stephen has used the NRSVA for these notes.

Sunday 19 August
Making demands of God

Read Luke 18:1–8

'And will not God grant justice to his chosen ones who cry to him day and night? Will he delay long in helping them?'

(verse 7)

Jesus' story challenges us to keep praying, hoping and crying to God even when we feel our voice is small or inconsequential.

My friend Katie came back from her time in Germany several years ago with a piece of the Berlin Wall. Something incredible had happened while she was there. Somehow relationships in Berlin had shifted, causing the world to be forever changed. From the east and west, people crossed the breach in the wall in order to meet friends and family members they hadn't seen for many years. Katie's piece of the wall was evidence of a huge political change. Hopes and prayers were answered and new possibilities emerged for Europe and for the people of Germany.

There have been other dramatic moments of change since, like Nelson Mandela's walk from prison and his election as the President of South Africa, or the end of sectarian violence in Northern Ireland. But the talk and the reality of new walls and fences indicate that divisions continue to form and harden. In these circumstances Jesus encourages us to persist in our prayers for justice and peace, and to believe that, by God's creative power, transformation will take place.

† Risen Christ, grant us the faith to persist in our prayers for justice and peace, even when faced with seemingly impossible difficulties. Amen

Monday 20 August
Job's lament

Read Job 3:1–11, 20–26

After this Job opened his mouth and cursed the day of his birth. Job said:

'Let the day perish on which I was born, and the night that said, "A man-child is conceived."'

(verses 1–3)

After seven days of silence with his three friends, Job's first words may shock us: 'I wish I hadn't been born!' What was Job saying about God when he cursed the hour of his birth? Did he really think that God was mistaken to bring him into the world? Job's perspective, his feelings of sorrow and despair, seem overwhelming, but then he finds his voice.

On the morning that Simon was due at work for his competency interview he didn't turn up. His boss, Brian, had triggered a process which could lead to dismissal because Simon was increasingly erratic in his work and missing important deadlines. While Brian was waiting for Simon to arrive, emergency services were called nearby to a very public suicide. Brian heard about this before he knew it was Simon, but somehow he guessed.

That afternoon Brian asked again and again what he could have done differently. 'If only I had known about Simon's feelings perhaps I could have dealt with this in another way.'

Faced with someone's overwhelming feelings of violence towards themselves, what can anyone do or say? For Job it is not his friends' advice that precipitates change, rather it is the expression of his overwhelming feelings to God.

Not all stories have the book of Job's positive ending. Overwhelming feelings, unspoken or unheard, can be destructive and have tragic consequences. Job and Simon's stories remind me of the need for people to bravely voice their feelings, even if they seem shocking, and also how important it is that stories from the heart's depths are listened to.

† God of compassion, you who hear our cries: we pray for all who have been affected in any way by suicide or self-destruction. Amen

For further thought

• Can desperate members of the human family find consolation and a new perspective through our willingness to listen to them?

Who cares? – Stephen Willey

August

235

A cry from the depths

Read Psalm 88:6–18

You have caused my companions to shun me; you have made me a thing of horror to them.
I am shut in so that I cannot escape; my eye grows dim through sorrow.
Every day I call on you, O Lord ...

(verses 8–9a)

'I've noticed', said a church member who lost her child in a tragic accident, 'that many people avoid me nowadays. They actually cross the street when they see me coming. It's as if I am now a bad luck symbol. I haven't done anything to deserve that, have I? I want their love and support but many of them seem to want me to disappear. That's why I struggle to go out sometimes.'

In the psalms, emotional pain and the experience of being shunned are often expressed without reserve or careful words. Here in Psalm 88 the psalmist speaks out against and blames God! Perhaps that opens up a way in which hope can be glimpsed. In their struggles, both psalmist and church member reveal frustration and anger, but also the need for dialogue and a refusal to be silent. 'It has helped to talk,' said the grieving mother. And the psalmist? Well, the writer of Psalm 88 continues to cry out and express eloquently how difficult life is when God's steadfast love seems far away. Does God actually shun the psalmist? On the face of it, that is what the psalm says, but notice that the psalm continues – and God allows this frantic and hurt voice to be heard.

Psalms like this one are not silenced and removed from the Bible. Quite the opposite! Thousands of years later this grief continues to be heard. So today, at least, we know that the psalmist has been heard by God, and the people of God.

† Bring to mind the voice of someone – perhaps in this week's news – who is despised by others or whose sorrows seem overwhelming. Ask God to hear their grief.

For further thought

• Does our thinking or speaking ever silence others? How can we hear more about people's hardship without hardening our hearts?

Healing among the tombs

Read Luke 8:26–39

The man from whom the demons had gone begged that he might be with him; but Jesus sent him away, saying, 'Return to your home, and declare how much God has done for you.' So he went away, proclaiming throughout the city how much Jesus had done for him.

(verses 38–39)

Having been completely excluded from contact with society as a result of his condition, the man at the tombs received restoration of hope and life from Jesus. Home, family, a place in society, clothes, sanity and freedom are all restored. His life is worth living again.

There are many ways in which people may need restoration. When you have experienced dementia within your family, there can be moments when you begin to wonder about the whole point of human existence, and hopes of restoration seem to diminish. Those with the disease may come to forget what was said or done almost instantly, but research suggests that emotions – feelings which may be triggered by forgotten events – often remain. These feelings are important aspects of a personality.

When the disease was quite advanced and it seemed like he was more and more distant from everyday society, there came a day when my father was in an awful mood. A long time before this, we had met together in the Taizé Community – we had prayed in the huge church together and sung the simple songs which are so much a part of the prayer there.

This day, in the nursing home, my wife and I hesitantly started to sing some Taizé songs with him. He seemed to relax and find some peace. I returned that evening with my mother. 'How are you, dad?' I asked. 'I have been to Taizé today,' he replied. My heart lifted to hear his response. He hadn't remembered my being there, but he had heard our prayer in his heart.

† Sing a simple but loved song of praise or say a poem or a prayer you have known for many years. Take notice of how it makes you feel.

For further thought

• What makes life worth living for people whose circumstances cause them to be isolated, ignored or even abandoned?

Who cares? – Stephen Willey

August

237

The struggle of Jesus and the prophets

Read Luke 13:31–34

'Jerusalem, Jerusalem, the city that kills the prophets and stones those who are sent to it! How often have I desired to gather your children together as a hen gathers her brood under her wings, and you were not willing!'

(verse 34)

Jesus, the one who went to Jerusalem for our sakes, was threatened, tortured and killed for being himself.

I was walking with a friend along a high street in the UK when a couple of men started to call me abusive names because I was with someone of a different ethnicity. The ones shouting at me wanted to separate me from my friend simply because of who he was. I was shocked and asked him afterwards how he felt about this. 'Oh, I'm used to it,' he replied.

Jesus is not shocked that people want his blood, but he offers a lament. He cries not for himself but for the prophets and for the refusal of the people in the city to allow the little ones – the vulnerable and weak ones – to be gathered in God's compassionate love.

I was not lamenting on the high street – I felt angry towards those racists and felt like pushing them away. On reflection, though, it was those ones whom I was separated from – the people who called me names and insulted my friend. Could I ever be reconciled with them? Could they be reconciled with my friend or others of his ethnicity? This feels unlikely. Perhaps I have found a lament in my heart too!

Whilst Jesus wants to gather Jerusalem's children into a place of warmth and safety, the city's powers conspire to kill him like the prophets before him were killed. But death fails to silence him and his laments (and our laments) continue to transform lives today.

† Jesus, you know how it feels to suffer on another's behalf. Grant that when I encounter others who are treated badly, I might share their lament with you. Amen

For further thought

• What have you or your community experienced that makes you lament? How can your lament be heard more widely?

Friday 24 August
Shunned and forgotten

Read Psalm 31:9–18

But I trust in you, O Lord; I say, 'You are my God.'
My times are in your hand; deliver me from the hand of my
enemies and persecutors.
Let your face shine upon your servant; save me in your steadfast
love.

(verses 14–16)

Early in my ministry I visited Beryl, a bedridden person who'd had a paralysing stroke and had been in that condition for several years. I went to give her support – to tell her that the church community were thinking of her, though they seldom came to her house. I expected her to be sad – distressed by a condition which prevented her from going outdoors and feeling the sun on her face. I knew that some people found visiting her hard. She had been an active woman and was not old when she was struck down. In a moment, as a result of the stroke, it almost seemed that Beryl had vanished from the face of the earth.

I was apprehensive as Peter, her husband, showed me into her room. There she was, lying quite still in a bed. How must it feel to see only those four walls with no one to talk with except her husband and an occasional visitor? Beryl smiled at me. It didn't take long for me to discover I was in the presence of someone with considerable faith. It seemed that God's face did shine on her, and I felt that God's steadfast love flowed through her. Somehow, mysteriously, her response to my visit made me feel supported, valued and even visited, myself. I thought I was the one visiting! Whenever I saw Beryl I had the same experience.

After suffering – shunned and ignored, despised and forgotten – the psalmist sings to God about the suffering, but also expresses something beautiful about trust in the God of steadfast love.

† Pray for a person you know who is bedridden or housebound, in prison or trapped. How might God's steadfast love be reflected in their lives?

For further thought

• Have I lost contact with someone who would like to hear from me? Why? Could I find a way to be reunited with them?

Saturday 25 August
Words from the whirlwind

Read Job 39:1–8, 26–40:2

And the Lord said to Job: 'Shall a fault-finder contend with the Almighty? Anyone who argues with God must respond.'

(chapter 40, verses 1–2)

'It isn't like it used to be in the 1970s; it was better then!' I am conscious that older church members sometimes feel a sense of fear and abandonment, even chaos, as familiar parts of life – friends, contemporaries, family members, favourite hymns, pews, church buildings – gradually disappear from their lives. It is possible to feel lost and alone after a lifetime of service.

Job's abandonment and misfortunes make him question his Creator. As he speaks, he reveals his heart to God's great heart. God replies, revealing a creator's heart: God, whose words have imbued meaning into what was meaninglessness; God who has breathed life into a chaotic void (as in Genesis 1); God who understands the elements and the elemental forces of nature; God who knows the animals and the whole of created existence. Such a God responds to Job's challenge! Then Job cannot find fault with the One who creates meaning, even though his experience is hard to bear. This revelation of God's creative heart becomes a blessing, as Job discovers a new meaning for his life.

Could God create new meaning in our lives even if we are losing what was familiar and are tempted to retreat into happy memories? In times of fear and loss, even chaos, is it possible that God's words could transform our present reality into a new time of hope and even joy? Rather than recreating what used to be, God creates something new with Job after his traumatic illness and losses. Job encounters the God who is breathing life into a future unimaginably rich and hopeful.

† Heart of the Almighty, create in me a new heart. Bless my past, present and future, and may my life richly bless your creation. Amen

For further thought

• How do you feel towards God about how things have changed in your life? How are God's creativity and blessings revealed today?

Who cares?
3 A community of care

Notes by **Liz Clutterbuck**

Liz is a curate in the Church of England, having trained at St Mellitus College. She works part-time in a North London parish and freelances as a researcher and writer. Her particular focus is on fresh expressions of church and how the impact the church has can be measured. She is also part of Matryoshka Haus, a missional community that eats together every week and intentionally works to build community in London. Liz is passionate about social media, film, baking and travel – and loves it when she manages to combine as many of her passions as possible! Liz has used the NRSVA for these notes.

Sunday 26 August
They shall be my people

Read Ezekiel 11:14–20

'I will give them one heart, and put a new spirit within them; I will remove the heart of stone from their flesh and give them a heart of flesh, so that they may follow my statutes and keep my ordinances and obey them. Then they shall be my people, and I will be their God.'

(verses 19–20)

The people of Israel were scattered across the Middle East when the Lord gave these words to the prophet Ezekiel. They had lost sight of their history and their role as God's chosen people. The prophecy Ezekiel received speaks of God reunifying this divided population in the land of Israel, but most importantly, emphasises that the community will have 'one heart'. This new, shared heart will be of flesh – the same flesh that was given to them in their Lord's image.

It is in community that the people of Israel will follow God's laws. It is in community that they will worship the one true God. It is in community that they will truly be God's people.

The theme for this week picks up where the previous two weeks left off, exploring the theme of caring, but specifically in the context of community. The Body of Christ has one heart with God, just as was promised to the people of Israel. That one heart binds us together and calls us to care for all who are made in the image of God.

† Lord, search my heart and if there is stone to be found within, turn it to flesh and join it with yours so that I may be one with you. Amen

Monday 27 August
Living in unity

Read Psalm 133

How very good and pleasant it is when kindred live together in unity!

(verse 1)

It seems to me that the psalmist celebrates unity because he knows just how difficult it is to achieve! It is indeed very good and very pleasant to live in unity with one another, but it is a rare event.

The history of the Church has demonstrated just how difficult it is for even the Body of Christ to live in unity. Our plethora of denominations, traditions and theologies are indicative of two millennia spent disagreeing and splitting, rather than living in the blessing that is unity.

Christian disunity is a pet peeve of mine. In an increasingly secular world, there are plenty of people keen to criticise the church. We don't do the Body of Christ any favours when we criticise each other publicly, without seeking to understand one another properly.

I trained in a theological college where 'generous orthodoxy' – the acceptance of different traditions and theologies within the one Church – was taught. Difference in practice and worship were celebrated, rather than allowed to divide the large body of students. It enabled me to appreciate the richness of the diverse Church, rather than fear those who were different to me. It was indeed a very good and pleasant united community!

It's been hugely valuable to my role in parish ministry. I've served my curacy in a parish that holds together a range of traditions and expectations about what 'church' should look like, adjacent to parishes who are very different to us in terms of their Sunday worship. But, by emphasising unity, these differences become a celebration rather than a tool for undermining Christ's people.

† Lord, fill your church with your Holy Spirit so that we may unite around our common bond in you. Would you protect us from division and heal our wounds? Amen

For further thought

- Where are there areas of difference or disunity in your local community? What would it take to bring about unity?

Tuesday 28 August
Feed my sheep and tend my flock

Read John 21:9–19

He said to him the third time, 'Simon son of John, do you love me?' Peter felt hurt because he said to him the third time, 'Do you love me?' And he said to him, 'Lord, you know everything; you know that I love you.' Jesus said to him, 'Feed my sheep.'

(verse 17)

The image of Christ as the shepherd of a flock of sheep is a familiar one. The flock is an obvious community, looked after by a shepherd who will go out of his way to rescue just one lost sheep.

In this resurrection appearance, Jesus is handing off the shepherding of his flock to Simon Peter. The role of the shepherd is twofold: to feed and to tend. It would be Simon Peter's responsibility to ensure that the words of Jesus were passed on to those who took up the challenge to follow him. In tending the flock, it would be Simon Peter's responsibility to keep them on the right track, to keep the flock united and to search for strays.

The first Christians were not to be a collection of individuals, they were to be a community of people, following Christ together, to be sustained and cared for by those whom Jesus had appointed to the role.

In your Christian community, who takes on the role of the shepherd? Who ensures that people are nourished and tended to? Many of us might assume that only church leaders can have this role, but it is actually a responsibility that can, and should, be taken on corporately. Do you keep your eyes peeled for those who are missing from your community for a few weeks and check in with them? Do you recommend nourishing books you've read to those around you? Do you encourage others in their spiritual life? Feeding the sheep is a task that the whole flock can undertake.

† Lord, I thank you that you are the Good Shepherd. May you equip and encourage me to feed and tend to those with whom I am in community. Amen

For further thought

• Pray about your role within your community. What particular role could you take on that helps to shepherd it?

Who cares? – Liz Clutterbuck

August

Wednesday 29 August
Building the next generation

Read Psalm 48

> *... that you may tell the next generation that this is God, our God for ever and ever. He will be our guide for ever.*
>
> *(verses 13b–14)*

As a student, I spent a year studying nineteenth-century missionaries. These were people sent from Britain to all corners of the British Empire and beyond, often making huge sacrifices to follow the call they felt God had given them. Reading their letters in the archives was often profoundly moving as they shared with those back home what they were experiencing. Over a century later, they were an inspiration to me in my own spiritual journey.

Something that scripture makes very clear is what our place as Christians is within the history of God's people. The Old Testament tells the story of the people of Israel – their exiles, the prophecy of their Messiah, and their regular failure to heed God's words. In the New Testament, we see how Jesus makes a new covenant with God, one that draws all of humanity into his kingdom. Two thousand years on, we are another piece of this epic history of God's salvation.

Christians reading this psalm today are the 'next generation' that is mentioned. Each generation that has followed has been guided by God as the psalmist describes. Each generation has experienced God's 'steadfast love'. Sometimes it is easy for us to get lost in the present day and forget that we are part of a community that has been taken care of and loved for centuries.

Our community is not just in this time and place. We have a God whose love for us has been demonstrated in generation after generation.

† Father of the generations, we give thanks that your love has been steadfast throughout salvation's history. Give us guidance as to how best to continue your work in our own generation. Amen

For further thought

- Is there a saint commemorated by the church, or an individual who had a significant impact upon a community known to you? Where would you be without that person?

Thursday 30 August
Caring behind the scenes

Read Acts 6:1–7

They had these men stand before the apostles, who prayed and laid their hands on them. The word of God continued to spread; the number of the disciples increased greatly in Jerusalem, and a great many of the priests became obedient to the faith.

(verses 6–7)

The beautiful thing about being part of a community of believers is that each of us has a unique calling from God. If everyone in the church was a skilled preacher or evangelist then it's likely that not much pastoral care would happen!

In the earliest days of the Church, the demands of both spreading the gospel and taking care of a growing community were in conflict with one another. The apostles had the gifts to do both, but they realised that it did not need to be all their responsibility, so they looked to their community to suggest those who could take on the role of caring for the needy in their midst.

Those chosen to care for the widows were not regarded as lacking in gifts that would make them skilled in sharing the gospel – far from it, for they are described as of good standing, full of the Spirit and wisdom. In fact, they were putting the gospel into practice, loving their neighbour as they would want to be loved.

Today, I think we have a tendency to emphasise ministries that are up front – preaching, speaking at conferences or writing intelligent books – and give much less credit to those doing the behind-the-scenes work of caring for the community. In fact, God commissions his people to a wide range of roles to ensure that everything is covered, and none are any less worthy of the Spirit than others.

† God, we thank you for those who, unnoticed, care for the most vulnerable in our community. Would you bless them and continue to fill them with your Holy Spirit? Amen

For further thought

• Consider how to set apart a time during Sunday worship, or even a service itself, for all those who are carers, to give thanks for what they do and to commission them publicly.

Who cares? – Liz Clutterbuck

August

Considering the weak

Read Romans 14:13–23

The faith that you have, have as your own conviction before God. Blessed are those who have no reason to condemn themselves because of what they approve.

(verse 22)

Division has been a persistent theme in the history of God's people. Despite all being one in Christ, differences have continued to have a negative impact upon the community. For the early Church, it was the theological conflict between those who had converted to Christianity from Judaism, and those who were Gentiles. Today, divisions are also social – split by class, wealth or race.

It is the opposite of the vision of the kingdom of heaven that we are repeatedly given in the New Testament. Paul says in this passage that the kingdom is not about food and drink, but Spirit and righteousness. I can imagine him saying the same to churches in the twenty-first century.

The church is a place in which all are welcome, but sometimes we unconsciously erect barriers to those who are different to us. Take the classic Christian pot-luck meal; this is a huge barrier for those for whom food is a big expense and there is no money for anything extra. A church I know in the East End of London intentionally acknowledges that some in its parish have much less than others, but encourages all to join in, even if all they bring is a small packet of crisps, because that can still be shared.

Perhaps we just find it easier to talk with and build relationships with those who are like us. Perhaps we're nervous around those who are different to us. We need to ask God to reveal these barriers to us and equip us to remove them so that the Body of Christ can truly be one body.

† Lord, would you reveal the divisions within our community to us and guide us through the process of healing them? Amen

For further thought

• Is there anything that your church might be doing that unintentionally discourages some in your local community from being part of the congregation?

Who cares? – Liz Clutterbuck

August

Saturday 1 September
Love builds up

Read 1 Corinthians 8:1–13

But when you thus sin against members of your family, and wound their conscience when it is weak, you sin against Christ.

(verse 12)

As the saying goes, we can choose our friends, but we can't choose our family. However, that's not how the Body of Christ works. Neither do we get to choose who is our family in Christ. As we explored yesterday, division is a common theme in the early Church, and this continues in this passage from Paul's first letter to the church in Corinth.

We do not get to choose who walks into acts of worship or church events. God and God alone has that right. Our role is to build relationships with whoever is sent our way, no matter how hard it turns out to be. The smaller the community, the harder it can be to avoid those we find difficult to be around.

However, just as it is God who sends people into our midst, so it is that God equips us with the love that we need in order to love them in return. Caring cannot happen without love. When we commit to loving and following Jesus, we commit to loving all who follow him too – no matter how different they are to us or how much they rub us up the wrong way. When we struggle with those who form part of our heavenly family, we do not need to look for our own human love to show them, but instead we must ask God to love them through us.

† Father God, fill me with your love so that I might share it out to those with whom I am in community, no matter how much I like or dislike them! Amen

For further thought

• Take some time to think about people whom you struggle to be around. Lift each of their names to God in prayer and ask for help in specific areas of your relationship with them.

Hosea
1 The Lord speaks

Notes by **Mandy Briggs**

 Revd Mandy Briggs is a Methodist minister who lives in Bristol. She is the Education Officer at the New Room (John Wesley's Chapel), which is the oldest Methodist building in the world. Mandy and the New Room are on Twitter: @mandbristol and @NewRoomBristol. Mandy has used the NIVUK for these notes.

Sunday 2 September
Introducing Hosea

> **Read Hosea 1:1–9**
>
> *When the Lord began to speak through Hosea, the Lord said to him, 'Go, marry a promiscuous woman and have children with her, for like an adulterous wife this land is guilty of unfaithfulness to the Lord.'*
>
> *(verse 2)*

If Hosea had a Facebook page, his relationship status would definitely be set to 'it's complicated'.

If you or I wanted to do something prophetic, we might think about joining in with a protest or signing a petition. God calls Hosea not just to take part in a one-off act but to live his whole life in a prophetic way. His marriage to Gomer, a woman with a bad reputation, is meant to symbolise God's love for the people of Israel, who have turned away to worship other gods, becoming corrupt in the process.

God's work through Hosea affects his children as well. Rather than calling them Michael, Bob or Stephanie, his whole-life prophecy means they are named Jezreel (scattered), Lo-Ruhamah (not loved) and Lo-Ammi (not my people). Like I said, it's complicated.

It is easy to react to the book of Hosea negatively. An unfaithful relationship is hard to reflect upon, even as a metaphor. It may bring up difficult feelings or memories.

Yet stick with it – if you look past the troubled relationships, there is much to think about regarding love, judgement and the deep relationship between God and his people.

† Loving God, as we are introduced to Hosea and his messy life, please help us to listen to what you might be saying to us. Amen

Monday 3 September
Tough love

Read Hosea 2:1–10

'Rebuke your mother, rebuke her,
for she is not my wife,
and I am not her husband.'

(verse 2)

My place of work, the New Room in Bristol, was featured in the second series of the popular BBC series *Poldark*. Built in 1739, the New Room fitted the historic period perfectly. It was transformed into an eighteenth-century courtroom, where the hero, Ross Poldark, was put on trial, facing charges of attempted murder and inciting a shipwreck.

Some theologians suggest that this part of the book of Hosea has elements of a divorce case in a courtroom. The relationship between God and Israel is described in terms of a statement in a lawsuit brought against an unfaithful wife and mother. There are uncomfortable echoes and reminders of what would happen if a woman was caught in adultery in biblical times. If unfaithfulness was discovered, the punishment was death by stoning (see for example John 8:1–11).

However, keep remembering that this is an analogy and God is really talking about his unfaithful people, Israel. As the people turn away to their other 'lovers' – other gods such as Baal – God directly challenges them, like a prosecution lawyer. The 'marriage' of the covenant is stretched to breaking point. No satisfaction will be found through chasing other religious practices.

The image of re-entering the wilderness is very strong. Israel may worship other gods, as a man or woman might chase after lovers, but this will lead them back to the desert, a place they thought they had left behind. And God, the one who has been abandoned, will allow this to happen, because the people have forgotten who brought them into a land of plenty.

† Pray for families who are involved in difficult court cases, including those dealing with custody and access, divorce settlements and domestic violence.

For further thought
• How can you support friends in challenging family situations?

Hosea – Mandy Briggs

September

Tuesday 4 September
Hope in the valley

Read Hosea 2:14–23

There I will give her back her vineyards,
and will make the Valley of Achor a door of hope.

(part of verse 15)

In 2006 I visited Kraków in Poland with a friend. We happened to be there at the same time as Pope Benedict, who had just succeeded Pope John Paul II.

We watched the TV coverage of Pope Benedict visiting the site of the WW2 concentration camp at Auschwitz. The sight of a German Pope praying in front of a line of memorials to those who had died there was very moving. And then, as we watched, we realised that a rainbow was quietly shining in the sky above him. It was a moment which could not be described in words, a moment full of hope.

When Hosea refers to the Valley of Achor in today's reading, he is referring to a place of judgement from Joshua 7. The Israelites are instructed not to keep any spoils of battle for themselves, but a man called Achan disobeys this rule. Israel lose the next battle, and when Achan is discovered, he is brought before Joshua and killed.

God's promise to Israel now is that the Valley of Achor will become a metaphor for hope and restoration. Despite the hurts of the past, a new covenant is possible, the relationship can be saved and renewed.

There is even the promise of a new betrothal – a new commitment between God and his people which before seemed impossible. Hosea speaks of hope beyond hurt and reconciliation beyond betrayal.

There is always a tension between the God who judges his people, as seen in yesterday's readings, and the God who loves his people and calls them back. Today, love wins.

† When I run far away from you, God, reach out to me with an everlasting love and call me back to you. Amen

For further thought

• How can you live out the phrase 'love wins' today?

Wednesday 5 September
Turbulent priests

Read Hosea 4:1–11

'The more priests there were, the more they sinned against me.'

(part of verse 7)

One of my favourite comedy shows is *Father Ted*. The hapless adventures of three slightly useless priests stuck on a small Irish island with a housekeeper and many eccentric visitors are guaranteed to raise a laugh.

The Catholic priests depicted in this sitcom are all flawed. Father Jack drinks and swears, Father Dougal is not the sharpest tool in the box and Father Ted smokes and has allegedly had 'money resting in his account'. However, as they are drawn in caricature, we become fond of them.

Not so the priests in today's reading. They are the villains of the piece. At first Hosea's complaint is, as usual, against the people of Israel, but as he warms up, his diatribe against the ordained becomes more pronounced.

The twenty-first-century media still declares itself shocked when a priest, vicar, rabbi or imam 'falls from grace', but it seems that in Hosea's time, they would have also had plenty to report. And yet the verses come full circle: 'like people, like priests. I will punish both of them for their ways and repay them for their deeds' (verse 9).

There is a warning here for all those whose responsibility it is to pass on to their people the message of God. However, at the end of this passage, it appears that Hosea is issuing a challenge to people to face up to what they are doing – whoever they are.

† It is hard to follow, Lord, and it is also hard to lead. Give wisdom and integrity to those in positions of leadership, whether political, cultural or spiritual. Amen

For further thought

• How do you encourage those people you know who are in Christian leadership?

Hosea – Mandy Briggs

September

A prophet's warning

> **Read Hosea 5:8–15**
>
> *'Among the tribes of Israel I proclaim what is certain.'*
>
> *(part of verse 9)*

Hosea now turns his attention to even stronger warnings. Things are now looking really bad for Israel as a result of their turning away from God.

Towns are under threat, particularly those in the southern part of the northern kingdom of Ephraim (Israel). Gibeah, Ramah and Beth Aven, towns on the border, could be ravaged one by one. Even the southern kingdom, Judah, is not safe, for they have shared in the same sins. Even the great king of Assyria, Tiglath-Pileser III, cannot help (although he may win a prize for one of the best names in the Bible!).

How do we deal with the image of God presented in this reading? God is angry because the people he loves have abandoned him; he wants to bring them back and allowing them to face destruction seems like the only way, the worst way, to get their attention. Yet in other passages, God yearns to receive his people back, to restore them and bless them.

Consider again the conflicting emotions that might run through someone's mind when they learn that their partner has been unfaithful – ranging from anger and a need for revenge, to grief, or maybe even the possibility of forgiveness and a commitment to a new start. The God of Israel portrayed in Hosea is all of these, and more.

This prophecy looks ahead to a turbulent time for Israel. The only hope for the people is to turn back to God.

† My heart says of you, 'Seek his face!' Your face, Lord, I will seek (Psalm 27:8).

For further thought

• What in Hosea would be helpful to victims of war or violence today? What do you think would be unhelpful?

Gossamer threads

Read Hosea 6:1–6

'What can I do with you, Ephraim? What can I do with you, Judah?
Your love is like the morning mist, like the early dew that
disappears.'

(verse 4)

I wonder if you have ever been outside early in the morning and spotted a spider's web. We often find them on the metal gate outside our house. Each strand has been delicately woven and is glistening with dew – and when it is really cold the dew freezes and produces delicate patterns of ice.

However, as soon as the sun rises the moisture on these beautiful threads will melt away and the web becomes – well, just a spider's way of hunting and surviving, no matter how attractive it looks.

Here is the dilemma in today's reading: at first the people of Israel seem to be responding to Hosea's prophecies. They recognise their wrongdoing, they consider the promise of God's restoration and healing and a new start. God is as reliable as day and night, as steadfast as the seasons; he will look after them.

But then, like the sun on gossamer threads, these promises of a new start fall away and God again addresses his people. God is not looking for empty promises and sacrifice done out of duty. Instead, God is searching to see a real change of heart in the people: 'mercy, not sacrifice, and acknowledgement of God rather than burnt offerings' (verse 6).

This story reminds me of the parable of the sower in Matthew 13, where seed falls onto rocky ground. The seed sprang up quickly but because the soil was shallow, the tiny plants were not deeply rooted enough and withered when the sun came up.

How do we make sure our commitments are rooted and grounded in God's love?

† The sun shines, and the dew melts; so may the Spirit of God keep us and encourage us as we seek to do the work of Christ. Amen

For further thought

• Look up the words of the hymn 'Will Your Anchor Hold' by Priscilla Jane Owens (1829–1907).

Hosea – Mandy Briggs

September

Saturday 8 September
Too hot to handle?

Read Hosea 7:1–10

All of them are hot as an oven; they devour their rulers.
All their kings fall, and none of them calls on me.

(verse 7)

My first proper 'Saturday job' as a teenager was in a local bakery as a shop assistant. When I arrived for work each morning, Andy the baker had already been there for several hours, preparing and cooking the bread, rolls and cakes needed for the day.

Occasionally we had to help him out by getting trays out of the very hot oven. For this task we had to wear special protective gloves because the ovens were so hot. There was no hanging around – otherwise you would get burned.

In Hosea's time, ovens were cone-shaped and the fire was lit at the bottom. Flat bread was baked on saucer-shaped hotplates which were placed over the embers. The loaf had to be turned over so that it could be baked on both sides. But as J.B. Phillips writes in *Four Prophets*: 'Ephraim is half-baked – scorched on one side and uncooked on the other!' (1963, p. 40).

In this analogy, Ephraim's (Israel's) passions and intrigues are inflamed and they are still a long way from God because of their corrupt behaviour. The implication is that the baking, with all its heat, will have an unsatisfactory outcome; Israel is being sapped of its strength but does not realise it. There may be a new king, but he is not a ruler chosen by God and does not call on God for help.

What lies ahead for Hosea and Israel? How will the story develop? Next week's notes continue the turbulent story.

† Though the flames of the world's passions rage around me, may I still listen for your voice, O God. Amen

For further thought

• How can Christians be the 'active ingredient', like the yeast in bread, in their local communities?

Hosea
2 Sowing and reaping

Notes by **Pevise Leo**

Pevise Leo is an ordained Church Minister of the Congregational Christian Church of Samoa. He graduated from Malua Theological College, Samoa in 2004 with a Diploma in Theology and is currently the Minister of a church in Brisbane, Australia named *Setima O Le Ola* – Brisbane Central. He is also a songwriter who has penned more than 100 Samoan contemporary and gospel songs. He lives in the small town of Inala, 40 minutes from Brisbane City, with his wife Shirley and three children. Pevise has used the NRSVA for these notes.

Sunday 9 September
Reaping the whirlwind

Read Hosea 8:7–14

For they sow the wind, and they shall reap the whirlwind.

(part of verse 7)

O le po'u e i'u ina papala is a Samoan proverb meaning, 'A small sore can become rot.' What starts out small can become uncontainable!

Everything we do has consequences. Good and bad deeds, our priorities in life, the choices we make, all have consequences. The consequences are often greater than the deed itself, just as a whirlwind is much greater than a wind.

Israel had abandoned the Lord, the source of life, and instead pursued the blessings of Baal. Hosea warns that these sins committed over time are like a little breeze here and a little breeze there. We forget about the sin much like we forget about the last breeze we felt. However, God sends punishment all at once, and when it comes, it hits us like a fierce whirlwind, a calamity that destroys the harvest, the reapers and anything that stands in its way. In other words, we will get much more than we bargained for.

As we read through the remaining chapters of Hosea this week, let us be reminded that the Lord was the source of Hosea's love – the love that will never let go.

† Gracious God, comfort us in love; do not visit us in anger. Cleanse our sins and spare us from the whirlwind. Amen

Lord of life

Read Hosea 9:10–17

*Once I saw Ephraim as a young palm planted in a lovely meadow,
but now Ephraim must lead out his children for slaughter.*

(verse 13)

I remember growing up in Samoa in the seventies. In my memory, beautiful greenery is surrounded by the blue ocean. Village life centred on fishing the lagoons and working the plantations. There was tropical weather and a cool breeze all year round, and no one had heard of abuse. The parents brought up their children in any way necessary to be good, respectable citizens. The disciplinary measures were sometimes extreme, but there was no abuse. Wisdom of Solomon says: 'Start children off on the way they should go, and even when they are old they will not turn from it' (Proverbs 22:6 NIVUK).

Discipline is a part of God's nature. In Hosea's view, the nation of Israel has been rebellious and stubborn about serving and obeying God. Instead, they worshipped Baal. Hosea is questioning the fertility of Baal, for there was only barrenness. The children born will be taken away in the slaughter. Israel is to have a miscarrying womb and dry breasts, a humiliating threat in the face of the fertility promised by Baalism. Baal means total barrenness; but YHWH is Lord of nature, and from him is life.

God's desire is not judgement; God seeks repentance and reconciliation. God promised not to go through with the destruction if they would turn back to him. We are reminded today that it is never too late to turn to God and enjoy his blessings, rather than to be the recipient of his anger.

† Compassionate Father, your grace transforms this world. We pray that you discipline us with your kindness, and never let us fall short of your mercy. Amen

For further thought

- What other 'gods' tempt you from dedication to the God of life?

Tuesday 11 September
Let it rain

Read Hosea 10:1–15

Sow for yourselves righteousness; reap steadfast love; break up your fallow ground;
for it is time to seek the Lord, that he may come and rain righteousness upon you.

(verse 12)

I remember watching my father plant our *taro* and banana plantations back in Samoa. I also remember the feeling during harvest seasons that the fresh produce was encouragement for all the labour of my father and older siblings.

My father was considered a great farmer, and to be a great farmer, one had to be aware of the seasons, the soil condition and the weather. Precipitation, especially rain, has a dramatic effect on agriculture, and the rains mentioned in the Bible refer to the blessings of God, who would also withdraw his blessings from his people.

The days of ease were over, and the time had come when Ephraim had to put her neck to the yoke. It was now time to seek the Lord, to sow righteousness and reap steadfast love. God would indeed come and rain salvation upon you.

Today we too must have the desire to allow God's Word and Spirit to produce righteousness in us.

Paul wrote: 'So let us not grow weary in doing what is right, for we will reap at harvest time, if we do not give up' (Galatians 6:9). The Holy Spirit will lead us in sowing for God's garden, and we will see the heavens open up and rain blessings on our farm. So, therefore, sow the right seed!

† Loving God, only you can grant our sanctification. Rain your love on us and bless your creation. Amen

For further thought

• What is some of the fallow ground around you that you must break up?

Wednesday 12 September
Beginning again

Read Hosea 11:1–11

Yet it was I who taught Ephraim to walk, I took them up in my arms; but they did not know that I healed them.
I led them with cords of human kindness, with bands of love.
I was to them like those who lift infants to their cheeks. I bent down to them and fed them.

(verses 3–4)

I have been moving from country to country, cities to towns, houses to houses for the past 35 years. The act of moving has the connotation of starting over, new atmosphere, new friends, new ways of living and so on.

The eleventh chapter is the most touching passage of Hosea's prophecy. In it he evokes the depth and power of God's relationship with his people. In earlier chapters, God has been, at times, an angry God, a God of wrath and of judgement, but the tone changes at this chapter. Yet despite the love manifested in the parent–son relationship, Israel strayed from it.

God wants to start again because God loves and cares for creation. God is profoundly compassionate because God is profoundly personal. God could have destroyed his people; they were such a disappointment. But Hosea heard God's heart, and it was a heart for change and renewal. God may have wanted to judge Israel, but more than that, God wanted to start again.

A very dear friend of mine turns 62 years old today, and will be retiring from the ministry in a few years. He talks with enthusiasm of how he will have to start over: ending one chapter of his life and turning over the next page.

When God starts over with us, God becomes again what he really was in the first place: a loving Creator.

† Creator God, thank you for your grace; grant us understanding so we may be willing to start again with you as our God and our Redeemer. Amen

For further thought

• What relationships that went sour have you started again? What about your relationship with God?

Thursday 13 September
Grasping the heel

Read Hosea 12:2–9

The Lord has an indictment against Judah, and will punish Jacob according to his ways, and repay him according to his deeds.
In the womb he tried to supplant his brother, and in his manhood he strove with God.

(verses 2–3)

There is a Samoan proverb that says: '*E so'o le Moasope i le Moasope.*' A *Moasope* is a rare chicken with an extra lock of feathers on its head, and only a *Moasope* can reproduce another. It simply means the child takes after the parent, either physically or mentally. A chip off the old block, some would say. The Samoan word for son is *atali'i* and derives from two words – *ata* meaning reflection or image and *ali'i* meaning man. So *atali'i* means 'reflection or image of the man'; that is, the father.

Hosea is contrasting Jacob with his descendants. Jacob took Esau by the heel in the womb in order to obtain, if possible, the privileges of the first-born (Genesis 25:22–26); his descendants disregarded God's promises and put their confidence in idols and foreign alliances. Again, by his strength, Jacob prevailed in wrestling with God for a blessing (Genesis 32:24–29); his descendants were the slaves of idols.

God made us in his image; we are his *atali'i*s. Who and what we are should reflect the perfect image of our Maker. When we go astray from the path of righteousness and God's will, the result is devastating. Jesus is God's perfect *Atali'i*, so we should lay hold of his heel. Having no right in ourselves to the inheritance, we must lay hold of the bruised heel of the crucified Christ, that it might secure for us a blessing from the Father.

† Sovereign God, help us to be your sons and daughters. Grant us the ability to reflect your holiness in our words and deeds. Amen

For further thought

• What kind of person was Jacob in the Genesis story? What kind of model for faith is he?

Hosea – Pevise Leo

September

Choose wisely!

Read Hosea 13:1–16

It was I who fed you in the wilderness, in the land of drought. When I fed them, they were satisfied; they were satisfied, and their heart was proud; therefore they forgot me.

(verses 5–6)

Life is full of choices. When will I get up? What will I eat? Who will be my friends? Where will I go on my holidays? And on and on. We become a product of our daily choices. Choices have consequences.

There is a Samoan proverb: *'Ua 'ai 'ulu, tuana'i ta'isi'* – when eating breadfruit, *ta'isi* is ignored. *Tai'si* is a traditional Samoan food prepared by cooking *taro* root in a Samoan oven. Breadfruit is harvested only at certain times of the year, and during the off seasons, the people enjoy the *ta'isi*; but when the breadfruit is harvested, they ignore the *ta'isi* altogether. This proverb simply means, 'You are happy to accept other people's help during bad times, but you forget them in your prosperity.'

God's people did precisely that. When they met afflictions and tribulations, they were happy to accept God's deliverance. But when all was well and life was prosperous, they forgot the Lord their God.

However, as so often in scripture, the thundering voice of judgement is followed by the loving voice of hope. Israel did forsake the Lord for idols and the Lord did bring upon his people judgements stated in his covenant. Israel had a choice, and they chose poorly. But today is a brand new day full of hopes and dreams. To fulfill them, we must choose wisely.

† Dear God, thank you for the gift of free will. We ask that you help us choose so we may inherit your kingdom. Amen

For further thought

• How can you choose life today (Deuteronomy 30:15–20)?

Saturday 15 September
A winning love

Read Hosea 14:1–9
*They shall again live beneath my shadow, they shall flourish as
a garden;
they shall blossom like the vine, their fragrance shall be like the
wine of Lebanon.*

(verse 7)

There is a Samoan myth about the origin of the coconut tree.
Once a girl named Sina befriended an eel. Every evening under the
moonlight they would swim together and talk. The eel told Sina
of how he was once a prince. As time went by, the eel grew larger
and more demanding of Sina's love. This began to frighten Sina so
she escaped, moving from village to village. The eel followed her
wherever she went. Sina told her uncle about her ordeal, so her
cousin went to confront the eel. During the battle, the eel's head
was severed. In his final breath, he asked Sina to bury his head,
and that in one day as a reminder of his love for her, a tree would
sprout from his head that would bear fruit with refreshing nectar.
The eel's face would be on the fruit, two eyes and a mouth, so that
each time Sina would drink from the fruit, she would in fact be
kissing him.

This myth in some way resembles God's winning love from the
book of Hosea. God's love followed Israel everywhere they went,
provided for them and even disciplined them. When they would
not listen to the words of his heart, God spoke with actions of
national crisis. Even then they chose to turn away from their loving,
heartbroken God.

With every disciplinary action, there is also hope. God gave his Son
for the sins of the world. Not the coconut tree, but the cross is the
reminder of God's love.

As we conclude the book of the prophet Hosea this week, let us be
reminded of God's winning love: the love that will never let us go.

† O Merciful God, thank you for your winning love, that you are willing to accept us
as fallible human beings. Amen

For further thought

• In what ways have you known God's winning love in your life?

Hosea – Pevise Leo

September

261

Balancing work and life
1 Work and rest

Notes by **Dafne Plou**

Dafne Plou is a journalist and social communicator who works on technology for development in an international organisation. Her work includes travelling to other Latin American countries to lead workshops and seminars and speak at conferences. She's a member of the Methodist Church in Argentina. In her local church, in Buenos Aires' suburbs, she works in the area of 'Community building and fellowship in liturgy'. She's also a women's rights activist and participates in the women's movement in her country. Dafne has used the NRSVA for these notes.

Sunday 16 September
Work and rest

Read Genesis 2:2–3, 15

So God blessed the seventh day and hallowed it, because on it God rested from all the work that he had done in creation.

(verse 3)

'It's my boss again asking for some data he needs urgently.' That lovely Saturday afternoon was ruined. Watching the Sunday evening TV show gets interrupted a dozen times by a buzzing phone. Even the minister has to kindly request parishioners to turn their devices off when service starts!

Have we become too fond of our screens? Is a new type of slavery growing quietly around us? It's hard to turn off our machines and not be on the alert and look casually through our screens every now and then. I've heard people saying, 'You can forget your wallet or purse at home but never your cellphone!' I look around my small studio and five machines reflect my image: desktop, laptop, netbook, tablet, cellphone. Can I stay away from them? Not for long …

What does it mean to observe the Sabbath on the seventh day? The Bible's central concern for work and rest is captured in this idea. Will we ever recover our blessed day? We begin our week's reflection on this note of urgency!

† Open my eyes and ears, God, to understand how invasive new ways of interaction can become. Keep my mind and heart free to become truly connected to others. Amen

Monday 17 September
Cursed is the ground

Read Genesis 3:17–19

Cursed is the ground because of you; in toil you shall eat of it all the days of your life.

(part of verse 17)

My grandmother once told me that when she was young, her mother wouldn't allow her or her sisters to walk in the sunshine without their parasols. She was brought up in the city of Montevideo, Uruguay, and lived very near the beach. Going to the seashore was not much fun for those girls. They had to wear long sleeves and skirts, plus hats and headscarves, and walk or sit always under their parasols. The sun was not to touch their skins! 'Why, Granny?' they asked. 'Because we're family girls, we're not to be confused with those girls that toil on the land.'

The land suffers this curse because of our misbehaviour. The way many have interpreted these words has pierced generations like a dagger and has brought not only terrible consequences for the land itself (destruction, contamination, pollution and exploitation of natural resources) but also the exclusion of many people. The Spanish conquerors of America thought that if they toiled the land, their status would be diminished, so they enslaved the native population to serve them and do the hard work. Is it possible to amend what we have done to the land and to others, and celebrate the harvest faithfully?

Recently some younger members of my family told us that they want to leave the city for the countryside, where they want to work the land and enjoy its fruits. They dream of farming free of chemical products and heavy use of technology. Let us all work for a harvest that does not discriminate or exclude, but brings joy to the lives of many!

† Creative God, thank you for all the fruits of your land. Help us to look after your creation and encourage us to confront rules and practices that hurt and damage your land and your people. Amen

For further thought

• What harvest traditions do you have in your culture? How are harvest festivals celebrated in your church?

Balancing work and life – Dafne Plou

September

Tuesday 18 September
Slavery and solidarity

Read Exodus 5:1–18

'Let heavier work be laid on them; then they will labour at it and pay no attention to deceptive words.'

(verse 9)

The neighbours were quite upset. They had been seeing these groups of people, foreigners, every day for some weeks walking around the block in pairs or small groups. They came out of the old factory that hadn't been in use for many years. They never spoke to anyone as they passed by; they just walked in silence for about half an hour every day at midday. What was going on there? One day, one of the foreigners crossed the street to buy some sweets in a small shop. 'Who are you? What's going on in the old factory?' he was asked. 'We work and live in the building,' he explained. 'We work for long hours and we're only allowed to come out for a short walk at midday, just for a little exercise.'

Like the Israelites, these migrant workers in the clandestine garment industry had heavy work laid on them. Their working conditions, their lack of good housing and proper meals, and their desperation for any wage at all didn't allow them to organise and demand for their rights. But the neighbours listened to their silent claim. In solidarity, they called the authorities who closed the factory, detained its owners and released the enslaved workers.

'Let my people go,' demands the Lord. Wherever we are, if we have eyes and ears, we are called to stand for people's rights, to build just conditions for all and to challenge the practices of the world.

† God of the Exodus, give us courage to stand against Pharaoh for workers' rights. Amen.

For further thought

• Find out more about the working conditions in the garment industry around the world, especially in the developing world.

Wednesday 19 September
Sabbath for today

Read Exodus 31:12–17

'You shall keep my sabbaths, for this is a sign between me and you throughout your generations, given in order that you may know that I, the Lord, sanctify you.'

(part of verse 13)

It is difficult to think of freeing up one day from our duties and our usual routine. There are so many things to do even in our so-called free time: shopping, going to the gym, meeting friends and family, catching up with those TV series we couldn't watch during the week, studying, bringing work home, cooking and freezing meals, taking the children to practise sports or birthday parties, going to church and so on … It seems this generation is skipping Sabbath!

Sabbath is not only a day to rest and get refreshed, as this Bible reading tells us God did. The deep dimension of Sabbath has to do with the fact that God has chosen a people and has promised to sanctify them throughout the generations if they keep faith, follow his commandments and consecrate a day to hallow his name. As believers, we are called to respond, keeping time to nourish our spirituality and grow in faithfulness.

How do we do this? Are we to create new rules and regulations that tell us how we should behave on a Sabbath, like the ones we find in the Bible? Or is it that God is expecting us to keep Sabbath's essence in a new way, in searching for new expressions of our faith, in service to others, in sharing the certainty of his grace and loving care?

Keeping Sabbath shouldn't be simply a chore, but rather a day of joy and dedication to announce the gospel in renewed ways!

† God of the Sabbath, teach us to renew our faith and spirituality so that we may announce your teachings and build bonds with those that don't know you. Amen

For further thought

• Where do you desire rest and refreshment in your life at the moment? How can you take steps to practise it?

Balancing work and life – Dafne Plou

September

Jubilee and justice

Read Leviticus 25:8–12

… and you shall proclaim liberty throughout the land to all its inhabitants.

(part of verse 10)

In autumn 2016, a horrible crime against a teenager in Argentina became the drop that caused the cup to overflow. A victim of rape, her body was thrown away like garbage. Twitter seemed to blow up in anger, sorrow and the need for action. Women came together to organise one of the biggest demonstrations in the country, and people of all ages and backgrounds got together in just a few days under the hashtag #NotOneLess (#NiUnaMenos) and marched silently one afternoon in cities, small towns and villages across the country. They wore black in remembrance of all who were victims of their partners, former partners, boyfriends … most of them killed at home, where a person is supposed to be safe. How shall we proclaim jubilee throughout the land when violence continues?

When God instructs the people of Israel to establish the year of jubilee, his directions are clear. It is a time for atonement and for building justice and peaceful relations with others and the environment. Could we, in contemporary societies, think of creating the conditions to celebrate such a year? Could we think of a time free of violence, where justice and peace prevail?

In Leviticus we find very detailed rules about how the people of God should proceed to live on the land securely (Leviticus 25:18). As Christians we are called to observe God's ordinances and let them permeate our society so that jubilee might come true for everyone. Living in just relations with each other, we feel safe, respected and cared for. Let this time of jubilee come!

† Listen to the cry of those who suffer, God, and encourage your Church and your people to work for a just society, a true jubilee! When everyone can feel free, be at ease, and enjoy your blessings. Amen

For further thought

• Discuss the reality of violence against women in your country and think of ways to support those who help survivors.

Friday 21 September
Unless the Lord builds the house

Read Psalm 127

Unless the Lord builds the house, those who build it labour in vain.

(part of verse 1)

Some years ago, when preparing the liturgy to celebrate the World Day of Prayer, South African Christians decided to share the meaning of an important traditional symbol in most of their families and communities: the three-legged iron pot. For them, this pot is a symbol of feeding, sharing and fellowship – of life in abundance.

Looking at this symbol through a Christian lens, these worship leaders reflected that just as this pot is anchored by three legs, so Christians are anchored in and are totally dependent on the Trinity. The pot, full of tasty food, also serves as a sign of God's invitation to build our lives in love and grace, believing in the gospel's teachings and in the strength granted by the Holy Spirit.

Listening to this vivid example from South Africa, the women celebrating the World Day of Prayer in a church in the suburbs of Buenos Aires thought that though there are not three-legged iron pots in Argentinian households, there are other ways of building fellowship and sharing God's grace. In Argentina we drink *mate*, a herbal infusion that we share with each other over long conversation, where we talk and listen with no rush.

Whether over a three-legged iron pot in South Africa, or over a cup of *mate* in Buenos Aires, it is in moments like this that God calls us to let his Spirit blow graciously to reach others. It is through interactions like these that God calls us to share the Good News and invite others to be nourished by it.

† Dear God, thanks for the gentle whisper of your Holy Spirit that reminds us that only when we ground our life in your hands will our efforts build true life and fellowship in your world. Amen

For further thought
• What would be the equivalent of the three-legged pot or *mate* in your own culture?

Balancing work and life – Dafne Plou

September

267

Saturday 22 September
Asleep at the screen?

Read Proverbs 6:6–11

How long will you lie there, O lazybones? When will you rise from your sleep?

(verse 9)

Doctors in Argentina are alarmed because as the years go by, children get fatter. They spend long hours lying on sofas or in beds, watching what goes on in their screens while they eat junk food. And their parents? Same story.

Many critics of our information society tell us bluntly that our relationships have been reduced to mere connections. If something happens, we go first to our phones, then to our friends. Some of these critics even say that we have become a generation of *'homo digitalis'*: people who interact online, but never think of real action, or of engaging sincerely with others. Have we become social lazybones? Should someone call us to rise from our sleep?

Could we announce the gospel only via messaging or online video? These can be useful tools, but Jesus showed us that even if he could preach at the pulpit of an important synagogue he was called to engage with the people face-to-face, visiting, healing, eating with them, sitting at the seashore, talking, listening, walking in the crowds and paying attention to people's needs, demands and cries for help. By his actions he showed us a new way to God, in commitment with each other, in justice, love and hope. Let us rise and follow him, looking up to build new communities where each of us matters and where relations are built on true fellowship.

† Dear Jesus, help us to understand the needs of our fellow men and women and follow your call to serve others with real interest, ready to listen, share and engage in actions and with causes that need our Christian commitment. Amen

For further thought

- What are the ways your church uses online media? What ministries of your church must be done with touch and physical presence?

Balancing work and life
2 Work

Notes by **Erice Fairbrother**

Erice Fairbrother is a Solitary of the Order of the Holy Cross Associates in New Zealand. Called to this work by her community, she is their Chaplain and leads the OHC Spirituality Centre in Napier. Her work includes teaching, leading courses in formation and in prayer and offering meditation and retreats. She is a published writer, pastoral supervisor and Anglican priest. She uses the genre of poetry to express contemporary theological reflection and critique. Her work includes editing, fostering local writing opportunities and publishing. Erice has used the NRSVA for these notes.

Sunday 23 September
Called to work

Read Proverbs 14:23–24

In all toil there is profit, but mere talk leads only to poverty.

(verse 23)

The well-being of a community (be it local, national or global) rests on equal access to resources and opportunities. In the novel *The Grapes of Wrath* the Joad family are discriminated against because they have no work, yet that lack of work lies not with personal inclination but with a society unwilling to ensure the basic human right to work and its profit.

Discipleship carries a similar responsibility; whether we are on our own or are part of a family, religious community or parish, our work is the same – to bring about the kingdom of God on earth. It means working for a world where there is equal opportunity for all to live together in peace, where none are denied the things that are profitable and where basic human needs are resourced and accessible.

Over this week we will explore the biblical wisdom around work as part of the divine desire for humanity, both the joys and the responsibilities this divine desire requires of us. For the godly life is an active life; it brings both sustenance and wisdom. We are all called to it; we are all called to make it possible for others to share in it also.

† Creator God, help us to see that all our work, whatever it be, is a sharing in the holy task of continuing as co-creators with you. Amen

God's business is for the happiness of all

> **Read Ecclesiastes 3:9–14**
>
> *I have seen the business that God has given to everyone to be busy with
> ... moreover, it is God's gift that all should eat and drink and take pleasure
> in all their toil.*
>
> *(verses 10, 13)*

Today we read that work is a gift, one that has been given so that
we might know life's happiness and pleasure. Producing the food
we eat and the joy we find in life's abundance are all part of what
God has designed and provided for us. It is not so much that we
are called to work to live, but that we are called to work to find the
fullness of life that comes from *God's* work of provision.

We read of this provision in verse 10: (there is a) 'business that God
has given to everyone to be busy with'. Growing up in a biblically
based religious environment gave me a childhood belief that the
work of God was about church work; being a missionary, a pray-er,
a preacher or leader of a faith community. After leaving home, and
beginning work in the marketplace, my childhood understandings
were challenged. I discovered there were Godly possibilities in the
everyday toil to put food on the table. That enjoyment and pleasure
were part of life, part of God's creative work of provision for us.

Currently the 'business' that God has given me is with writers
and artists and the provision of events enabling their work to be
enjoyed. It is work that comes from creative toil and gives rise to
pleasure and ongoing reflection, crossing divides between the
'secular' and the 'religious' spheres. It has caused me to reflect that
the 'business' that God gives us does not occur within such neat
categories. God's work is not exclusive. God's provision is for all.

† God of creation, give me a heart to find you wherever your 'business' for my life
takes me and to welcome all who come and share in it with me. Amen

For further thought

• Take time to meditate on what kind of work brings enjoyment
and happiness to you and to your community. What might it tell
you about God's provision for you?

Working together: a social priority

Read Ecclesiastes 4:6–12

Two are better than one, because they have a good reward for their toil …
A threefold cord is not quickly broken.

(verses 9, 12b)

A recent magazine interview covered the story of a young woman who left home at 17. Alone, without support, she tells how she was willing to take any work at the local takeaway even though it was irregular, and the wages below the minimum standard. As one meal a day was provided while at work, her hunger saw her taking short shifts at any and often risky hours, just to eat, just to survive. Approaching her union was to risk being laid off. Such exploitation of the vulnerable in the workforce is not new. Work that can sustain a reasonable standard of living is all too often a privilege that is taken lightly.

The scripture today suggests that people working together is an approach to work that allows for support, mutual benefit and companionship. Some years ago I had a role within my workplace as a union delegate. Our work meant we were able to stand together so that exploitation in terms of working conditions and pay could be resisted. It witnessed to the truth in verse 10, that if one falls (or is disadvantaged) they will find support.

This is, after all, the gospel model. Jesus called his disciples to work with him, forming a community of friendship that was tasked to build God's realm on earth; a realm where personal gain at the expense of others, and exploitation of the poor could have no place. It is a promise that will be realised when you and I make working for God's justice and peace a social priority.

† Pray that God's realm will come through your commitment to justice and peace for God's world.

For further thought

• Find out about local needs among the young, the vulnerable and the unemployed. Is there some way your faith community can assist in making changes?

Balancing work and life – Erice Fairbrother

September

Working in the now

Read Ecclesiastes 9:7–10

Whatever your hand finds to do, do with your might; for there is no work or thought or knowledge or wisdom in Sheol ...

(part of verse 10)

It is right and good to work hard; work is what makes our life possible and provides us with what we need. Indeed we are told to work 'with might'. Yet it is more than gaining an accumulation of things, for work can also be a source of freedom from worry. It is a blessing to be valued, but there is a warning against turning an appropriate valuing of what we gain into misplaced pride. Pride leads us to imagine that all we have is of our own making. It leads us to imagine it will last forever. On the other hand, a true work ethic is one that begins with a thankful heart, and whose benefits we share. It does not leave God out of the equation, nor does it neglect our neighbour.

Once, while leading a seminar on a theology of poverty, with students preparing for ordination, anxiety began to surface. Was I saying, one student queried, that to have two cars was wrong? The discussion then turned on the issue that it is not what we get out of our work, but what we do with the benefits it brings that should concern us. It is OK to enjoy the fruits of our labour. What is not OK is when we imagine that our work gives us the right to live in ways that deprive others of having a beneficial life. Resisting taking work for granted in the first place is a holy task that leads to a spirit of thankfulness and a social responsibility that creates communities of mutuality and respect.

† Giver of all good things; help me to remember that you are the true source of all I have and keep me generous, as you are generous in this life to me. Amen

For further thought

• Consider how the things that we have surrounded ourselves with might hold us back from being generous.

Thursday 27 September
Lasting investment

Read Matthew 25:14–29

For to all those who have, more will be given, and they will have an abundance.

(verse 29)

Most of us, I imagine, connect investment with money. However, the work of God is not always measurable or evaluated in financial terms. Generosity, for example, is a gospel value and a spiritual gift. Perhaps the accountability in our reading today touches on such valuables, more than on financial wealth. What if governments were to invest in generosity? Would it build a better world? Could it bring real benefit to everyone? What would it look like?

In recent years New Zealand has experienced devastating earthquakes. They have caused fatalities, they have brought down commercial centres and they have ruptured workplaces, from homes to urban sprawls, to farms, to sea-dependent communities. The impact has been social and psychological as well as economic. Many organisations have given much to the work of relief. But movingly, it has been the neighbourly gifts of time, the opening of homes, the giving from the heart and loving support that are unforgettable. It was a time when even the least of 'talents' and resources were shared, bringing very real benefits of companionship, warmth and comfort. It was a time when abundance was seen to be as much about the heart as about income.

Gospel abundance is about generosity and relationships rather than dogma or creed. The call to build the community of God on earth is a 'talent' we all receive for investing. It is an investment of hope, of faith and of justice. It is an investment that will create richer and whole communities. It is an investment for which we will all be held accountable by future generations.

† Grant that I may invest wisely and well, on a theology of poverty, the talents and resources that I have received. Amen

For further thought

• Where do I invest most of my energy and time? Does it help build a stronger, safer community?

Friday 28 September
Making trust possible

Read Luke 12:22–34

'Therefore I tell you, do not worry about your life … Instead, strive for his kingdom, and these things will be given to you as well.'

(verses 22a, 31)

No one in the helping professions would say to someone who was depressed, 'pull yourself together', nor would anyone working with a father of six who has been made redundant say, 'don't worry'. In a world of poverty, unemployment, oppression and exclusion from having enough through inequitable economic policies, this reading today begins to sound like advice for the privileged.

The spiritual issue that lies at the heart of social inequity is in fact highlighted in this passage. When there is not enough to go around, where suffering is not being addressed in real terms, the human spirit becomes depleted and faith is diminished. Inspirational leaders like Mother Teresa, Catherine of Genoa, or Mother Aubert here in New Zealand have helped us to see that commitment to the work of God cannot be separated from the commitment to work with the real needs of the deprived, needy and sick. They set about building God's realm on earth through practical work: the provision of shelter, medical help, food and support.

I'm not sure there is any immunity from worry, for we all get a share of it over our lifetime. Perhaps when Jesus asks us not to worry, it is more about a call to trust than to ignore reality. When we act for others, or advocate for the disadvantaged, the trust we have becomes visible. Where there is alleviation of earthly worry the words of Jesus emerge as life-giving and trustworthy. Life's pressures may remain, but what we do in the face of them, for ourselves as well as for others, makes all the difference.

† O God who meets me in my needs, keep me ever mindful of the needs of others. Amen

For further thought
- Find out about what's happening in your community, such as the arrival of new refugees, and explore ways of giving ongoing practical support.

No excuse for not contributing

Read 2 Thessalonians 3:6–13

… we were not idle when we were with you, and we did not eat anyone's bread without paying for it; but with toil and labour we worked night and day …

(part of verses 7–8)

It is considered prudent to look ahead and make provision for the future. Society encourages us to keep our eyes on what's coming up, exhorting us to plan for everything that might possibly happen. Such planning has its place and a wise person is diligent in making sure that no one in the future is disadvantaged by lack of forethought. Thinking ahead can also be a matter of safety.

I grew up knowing regular earthquakes, in a house that was at one stage partially damaged by one. As a result, my mother would every night ensure that her clothes were at hand so that she would be prepared to get us out in the event of another 'big one'! Today I, like many others, have an emergency pack nearby. We are a nation that lives prepared for what might come next.

The danger, however, is that living with an eye to the future can remove our focus from the needs and responsibilities of the present. The Thessalonian Christians were tempted to stop working while waiting for the return of Jesus. Paul reminded them that even he did not neglect his responsibility to work. Our Christian faith is no excuse for not contributing to society. Like Paul, our commitment to ensuring life will be well for all, begins with contributing to society's financial, political and social realities. Our work, the way we go about it, and the way we live relationally because of it, will shape and form God's kingdom on earth. Working faithfully in the present will bring us safely into what God has already prepared for us.

† Pray the Lord's Prayer slowly.

For further thought

- Meditate on the phrases concerning the 'kingdom come' and 'our daily bread'. How do they affect your approach to your daily work?

Balancing work and life
3 Rest

Notes by **Carla A. Grosch-Miller**

Carla A. Grosch-Miller is a freelance practical theologian, theological educator and poet. She lives in Northumberland, UK, where wild winds blow clutter from the mind, cloudscapes delight and light astounds. She is in love with the Grounding Mystery, curious about Reality and desirous of Living Aright on the earth. To this end she strives to be awake and to pay attention. She is the author of *Psalms Redux: Poems and Prayers* (Canterbury Press 2014) and articles in Volume 20:3 of *Theology and Sexuality*. In her dreams she is a mermaid. Carla has used the NIVUK for these notes.

Sunday 30 September
The end of anxiety

Read Exodus 33:12–23

The Lord replied, 'My Presence will go with you, and I will give you rest.'

(verse 14)

Confession: I am rubbish at resting, despite a decade-long infatuation with the idea of Sabbath. A few days ago I sat in an earnest room with other spiritual seekers, eating lunch and watching a cat languorously stretch out before the fire with a slow slap of her tail. How I would have liked to join her on the small rug before the hissing grate! I realised that to my mind I need an excuse to rest. I will work until I literally drop. A few years ago the strain of multiple bereavements and unhelpful work habits brought me to the limit and I was forced to stop, signed off sick. It was a humbling experience that in time became life-giving. I am learning to listen, to trust and to honour the sacred rhythm planted within.

This week we will explore God's offer of rest and our anxious striving. Moses was highly anxious; he was leading a stiff-necked, wayward people. He wanted to do the right thing and he knew he needed God's companionship to do that. God promised His presence and spoke to Moses' deepest unspoken need, saying, 'I will give you rest.'

† Holy One, You know me better than I know myself. Grant me faith to rely on Your presence and humility to accept Your offer of rest. Amen

Monday 1 October
A yoke of light

Read Matthew 11:25–30

'Come to me, all you who are weary and burdened, and I will give you rest. Take my yoke upon you and learn from me, for I am gentle and humble in heart, and you will find rest for your souls. For my yoke is easy and my burden is light.'

(verses 28–30)

'Yeah, right,' my shattered soul says. It's Your work, Jesus, that makes me weary and burdened. Your people wear me out. Your insistence that I love everyone, even my enemies, weighs me down. Your vision of a better world keeps me up at night. No way is Your yoke easy and Your burden light.

Unless You know something I don't know. Like the fact that no one, not even You, has to carry their burdens alone. And that actually I am not God and I am not in control. I don't have to know, understand or do everything. Maybe it is my arrogance that is making me feel over-responsible, my stoicism that is keeping me from asking for help and my ignorance that has blinded me to another way of being.

You watched Your father make yokes from green wood; perhaps You made them Yourself. You know that two oxen yoked together are far stronger than one. Are You offering to be my yokefellow? Are you asking me to trust You to lead me? To let go of thinking that it is all down to me? Are You inviting me into a communion that will infect me with gentleness and patience and enable me to walk with a spring in my step and the assurance that all shall be well?

I open my hands and let the burdens fall where they may. I pick up Your yoke: it is light – it is made of light. I lift my head and see the world and myself anew.

† Free me from myself. Make me like green wood and shape my life to wear Your yoke joyfully and gratefully. Amen

For further thought

• Sing the hymn 'I Heard the Voice of Jesus Say' by H. Bonar (1808–89). Let the song carry you through the day.

Balancing work and life – Carla A. Grosch-Miller

October

Enough already

Read Matthew 14:13–21

When Jesus heard [that John the Baptist had been killed by Herod], he withdrew by boat privately to a solitary place. Hearing of this, the crowds followed him on foot from the towns.

(verse 13)

I once heard someone say that if you read the Gospels carefully, you will see that Jesus often takes Himself away from the disciples and the crowds. I didn't believe it (which says something about me) until I combed the sacred text myself. This story of frustrated solitude was the only one I had remembered unaided.

The story speaks to me of expectations: ours and others'. The Gospel writer tells us that Jesus put aside His grief and weariness to heal and to feed. In the past I heard in this story that I was expected to do the same, ignoring personal basic needs in order to serve others. And so I did, until I learned the hard way that when the well is empty, what I attempt to give will not satisfy anyone and can cause damage. What I know now is that I can't give what I don't have. I need to separate myself from the crowd and drink deeply and often from the well in order to share living water with others.

The requirement of self-love and -care is hard to accept if one has been trained from a young age to meet others' needs and/ or has absorbed a theology of self-negation. Hear again the Great Commandment: Love the Lord your God and love your neighbour as yourself. We are not expected to give something we don't have, even if they are asking for it. Instead we can trust that God will use what little we do have and it will be enough.

† Call me away from the demands of others that I might find myself again in You and drink deeply from the well of salvation. Amen

For further thought

• Review your commitments. Which cause you dread? Which make your heart sing? Is there a clue here to what God may be asking of you?

Balancing work and life – Carla A. Grosch-Miller

October

Wednesday 3 October
Grace under pressure

Read Philippians 4:1–9

Do not be anxious about anything, but in every situation, by prayer and petition, with thanksgiving, present your requests to God. And the peace of God, which transcends all understanding, will guard your hearts and your minds in Christ Jesus.

(verses 6–7)

Paul wrote this letter to his beloved church in Philippi whilst in prison. That little church, the first planted on European soil on a main east–west road in the Roman Empire, was not popular with its neighbours. The city was hostile to the upstart community and made life difficult for the Followers of the Way. Moreover the church had its share of internal disagreements. Trouble within, trouble outwith – it was a community under pressure.

Paul in prison commands the church to 'Rejoice!' I would like to think that if I were imprisoned, I would rise to the occasion and become the best I could be (à la Nelson Mandela). But I know how small frustrations derail me. I know how the hostility of the outside world can have me doubting my community and myself. Call it internalised Christianophobia. On the one hand, doubt strips away assumptions and ideas that don't hold water. It can be a friend that helps me to make sense of faith and take reality seriously. On the other hand, doubt can fool me into thinking that faith is all about rationality and blind me to other kinds of knowing – intuitive, kinaesthetic, emotional, spiritual.

Knowing is at the centre of this passage. Knowing that God is. Knowing that our job in the grand scheme is to keep the faith, as one keeps a flame alight in the wind, taking one step at a time and entrusting the outcome to God who knows more than we ever can. Knowing that the fruit of surrender is the greatest of gifts: peace that passes understanding.

† You are God, not me. Open my hands and take every anxiety. Hear the prayers I dare not speak aloud. Bless me with the wisdom to trust and accept Your gift of peace. Amen

For further thought

• Look up Dietrich Bonhoeffer's poem 'By Gracious Powers so Wonderfully Sheltered', written in prison a few months before he was murdered by the Nazis.

Balancing work and life – Carla A. Grosch-Miller

October

Thursday 4 October
You can't take it with you

Read 1 Timothy 6:6–10

But godliness with contentment is great gain. For we brought nothing into the world, and we can take nothing out of it.

(verses 6–7)

Years in parish ministry taught me that people with the least were often the most generous. In their relative poverty they had learned what is of most value – that life was a gift to be shared, that vulnerability and tragedy haunt every doorway, that kindness is the currency of the kingdom.

We arrive, brand spanking new, in our birthday suits and spend the next days, months and years growing into ourselves and learning these things if we are lucky. Many distractions divert our attention. The shininess of things, the slipperiness of security, the seduction of more. We reach for the golden ring only to discover it is cheaply plated and breaks under pressure. All too often we only learn what is of most value when it is under threat or we lose it altogether.

The focusing question is: what is the purpose of your life, of my life? We bring nothing in but potential; we take nothing out but our death rags. In between we struggle and strive to make the most of it. The epistle writer counsels a simple focus to order life aright: godliness with contentment. Godliness – to live awake and responsive to the Holy; contentment – to have the wisdom to know what is worth struggling and striving for and the humility to be satisfied with one's life and effort. There is breath in this advice and nourishment. Life requires effort, yes, but there is contentment too.

† Focus my heart, Great God, on that which is of the most value so that I might lie down at night content with the day's choices and efforts. Amen

For further thought

- Open your bankbook. Note where your money goes each month. What does it say about what you value most? What would you like it to say?

Friday 5 October
Thou shalt rest

Read Hebrews 4:1–11

There remains, then, a Sabbath-rest for the people of God; for anyone who enters God's rest also rests from their works, just as God did … Let us, therefore, make every effort to enter that rest, so that no one will perish by following their example of disobedience.

(verses 9–11)

God commands Sabbath-rest. I forget this. I think of observing the Sabbath as good advice on a par with healthy eating and exercise: things that are good for body, mind and spirit. So it is … but it is also one of the Ten Commandments.

At the start of the new century I spent three weeks in Jerusalem and its environs, visiting a friend who was studying to be a rabbi. Leah lived in an Orthodox Jewish neighbourhood in a flat with a rooftop patio and large windows to let in the cooling breeze. Every Friday before evening fell, a neighbour began to sing a love song to welcome the Sabbath, the 'Queen of Days', his gorgeous tenor wafting in through our open windows. I was captivated, seduced. As he sang tension melted from my shoulders and a prayer of gratitude rose in my heart. I would spend Saturdays draped on the sofa, sampling Jewish devotional texts and enjoying the simple pleasures of long-time friendship and food. Saturday evening, Leah, her fellow students and I would climb the stairs to the rooftop patio, light the *Havdalah* candle and sing the end of Sabbath blessings.

The great rabbi and activist Abraham Joshua Heschel wrote a slim volume titled *The Sabbath,* first published in 1951. It too is a love song that woos our souls, naming the Sabbath as the greatest gift God has given to humankind and unravelling some of its mysteries.

These days, time seems to pass ever more quickly, each day full to the brim with opportunities. Deep in my soul, I hear the command of Sabbath-rest and I give thanks.

† May my voice join the great choir that sings in praise for the Sabbath and may my worshipful rest be pleasing to You, God of All Time and Space. Amen

For further thought
- How do you honour the command of Sabbath-rest? How will you do so in days to come?

Balancing work and life – Carla A. Grosch-Miller

October

Eternality

The world and its desires pass away, but whoever does the will of God lives for ever.

(verse 17)

I love the world. I cannot not love it. I love the slick leaves that will soon be underfoot as trees shed their colours. I love the billowing clouds that sail past my study window, the warm sun that fills the lounge in the morning and the garden in the afternoon, the burst of brightness in the flower tub outside the kitchen window. I love every season in its particularity. I stop and sniff roses as I walk to the postbox, breathe deeply as I bike to the pool and greet leashed dogs out for their morning constitutional. I am gaga over the earth and all that dwells upon it.

And knowing that it is temporal, and that I am too, makes it all the more precious.

Early Christianity was formed in a philosophical crucible of strong dualisms: matter = bad, spirit = good; female = bad, male = good. Desire was feared as something that tended towards evil. Some of the language of the epistles can lead us astray if we don't know that. Recent generations have rejected the dualisms and reclaimed desire as something that (discerned rightly) may also lead us to God. Despite the limitations of some of the language in 1 John, this last verse points to something unlimited and profoundly true: that in throwing oneself into the great flow of the river that is the love of God, we become part of something that is utterly unending. Our lives are part of the blessing flow, creating and recreating, as we are carried homeward bound. How can we keep from singing?

† I throw myself into Your great river, letting it carry me as it rushes through the earth, bringing life. May this river never cease to flow. Amen

For further thought

- Let go, let God … today and every day. If it may help, write down all your worries and concerns and place them in a prayer bowl or basket. Once they are in there, they are God's, not yours.

October

Proverbs
1 A tree of life

Notes by **Anthony Loke**

Dr Anthony Loke is an independent researcher, freelance author and educator in the area of biblical studies. His PhD, from the University of Wales, was on the 'Fear not' oracles in Deutero-Isaiah. He was formerly teaching in an ecumenical seminary in Malaysia for 19 years and a pastor with the Methodist Church for 32 years. He and his wife have two grown-up children and two guinea pigs. Anthony has used the NRSVA for this version.

Sunday 7 October
The fear of the Lord

Read Proverbs 1:1–7

The fear of the Lord is the beginning of knowledge; fools despise wisdom and instruction.

(verse 7)

We live in a world of knowledge and information. With these at our fingertips, we should be wiser than our forebears but this is often not the case. Surrounded with constant information overload, we find that true wisdom is in short supply and often lacking in the crucial areas of life.

There is a vast difference between knowledge and wisdom. Knowledge is facts but wisdom is the ability to put knowledge into good use. Many young people today are tech-savvy. They are full of information and data but it is another thing to be able to know how to use it. Wisdom is not really about the amount of grey matter in our brains. The ancient Hebrews knew this difference and sought to accumulate their wisdom, gathered through the centuries from wise sages who observed life in all its intricacies. This body of wisdom is to be passed down to the next generation who adds on their wisdom. Proverbs is a prime example of this type of wisdom. It is a wisdom that comes with age, like fine wine that is carefully aged.

Proverbs begins with a reminder to seek after wisdom (verses 2–7) because the aim of wisdom is to fear God and live a life that is pleasing to him.

† Lord, the world has much knowledge but greatly lacks wisdom. May people seek out your wisdom and live. Amen

Heed your elders

Read Proverbs 1:8–19

Hear, my child, your father's instruction, and do not reject your mother's teaching.

(verse 8)

Parents will know it is sometimes difficult to speak with their teenage children. The latter often think they know more than their parents. In a sense, they are right and not right. There is a Chinese proverb which says, 'I have eaten more salt than you have eaten rice.' It means there is a type of wisdom that only comes with age and experience and parents have lived longer than their children and have garnered some of that wisdom.

The Bible calls those who despise wisdom 'fools' (Psalm 14:1). Thus, we can note the urgency in the father's plea to his children (the Hebrew plural of 'sons' can include daughters) to heed his wisdom as well as their mother's wisdom. Because young people are prone to listening to their friends and easily succumb to peer pressure, they would prefer not to listen to their parents' advice. Without the benefit of a wisdom learned through years of 'trial and error' and a wisdom matured by the ages, young people can be easily enticed to go astray by mixing with bad company (verses 10–19). The voice of the parents is like the voice of Wisdom. They beckon their children to listen to the voice of experience: 'we know that is not good for you' (verse 10), 'we can see the outcome if you do this' (verse 19).

† Lord, help us to heed the advice of those who are older and wiser than us, so that we may learn from their mistakes and avoid repeating their errors. Amen

For further thought

• Those who are parents have to seriously consider how they can get their children to listen to them without coming across as domineering or as saying 'We know everything!'

Proverbs – Anthony Loke

October

Listen to Lady Wisdom

Read Proverbs 1:20–33

*'But those who listen to me will be secure and will live at ease,
without dread of disaster.'*

(verse 33)

These verses form the first of three addresses by Lady Wisdom.
The ancient Hebrew sages chose to personify abstract qualities like
wisdom and folly. This was a unique way to get their hearers to pay
attention to these two voices. Lady Wisdom and Lady Folly are two
competing voices calling out to the young people, and there is a
sharp contrast between choosing the life offered by Wisdom and
the life offered by Folly.

Lady Wisdom calls out in the crowded city street (verse 20). Her
audience is the 'simple ones' (verse 22). In modern terms, these
people are the naïve and simple-minded, prone to follow without
discerning. Lady Wisdom cajoles and reasons with them (verses
22–27) but they choose to ignore her (verse 24). They prefer to
follow the alluring voice of Lady Folly (9:13–18). People are prone
today to hear and follow the voice of foolishness rather than the
voice of wisdom. How often we regret our actions after that!

The consequences of not heeding wisdom are spelt out in verses
31–32. They will reap what they have sown. To reject the voice
of Lady Wisdom is actually to reject God (verse 29) because true
wisdom comes from God (verse 7). It is not too late for young
people (and old) to acknowledge and abandon their foolish ways
and seek after true wisdom. Even the prodigal son in Luke 15
realised his mistake and returned to his waiting father.

† In the midst of the competing voices we hear in the world, help me, Lord, to
distinguish the voice of Wisdom, follow after her and walk in her path. Amen

For further thought

• How can you learn to clearly distinguish the two voices of
Lady Wisdom and Lady Folly?

Proverbs – Anthony Loke

October

285

Seek wisdom and find safety

Read Proverbs 2:1–15

Then you will understand the fear of the Lord and find the knowledge of God.

(verse 5)

The father speaks to his children to encourage them to strive for wisdom (verses 1–2). The parents' words are like the commandments (the Torah) and the latter will incline their hearts to understanding. Each person must make his or her own quest to discover wisdom. Their quest will not fail because wisdom comes from God and he will give wisdom to those who actively seek for it (verse 6).

But is the quest for wisdom still relevant today? Young people are on their own quests to make money, get their degrees, become famous and find the good life. So we constantly equip ourselves with skills and knowledge for specialised areas of work. We attend courses and seminars to prepare ourselves to face new challenges in our workplace. Who really wants to go on a personal quest to be a wise man or wise woman?

In chapter 2, we see the value of wisdom and education. The quest for wisdom is not a self-centred esoteric pursuit but one that leads to wisdom and ethical behaviour as the goal. We pursue wisdom in order to learn to live uprightly before God and humans (verse 7). We do so in order to become good citizens in our society with a concern for the welfare of others, to preserve justice and righteousness (verses 8–9). The converse of this are the wicked who rejoice to do evil and delight in it (verses 13–15).

† Lord, direct my life towards seeking you, the true Wisdom. Amen

For further thought

• There is safety in finding wisdom. Do we place as much concern on this quest for wisdom as we do on other things in our lives?

Wisdom as a moral safeguard

Read Proverbs 2:16–22

You will be saved from the loose woman, from the adulteress with her smooth words.

(verse 16)

In chapter 2, we are told that the second value of wisdom is to protect ourselves from one of the enemies of Lady Wisdom: the deceptive woman (verses 16–19). Some people will find this negative portrayal of the 'adulteress' or 'loose woman' offensive. Because the prime target of the ancient Hebrew sages was the young men in Hebrew society, the sages used this portrayal to get across the urgent message. The young men were the future leaders of the family, society and the nation and if they failed by being tempted to go sexually astray, all the units of family, society and nation would be affected. Hence, the urgent warning in these verses not to fall into the wiles and charms of the 'adulteress' or 'loose woman'. If the message had been addressed to the daughters, then the equivalent would be the 'smooth operator' or the 'Casanova'.

The lesson here for young men (and young women) is that it is easy to succumb to sexual temptations. When they commit sexual and moral infidelity (especially if they are already married), that fatal mistake can destroy the very fabric of family, society and nation. Wisdom can be a moral safeguard here for the young. Wisdom will jealously guard their paths and help them keep to the paths of the just (verse 20). Be counted among the upright and innocent, not among the wicked and treacherous (verses 21–22).

† Lord, help me to guard my path so that it does not lead to wickedness and evil but to justice and uprightness. Amen

For further thought

• How can young people keep their way pure? By guarding it according to your word (Psalm 119:9).

Proverbs – Anthony Loke

October

Happy are those who find wisdom

Read Proverbs 3:13–26

She is a tree of life to those who lay hold of her; those who hold her fast are called happy.

(verse 18)

Those who find wisdom are called 'happy'. In some translations, the word 'blessed' is used which reminds us of Psalm 1:1: 'Blessed is the man.' The person who finds wisdom is indeed a happy person because true wisdom is firstly a hard-won possession more profitable than silver and gold (verse 14) or jewels or anything we desire in life (verse 15). Secondly, wisdom is a tree of life to all who find her (verse 18). With wisdom one finds long life on one hand and honour and riches on the other hand (verse 16). Armed with wisdom, one can ensure that one's life will be more at ease and reap the benefits that wisdom offers.

The father's voice appears again in verse 21 reminding his children to keep sound wisdom and prudence. The benefits of keeping sound wisdom and prudence are spelt out in the rest of the verses. How sad it is today that young people are often not interested in this pursuit of biblical wisdom. Safety and security come to those who actively pursue after wisdom. How many times have we done something hastily and unwisely and after that lived to regret our actions? If our actions have been wisely informed, we would not have been caught unawares (verse 25). Because wisdom comes from God who is the true giver of wisdom (verses 19–20), he is also our source of true confidence (verse 26). Indeed, the blessed person is the one who through wisdom puts his or her trust in God and fears him.

† Can we trust you, God, in everything including times of adversity and suffering? Help us to trust. Amen

For further thought

• In times like these, how can one continue to be 'happy'?

Saturday 13 October
A father's example

Read Proverbs 4:1–13

> Listen, children, to a father's instruction, and be attentive, that you may gain insight.

> *(verse 1)*

In the old days, a father would teach his children what he himself had learned from his father. It is interesting to note the linking of three generations (children–father–my father) in the process of acquiring and passing on wisdom (cf. Deuteronomy 6:1–8; Psalm 78:1–8). This is also the pattern here in Proverbs (verses 3–4). The father tells his children to pay attention to his words as he is speaking from his experience. This type of wisdom cannot be learned from books but from the 'school of life' (or as someone candidly puts it, the 'school of hard knocks'). Only when a person has gone through the different seasons of life (childhood, adolescence, adulthood, old age) can he or she speak with experience and knowledge on certain matters.

Listening is the first step to gaining wisdom (verse 1). Only when we really listen and pay attention to the words can we begin to acquire wisdom. Listening to the words from our forefathers is one good way to deepen our wisdom but we often hastily dismiss such stories as 'old wives' tales'.

The father, in exhorting his children to listen to his words, is bringing them to a higher level – contact with Wisdom herself (verses 6–9). When they engage in the pursuit of wisdom, they are actually pursuing Lady Wisdom who, like a good companion for life, will bestow upon them honour, protection and even life itself (verse 13).

† Lord, if I can spend so much time in the pursuit of things that ultimately don't matter, help me then to pursue Wisdom and receive from her the things that matter. Amen

For further thought

• How can we ensure that we pass down the body of family wisdom accumulated within our own family circle to the next generation?

Proverbs – Anthony Loke

October

Proverbs
2 You are my sister

Notes by **Jane Gonzalez**

See p. 190 for Jane's biography. Jane has used the NIVUK for these notes.

Sunday 14 October
The university of life

Read Proverbs 5:1–14

> You will say, 'How I hated discipline! How my heart spurned correction!
> I would not obey my teachers or turn my ear to my instructors.
> And I was soon in serious trouble in the assembly of God's people.'

(verses 12–14)

Self-help and self-improvement books, programmes and apps are big business nowadays. While the section on 'Religion' in our local bookshop shrinks steadily, the one containing books to help us cope with the stresses of modern living expands all the time. Television programmes abound with experts on every subject, advising us on how to declutter our lives, bring up children and be happy. It seems that we no longer trust in the wisdom of the past or in our own judgements.

Our readings this week come from the self-improvement manual of the Hebrew people. The book of Proverbs is a distillation of life experiences with the practical aim of enabling people to live successfully: that is, to seek wisdom, and live righteously and in proper relationship with God and each other. To be called foolish in those days was not to be thought merely silly, but to be sinful.

For a Christian, conversion – self-improvement – needs discipline and takes time. The root of the word 'discipline' lies in the Latin for 'learning'. Discipline is a means by which we learn, through reflection and instruction. A hard lesson for us to take in and one which takes a lifetime to comprehend.

† Father, help me to heed your call to conversion. Give me a heart willing to learn and the wisdom to follow your ways in all things. Amen

Monday 15 October
Someone to watch over me

Read Proverbs 5:15–23

The evil deeds of the wicked ensnare them; the cords of their sins hold them fast.
For lack of discipline they will die, led astray by their own great folly.

(verses 22–23)

As a family we enjoy watching films together. One of the favourite ones recently has been *The Lives of Others*. It is set in East Germany during the years of communism when the population was under constant surveillance by the security forces. Today, in the UK, it appears that this is the case for us. Apparently, we are the most snooped-upon nation on earth, with an enormous number of CCTV cameras watching our every move. This keeps us safe but questions are often raised about our privacy. Can we have security without intrusiveness?

It is a sad fact that, for many people, God appears in this light. He is a stern judge, ceaselessly monitoring the intelligence tapes in search of misdemeanours or mistakes. He listens in to our conversations, tapping the phone, looking for unorthodox views or bad language. Passages like the one we read today might seem to bear this out. And indeed we know that one day we will be called to account for our lives.

A more fruitful way of looking at this passage might be to concentrate on how God watches over us, not marking where we trip up but catching us as we fall. He doesn't set snares for us; rather he helps clear them. Wisdom invites us to learn from the stumbles on the path – this is the discipline that enables us to change and grow as people – in the knowledge that we are not monitored as potential wrongdoers but rather watched over with love.

† Father, I thank you for your all-embracing love and care for me. I know that I walk always in your presence and I am grateful for it. Amen

For further thought

- What is your image of God? Reflect prayerfully on Psalm 139: 'O God you search me …' Does the God described here worry or reassure you?

Proverbs – Jane Gonzalez

October

Tuesday 16 October
It's a family affair

Read Proverbs 7:1–5

Say to wisdom, 'You are my sister,' and to insight, 'You are my relative.'
They will keep you from the adulterous woman, from the wayward woman with her seductive words.

(verses 4–5)

This summer my husband and I celebrated 39 years of marriage. Although not a significant number in terms of anniversaries, we marked it in a very special way, with a short ceremony of blessing at the church we attend in Spain. We gave thanks for the gift of each other and recalled the vows that we made on our wedding day.

Promises are sometimes easily made and as easily broken. The increasing number of marital break-ups may cause us to wonder if people take their vows lightly or fail to work at maintaining relationships. We are all familiar with some business practices whereby promises are made to keep factories open or enterprises running, and then these are set aside, often with the flimsiest of excuses. In parish life, no less than in our personal lives, we may notice a reluctance to commit on the part of many.

The book of Proverbs praises the wisdom shown by those who keep their promises and honour their commitments. This is a hard-won fidelity – it takes courage and resolution to be faithful to a relationship through all the ups and downs of life when the temptation is to give up. Of course, some struggles prove too much no matter how hard people try.

We are not alone in our adversity – the Spirit is with us. The intimacy of that relationship means that we are not friendless or without resources. No matter what comes our way, in the way that a loving family rallies round when one of its members is in need, we will not be left as orphans (John 14:18).

† Father, increase my faith in you. When troubles come, and I am tempted to give up, give me the strength to carry on. Amen

For further thought

- Consider the initiatives and projects that run in your church or faith community. Can you commit yourself to one of them and pledge your time as well as your money?

Wednesday 17 October
Fools rush in

Read Proverbs 7:6–23

With persuasive words she led him astray; she seduced him with her smooth talk.
All at once he followed her like an ox going to the slaughter ...
like a bird darting into a snare, little knowing it will cost him his life.

(verses 21–22a, 23b)

A friend is having his kitchen remodelled at present. Of all the improvements, the thing of which he is proudest is the built-in, state-of-the-art coffee machine. It's something he uses daily, many times during the day, in fact. I'm not sure how many of the other gadgets will be as frequently used! How many of us have cupboards cluttered with juicers and bread machines, or sheds containing exercise bikes and sports equipment – many purchased because the advertisers sold us a dream, an idea of fitness or health or the easy life? Advertising works by seducing us into buying what we don't need or want.

Many of the readings from the book of Proverbs warn against the temptation presented by beautiful and seductive women who can easily lead callow young men astray. The first nine chapters of Proverbs, in particular, are very much a call to seek out the beauties of Wisdom and to avoid being tempted from her by other attractions. So, while it is right to speak out against adultery we should not interpret the today's passage in too narrow a sense. There are many infidelities that can distract us from the path of wisdom. They can lead us into sin, and if we are not careful, into vice.

Jesus emphasises this. In Matthew 5:21–28, he tells us to keep to the spirit of the Law rather than the letter. We may not be guilty of adultery as such but where are the betrayals in our lives? What seduces us from doing right? Whom do we let down by our lack of commitment?

† Father, keep me focused on the right path. Lead me and guide me in the way of righteousness. Amen

For further thought
• Are there situations in our life where you feel betrayed or let down? Spend some time in prayer for those who have hurt you.

Proverbs – Jane Gonzalez

October

Thursday 18 October
Easy come, easy go

Read Proverbs 8:1–12

Choose my instruction instead of silver, knowledge rather than choice gold,
for wisdom is more precious than rubies, and nothing you desire can compare with her.

(verses 10–11)

In these days of easy credit and access to loans, the notion of saving up for anything can appear strange. I can remember my mother arranging for us to have new bedroom furniture when we were young and my father's horrified reaction when she told him that it was all being done on hire purchase. His was a generation that saved. It is pleasant not to have to wait a long time to acquire the things that we desire but instant gratification has its pitfalls. Things that come to us easily are just as easily discarded. There is no sense of achievement or satisfaction in having worked hard for something.

In the book of Proverbs, wisdom is the 'pearl of great price'. Wisdom cannot be bought, however. It can only be learned through instruction by those who have walked in wisdom's ways, and by learning from one's own mistakes. The acquisition of wisdom entails application and discipline. There are no get-wise-quick schemes. Like saving up, acquiring wisdom takes time.

Taking time sits uneasily with many of us today. Sacrifice is a difficult concept to understand when we have got used to next-day deliveries from Amazon. Our faith, however, is one which asks us to be patient. There is a cost and we are asked to pay it. Jesus tells us of a merchant who sells all he has to possess a gem, or someone who buys a field full of buried treasure again by selling everything he owns (Matthew 13:44–46). The wise person knows the cost and willingly pays it.

† Father, help me to be wise. Give me the strength and the patience to store up treasures in heaven. Amen

For further thought

- Make a gesture of sacrifice today. Give up the internet or your mobile phone. Switch off the computer or the television. Use the time you save wisely.

Life's rich tapestry

Read Proverbs 9:1–6

'Let all who are simple come to my house …
Come, eat my food and drink the wine I have mixed.
Leave your simple ways and you will live; walk in the way of
insight.'

(part of verses 4–6)

The word 'simple' is one with many connotations. From unsophisticated to foolish, there are many meanings. My father was a simple man – in the best meaning of the word. He wasn't uncomplicated – no human being is; nor was he foolish or gullible. He was modest, unaffected and unassuming. I would say that he was wise – in the way that Proverbs sees wisdom. He had a rich experience of life that had left him with a calm and practical acceptance of his lot and the ability to see the good in all. He was a man who valued common sense.

In our passage, Wisdom is not calling to people like my father. She summons the naïve, the credulous, those whose inability to learn from life's experiences may lead them away from God. She challenges us all to learn from her: to seek a proper simplicity. We overcomplicate our lives because we are often worldly rather than worldly-wise. The values of the world, if we are not wary, may contaminate us. For this reason Christians have often had an uneasy relationship with the 'world'. It has been seen as a place to flee from; the realm of darkness where the forces of evil lurk in wait for the unsuspecting. Wisdom offers us a way of resisting and of remaining true to the gospel.

The world is the arena of our activity. We live in it, we make mistakes in it, and if we follow the paths of wisdom, we learn from it, gaining insight and true simplicity of heart.

† Father, give me a childlike, simple faith which trusts you in everything. Keep me pure in heart and focused only on doing your will. Amen

For further thought

• Live simply, that others might simply live. Have a look at CAFOD's 'Live Simply' campaign on their website. How might you rise to this challenge at home and in your parish?

Proverbs – Jane Gonzalez

October

Saturday 20 October
A hard act to follow

Read Proverbs 31:10–31

'Many women do noble things, but you surpass them all.'
Charm is deceptive, and beauty is fleeting; but a woman who fears the Lord is to be praised.
Honour her for all that her hands have done, and let her works bring her praise at the city gate.

(verses 29–31)

I was talking to a friend not so long ago about the stresses faced by young families today. Being female, we also touched upon the intense pressure that many women face to be 'superwomen'. This was a term made famous by Shirley Conran in the 1970s. Since then she has said that life is, in fact, 'too short to stuff a mushroom', but many women feel compelled to be all, do all and have all: to be the perfect wife, mother and homemaker while pursuing a full-time career. Expectations are high and not necessarily achievable.

On the surface, today's passage (an acrostic poem in the original Hebrew) seems to set out a pattern of womanhood, a model for women to follow – in so far as we can, many centuries after the original was penned. It speaks of a paragon of virtue, whose grasp on both domestic and business matters is second to none. She sounds like the original superwoman. Most women, both then and now, would find this lady a very difficult act to follow.

A closer reading reveals that this is less about upholding an ideal for us to emulate than a hymn of praise by a husband for his wife. He is respected, supported and honoured by the high esteem in which she is held. He looks at her with love and sets out a personal record of the blessings she has brought to him. These are the particular attributes of one woman. All of us, male and female, however, might learn from the wisdom of her ways.

† Father, help me to seek perfection by following your ways and not the ways of the world. May I emulate Mary, the mother of Jesus, in a life of service and commitment. Amen

For further thought

• Think about your favourite biblical woman or female saint. What can you learn from them and put into practice in your own life?

Proverbs
3 The golden earring

Notes by **Deseta Davis**

See p. 169 for Deseta's biography. Deseta has used the NIVUK for these notes.

Sunday 21 October
Where is your trust?

Read Proverbs 11:28

> *Those who trust in their riches will fall, but the righteous will thrive like a green leaf.*

> *(verse 28)*

A common British proverb today is, 'Money does not buy happiness.' Yet it would seem quite a false proverb. In this celebrity-driven world, which is all about externalities, a person is judged by what they are wearing, what they are driving and where they live. The bigger the bank balance the better, as the gap between the rich and poor grows ever larger year-on-year.

There seems nothing good about being poor; but Jesus says 'the kingdom of heaven belongs to them'. The elders in my church tell us many stories of their life in the West Indies. A common story is where they had no food for their young children, so they would fill a saucepan with water and set it to boil. They would then pray that God would provide the food. They were never disappointed. The knock would come on the door and someone would bring a few potatoes or some flour or some other food and their children and household were fed. God truly blessed them and they flourished.

Psalm 62:10 tells us not to make our living by extortion or stealing, and if riches increase, not to set our heart on them. Throughout the Bible we are warned against making riches the centre of our lives. Money is not bad in itself; it depends on whether our trust is in riches or God!

† Thank you, God, for all your good gifts. May we trust in you rather than your provisions. Amen

Proverbs – Deseta Davis

October

Monday 22 October
Sticks and stones

Read Proverbs 15:1

A gentle answer turns away wrath, but a harsh word stirs up anger.

(verse 1)

When my children were called names at school, I always told them to repeat the little rhyme, 'Sticks and stones may break my bones, but words will never harm me.' How wrong I was! Words can cut just as deep as a sharp instrument, if not more. They can be used for beneficial or destructive purposes. How you answer a person can incite anger or calm them down, heal or inflict pain. We can carry words with us throughout our lives and when we least expect it, they come back to haunt us.

Belonging to a family of five children there was always something to fight and argue about. My mother, ever the peacemaker, often quoted this proverb. This did not stop me from trying my hardest to cut deep with my words, going straight for the jugular.

I am grateful that as I have grown older, I realise how much words can hurt and now try to speak into a situation a little more calmly and in a more measured way. As a prison chaplain, I deal every day with men who are very angry. Some are ready to fight over the simplest things. When meeting with them, it is important that I remain calm and keep the situation peaceful. I cannot play up to their anger. I am so often amazed how speaking to them gently and calmly generally quiets their rage and towards the end of the session I have a very different man sitting in front of me than the one that first came in.

† Dear God, forgive us for hurting one another with our words. May we make it right with each other. Amen

For further thought

- Think consciously of the words you speak today. Try and make them wholesome and healing.

Children learn what they live

Read Proverbs 17:1

Better a dry crust with peace and quiet than a house full of feasting, with strife.

(verse 1)

Today in the West we believe that the mark of success is in the abundance of things that we own. However, the Bible teaches us that 'godliness with contentment is great gain' (1 Timothy 6:6). Therefore true success is contentment with the things we have. This helps us to break out of the pressure of living to constantly gain more.

As the writer of Proverbs is prone to do, he turns popular culture on its head. The household with little but which lives in peace is superior to the one that is filled with feasting yet also conflict. The family with little shows their contentment with what they have and are able to live without conflict. Their peace and love for one another bring happiness within the family even though they have nothing else in the world. Yet a family living in the middle of luxury can live a life of misery when differences and bitterness have crept in.

It is well documented that a house of conflict is a dysfunctional household. Children grow up to believe what they see; they believe that is how life is. They bring it into their adulthood and it continues into their new family.

Riches do not protect from conflict, rather they have the tendency to cause more conflict and wars. But peace can be found in the household of those who have very little.

† Bread of Life, may we be content with what we possess and live in peace with each other. Amen

For further thought
- Find the poem 'Children Learn What They Live' by Dorothy Law Nolte. What can you learn from it?

Proverbs – Deseta Davis

October

The least of these

Read Proverbs 21:13

Whoever shuts their ears to the cry of the poor will also cry out and not be answered.

(verse 13)

There are many stories in the Bible about the rich not getting benefit in their time of need, such as Lazarus and the rich man in Luke 16. The surprising thing about this proverb is that it talks about a man rather than a 'rich' man. It lets no one off the hook, everyone is responsible. Most people, if asked, would not say they were rich; but if we are honest, there are many people poorer than ourselves. Is this proverb talking about us?

If we own a business and pay the lowest wages possible, if we neglect to do justice, if we do not help to relieve those in distress according to our ability to do so – we are stopping our ears to the cry of the poor.

Jesus in Matthew 25 puts a curse on those that did not look to the care of others, saying, 'I was hungry and you gave me nothing to eat, I was thirsty and you gave me nothing to drink, I was a stranger and you did not invite me in, I needed clothes and you did not clothe me, I was ill and in prison and you did not look after me.' Going on, Jesus said, 'whatever you did not do for one of the least of these, you did not do for me' (Matthew 25:42–45).

When we shut our ears to the cry of the poor and others who are oppressed, we shut our ears to Jesus, for he is among the least of these and will not hear us in our time of need.

† Loving God, may I not stop my ears to the cry of the poor. Help me to be the hands and feet that you use to help them in their time of need. Amen

For further thought

• Jesus said, 'Blessed are the merciful, for they will be shown mercy' (Matthew 5:7). Whom can you show mercy to today?

Thursday 25 October
Speak, Lord, your servant is listening

Read Proverbs 25:12

*Like an earring of gold or an ornament of fine gold is the rebuke
of a wise judge to a listening ear.*

(verse 12)

Recently in a course we learned about active listening. If you are like me, I am not very good at listening. I am always ready to give an answer. I always have something to say. I have chastised myself many times for 'putting my foot in it', i.e. speaking without thinking and getting myself into trouble. This shows a lack of wisdom in many respects.

Listening is an important part of life. We are told that we have two ears and one mouth in order to listen more than we speak. It could be said that he who willingly gives heed to wise chastisement does a better service to his ears than if he adorned them with the finest gold and with genuine pearls. Just as gold is purified in the fire to burn out dross, so a rebuke or criticism from a wise person, although not something that we like to hear, helps to make us into a better person, if we apply it to our lives.

Wisdom comes from God, so a wise person knows how to rebuke and warn in a discreet and prudent way. They choose the occasion and their words carefully. The listening ear is a ready hearer who appreciates the value of rebukes and is not stubborn or rebellious. Listening is more than hearing, it's about learning and applying what has been heard. As God speaks through others into our lives, we can join with Samuel and say, 'Speak Lord, your servant is listening.' May we not be forgetful hearers.

† Wise God, may I be quick to hear, slow to speak and slow to anger, knowing that you have put your wisdom in others to help make me the person you want me to be. Amen

For further thought

• How are your listening skills? Look into a course that will help to improve them.

Proverbs – Deseta Davis

October

Self-control!

Read Proverbs 25:28

Like a city whose walls are broken through is a person who lacks self-control.

(verse 28)

When a city was built there were strong fortifications and gates with great walls. These walls also had towers constructed as part of the wall. At the point of the tower, the walls were built higher and served as a fortification. The wall was a protection for the city. The approach of the enemy could be sighted from the tower and weapons hurled down upon the enemy who attempted to take the city. Almost every gate of any consequence would have a tower over it.

When a city was invaded the wall was broken down and destroyed, the city became exposed, vulnerable and defenceless. It was then at the mercy of the enemy who would come and destroy the city.

The proverb today tells us that a person who lacks self-control is like an unfortified city at the mercy of the enemy, vulnerable and defenceless. It is said that the greatest battle is against one's spirit.

Many people today lack self-control to some degree or other – this may be through affections, appetites, passions, desires, inclinations, resentments and much more. Working with those in prison, lack of self-control is evident every day. Many give themselves over to their base desires and passions and being like an unfortified city, they become vulnerable and end up in prison.

Self-control is one of the fruits of the Spirit. It is easy to lose self-control but with the help of the Spirit we can overcome. The old saying is apt in this situation: 'A man who conquers himself is greater than a man who conquers a city.'

† Dear God, give me grace to control myself in all aspects of my life, through your Spirit. Amen

For further thought

• Reflect on yourself – where do you need more self-control? Try working on it.

Saturday 27 October
What is stealing your sleep?

Read Proverbs 26:14

As a door turns on its hinges, so a sluggard turns on his bed.

(verse 14)

A door moves back and forth and from side to side but never goes anywhere. It keeps things in or out. A lazy person is seen in the same way. This proverb condemns the attitude, action and character of a lazy person. A sluggard will do anything but work.

Although sleep is very important for health and well-being, too much can also be detrimental to health. According to Proverbs 20:13, too much sleep can bring a person to poverty. The benefits system in the UK allows people to live without working, whereas in many other countries if a person does not work, they cannot live.

In our modern world, the benefits of electricity and the continued access to electronic devices like televisions, computers, game stations and smartphones steal our time more aggressively than sleep. I know of some people so addicted to social media that they cannot go to sleep without checking what has happened. This continues late into the night, night after night and affects everything that happens the next day. The nights become longer and the days become shorter.

The advent of computers was also supposed to make life simpler at work. In the UK there was supposed to be a shorter working week and a paperless office. Contrary to this, people now work from home well into the night and paper is used much more than ever. Sleep is then eroded and taken where it can be. The work–life balance continues to deteriorate. In the UK many times we live to work, whereas in other countries, they work to live!

† Blessed God, help me to slow down if I am employed, and to find work if I am unemployed. Also help those who work very hard for very little each day, please provide for them. Amen

For further thought
• What is your relationship with technology? Does it help your work–life balance, or hurt it?

Proverbs – Deseta Davis

October

Readings in Mark (3)
1 Watch and wait

Notes by Jarel Robinson-Brown

Jarel Robinson-Brown was born in London and is currently a Methodist minister in the Cardiff Circuit in South Wales. He has the privilege of working with many ages and preaching to varied congregations as well as ecumenically in Wales. As someone passionate about issues of justice and equality, Jarel finds his rooted-ness in sacramental Methodism and Benedictine Spirituality. He enjoys spending time at the piano, or with his Jack Russell enjoying the Welsh outdoors! Jarel has used the NRSVA for these notes.

Sunday 28 October
The power of Jesus' words, and our own

Read Mark 13:1–8

As he came out of the temple, one of his disciples said to him, 'Look, Teacher, what large stones and what large buildings!' Then Jesus asked him, 'Do you see these great buildings? Not one stone will be left here upon another; all will be thrown down.'

(verses 1–2)

I've often found myself whilst walking Seb (my dog!) saying things in conversations to strangers without really thinking. In this passage, we are left asking, What exactly did Jesus want to get across? What on earth was Jesus thinking?! Perhaps he wasn't thinking much at all – in that post-worship state of mind. We all know what that can be like! Words always have the potential to be explosive, and we ourselves may recall moments when potentially explosive words flew out of our mouths, or out of the mouths of others towards us. Jesus' words here in Mark's Gospel are explosive, but they are also necessary.

Necessary, not just because they were true, but also because their message was urgent and pregnant with meaning. Peter, James, John and Andrew need not be consumed by worries about the Temple, but rather about the falsehood and dishonesty of those who say they are of Christ. What the disciples need to know is that Christ alone is trustworthy, and the destruction of any earthly thing cannot change that. Evil may have its hour, but God shall have his day!

† Lord Jesus Christ, tame my tongue this week, that in all that I say and do it might bring glory to God. Amen

Monday 29 October
Promise keeper

Read Mark 13:14–27

Then they will see 'the Son of Man coming in clouds' with great power and glory. Then he will send out the angels, and gather his elect from the four winds, from the ends of the earth to the ends of heaven.

(verses 26–27)

I love the hymns of Charles Wesley for their real, but heavenly descriptive power. Every Wesley hymn is a work of magnificent poetry – and each hymn by Wesley lands us in heaven, regardless of where we begin in the opening verse.

Scripture has a habit of dressing Jesus up in a whole load of unhelpful paraphernalia. Here, in Mark's Gospel it is Jesus himself who gives a glorious account of his coming at the end of time. We might think of that great Advent hymn by Charles Wesley, 'Lo He Comes with Clouds Descending!' Sadly, in our world today, it isn't difficult to imagine a darkened world full of famine, war and suffering. Yet we very seldom remember to give thanks for the good, the love and the peace which we do experience. What we have to remember is that the one who has made the promise is trustworthy, and Jesus has promised that he shall come again – and when he does all that is wrong with our world will be put right. The hard part is keeping mindful of the promises of Jesus, of holding on to the promise that daylight truly does come in the morning – that the light which shines in the darkness will never be overcome, and that the mystery of faith, which is great, stands firm: that Christ has died, Christ is risen and Christ shall come again.

† Lord of heaven and earth, you call all things into being – and through your Son Jesus Christ order both heaven and earth. Bring peace, hope, and light to our world, in us and through us. In your name, amen

For further thought

• Are you a light in the darkness of others? Maybe there are ways you can brighten up someone's day with a simple phone call, or a word of encouragement this week.

Readings in Mark (3) – Jarel Robinson-Brown

October

Tuesday 30 October
Be watchful – not worried!

Read Mark 13:32–37

'But about that day or hour no one knows, neither the angels in heaven, nor the Son, but only the Father. Beware, keep alert; for you do not know when the time will come.'

(verses 32–33)

Jesus is coming – look busy!

Something that St Benedict would despise in me is perhaps my tendency to be 'busy'. Not because busyness is bad in and of itself, but because to be busy means that many things are pushed outside of our attention. I once made a retreat at Douai Abbey in Reading, for a whole month over August – I thought I would find it immensely difficult, and at times it was, but I was amazed at how my mind, body and soul were able to be much more attentive to those things which really mattered.

I have lost count of the number of times that I have seen someone with a variation of a sign like this. Usually the sign reads: 'Jesus is coming: Repent or Perish!' – often on a street corner with an almost overpowering apocalyptic-sounding megaphone. These warnings have their place in certain parts of society, though the content and its delivery might need refining. The danger is always that rather than investing in the here and now, we invest in the hereafter – but the awareness of the world to come is of use right now, today. In this passage, Jesus is reminding us of the need for watchfulness in our lives. It's very easy for our watchfulness to clothe itself in panic. But being watchful and living in panic are not quite the same thing! When we panic, what we actually do is take our eye off the goal, we actually focus on the obstacle rather than the prize. When we panic, we lead ourselves down the road of foolishly believing that we have the power to save ourselves … and when we do that, we are as close to perishing as we can be.

† In the hustle and bustle of life, like a lighthouse on a stormy sea – help us to focus our eyes, minds and hearts on you, O Lord. That you may bring us back to the fold in safety and peace. Amen

For further thought

• Perhaps it's time to pause? To simply thank God in prayer, for who God is and not for what God might do. Give busyness a break.

Wednesday 31 October
The smell of death

Read Mark 14:1–9

'But Jesus said, 'Let her alone; why do you trouble her? She has performed a good service for me. For you always have the poor with you, and you can show kindness to them whenever you wish; but you will not always have me.'

(verses 6–7)

Every Good Friday, during our walk of witness, we somehow manage to either get heckled or receive some very strange reactions here in Cardiff. It would be easy to think that that was a knee-jerk reaction to Christian witness, but I happen to think something deeper is at play. There is nothing like a giant cross moving through a busy street to remind people of their own mortality, or more profoundly of the vulnerability of God in Jesus. It is effective, and for me a highlight of Holy Week each year.

I often wonder what was really going on in this part of Mark's Gospel. On one level, the disciples and guests are agitated and uncomfortable with the intimacy that this woman has sought in this encounter with Jesus. We hear in Mark's Gospel that not only were the guests uncomfortable, but they were angry! The focus moves away from the woman's act of generosity and adoration of Jesus to an argument about the waste of pouring ointment on Jesus' feet; a sort of false righteousness, as people claim how much the poor could have benefited from the ointment's sale! But I think what's actually going on here is that Jesus' inner circle are disturbed by the signal this ointment is giving, for it points boldly to the cross. The issue here beyond all others is that this woman is preparing Jesus for his burial, and the smell of that ointment will linger in that house and in their memory for days as a lasting reminder of that harrowing fact. Christ's anointing is a very unavoidable reminder of our own mortality – that death is not something which we can escape – but when faced with faith in Christ, even death has the capacity to be life-giving and hope-filled.

† Lord God, help me to be mindful of my own humanity and vulnerability, particularly on those days when I act as though I can rely on my own strength, and not on yours. Amen

For further thought

- Ponder on the things that really matter to you – what might facing eternity at the end of our lives actually feel like? Give that thought some time today.

Readings in Mark (3) – Jarel Robinson-Brown

October

Thursday 1 November (All Saints Day)
Faithful to the end

Read Psalm 43

O send out your light and your truth; let them lead me;
Let them bring me to your holy hill and to your dwelling.
Then I will go to the altar of God, to God my exceeding joy;
And I will praise you with the harp, O God, my God.

(verses 3–4)

I was raised almost single-handedly by my grandmother, who when I was six took my sister and me under her wing due to our mother's bipolar disorder. My grandmother is a saint, not just because she is my grandmother – but because she is the fullest embodiment of Jesus Christ that I have ever known, and the most faithful Christian I have known. As an orphan herself, she knew what it meant to be parentless, and my moral compass and deep convictions are due to her.

One thing our world needs more than ever is people who are faithful – people of integrity, people with conviction. Commitment builds trust, and where there is trust there can be friendship, and even love. Whether our commitment manifests itself in being faithful to our families, our work, our vocations, our studies – or a position for which we have been elected, we need people who are committed. Commitment changes the world, because it proves that there are some things worth making a sacrifice for – some things worth saying 'no' to earthly joys for. The true saints always point away from themselves to the image of Christ: Christ crucified, risen and ascended. Because it is Christ alone who has the power to save us – and he alone who enables us to become saints, day by day, through his awesome grace. We need not be afraid of the call to be holy, or the call to live a life of holiness, for that is the life and way and path of Jesus. Through him, with him and in him, all things are possible!

† God of all power and truth and grace, we thank you for the saints. Help us to see a vision of your glory, that we might grow day by day, moment by moment into the stature of your Son, our Saviour Jesus Christ. Amen

For further thought

• Some things are worth saying 'no' to. What things are getting in the way of our relationship with God? Be bold and courageous, and say the words that will make a difference.

Friday 2 November
Dying to live

Read Mark 14:10–31

Peter said to him, 'Even though all become deserters, I will not.' Jesus said to him, 'Truly I tell you, this day, this very night, before the cock crows twice, you will deny me three times.' But he said vehemently, 'Even though I must die with you, I will not deny you.' And all of them said the same.

(verses 29–31)

How could they have prepared themselves for their worst nightmare? None of the disciples could have truly prepared themselves for the swift scene change that was to come. For them, the man they had followed and journeyed with was heading for the cross on Calvary.

Yet before all this, Jesus has one very important thing he needs to do with them. And so they meet and share together the Last Supper, when Jesus gives himself to them in bread and wine, his body and his blood, and commands them, and therefore us, to do so in remembrance of him. This is Jesus planting sacrifice at the heart of Christian worship and life and mission. When Jesus breaks bread and wine in the heart of this troubled and troubling gospel scene, he is reshaping the whole purpose and vision of his inner group. For they are to be broken and they are to be poured out – in all the ways which God in Christ Jesus wills – so that the world may believe.

† Help me, O Lord to be faithful to you – not just in the big things, but in the mundane everyday things of life – so that when you come in glory, you may find me worthy of your promises. Amen

For further thought

• Is there a way that we can deepen our communion with God? Are we as faithful to God as he is to us? It's always a good thing for us to evaluate our relationship, and then do something to improve it.

Readings in Mark (3) – Jarel Robinson-Brown

November

The human Jesus

Read Mark 14:32–42

And he said to them, 'I am deeply grieved, even to death; remain here, and keep awake.' And going a little farther, he threw himself on the ground and prayed that, if it were possible, the hour might pass from him.

(verses 34–35)

The night before my first day in office here as a minister in Cardiff was perhaps the longest night of the year. My friends who had helped me move in and settle down had returned to London and the sudden awareness that I was both alone and available to the community in my role sharply hit me. They left, and when I looked at the wall in my study, there was a note, which is still there today, four years later: 'We love you, you can do this! Melissa and Reema x.' It settled me enough to get on with the task the following day, and now it seems like a walk in the park in comparison. We should never underestimate the power of friendship.

Every now and then in the gospels we see Jesus at his most human. Here, Jesus is deeply troubled, he is anxious and bewildered – he probably feels abandoned by all of those closest to him, just at the point where he needed them. For me, seeing Jesus display such human characteristics is deeply encouraging – it shows that we have a God who in Christ knows the depths of human experience. So when we come before God in prayer, we can be confident that God knows the feelings in our hearts. The God who made us and loved us into being calls us to be real in our prayer with him. Because if we cannot be ourselves before God who made us, when, and with whom can we be?

† Lord God, help me to be myself with you, to love and trust you as a friend and saviour. Today, and always. Amen

For further thought

- Is there something we need to tell God that is hidden deep in our hearts? Well, now is as good a time as any – be honest with God, God can take it!

Readings in Mark (3)
2 The final word

Notes by **Noel Irwin**

 Noel is a Belfast boy and a Methodist Minister. In 2000 he moved to Sheffield, firstly working for the Church of England as a community outreach worker, then as Superintendent of the Methodist Mission in the city centre. After working as Director of the Urban Theology Unit in Sheffield, he is now Tutor in Public Theology at Northern College, Manchester, and trains Church Related Community Work Ministers for the United Reformed Church there. In his spare time he enjoys running and martial arts. Noel has used the NRSVA for these notes.

Sunday 4 November
Loyalists and traitors

Read Mark 14:43–52

All of them deserted him and fled.

(verse 50)

One of the greatest sermons I have ever heard was delivered by a terminally ill Baptist Pastor who suggested we should aspire to be 'honest hypocrites'. Both Judas and the disciples are seen as being (for different reasons) traitors who betrayed Jesus and left him in the hour of his need.

In his review of Amos Oz's recent novel *Judas*, Rowan Williams wrote in the *New Statesman* of how we should not think of the world as being split between loyalists and traitors. For Williams there are only 'different kinds of "traitors"'. I would term them as 'honest' and 'dishonest' traitors. He says, 'There are those who betray the vision by allowing it to engage with the raw facts of history, and there are "traitors" who put what seems the essence of the vision at risk in order to make it more than just a vision.' Did Judas betray the vision in order to push Jesus to do something amazing to actualise the vision? On the motivation of Judas we can only speculate. But the dilemma between power or principle and credible or radical is an eternal one, as we see today in both political and church life.

† Lord of my heart: be thou my vision. Amen

Mind your language, please

Read Mark 14:66–72

'Certainly you are one of them; for you are a Galilean.'

(verse 70b)

The story of Peter's denial of Jesus begins in 14:54 when he follows Jesus into the courtyard of the High Priest. Jesus' prediction that the disciples would betray him (14:27) has been fulfilled. They have all fled … well, all except Peter. We forget that Peter went further to follow Jesus than his compatriots did; we need to remember only Peter put himself in a position to have his loyalty tested.

Recall, as well, that Peter is standing very close to where his Master is being abused and tortured. It is not surprising Peter is afraid of being recognised, identified with the one who is accused, then being hauled off to share his fate. What lets him down? How does he get caught out? His accent. Being from Northern Ireland I pronounce the words: power, flower, car, shower, in a very different way from my English wife and children. When I was in England during times when Irish terrorists bombed English cities, sometimes I would be challenged and abused because of my accent. I would often react strongly, cursing the people who would do such things, hoping to protect myself from the abuse and its possible physical consequences. Peter curses the one who had never used violence and only brought God's love. Peter realises what he has done and is devastated.

Both Judas and Peter are traitors. However, even though for the 'special one' there has been a 'special failure', later (16:7) there is a 'special message' which will lead to new hope for Peter.

† Lord, we often slip easily into condemnation! Let us learn from Peter's experience. Amen

For further thought

• Failure, sorrow, restoration: ponder how these words apply in your life.

Who is the revolutionary?

Read Mark 15:1–15

They shouted back, 'Crucify him!'

(verse 13)

Jesus is condemned by the religious authorities and now he goes before the real power in the land: that of the Roman Empire. Pilate is not interested in any of the religious accusations. It is only the political charge of kingship that he wants to pursue. Jesus says very little, and Pilate is 'amazed' (verse 5); he cannot understand how anyone could be threatened with the appalling threat of crucifixion and not present any defence, or plead for mercy.

We then move on to the incident with Barabbas. In Mark 6:34 we are told Jesus had compassion for the crowd 'because they were like sheep without a shepherd'. In verse 8 the crowd are reintroduced. Here the crowd are asked to choose between two competing visions: the radical, upside-down, non-violent kingdom which Jesus proclaimed and lived, and the backwards-facing, violent one of Barabbas the terrorist. I very much picture the chief priests and others in the background manipulating the crowd, while Pilate eggs them on from the front. So while recently the crowd was listening to Jesus 'with delight' as he took on the scribes in the Temple (Mark 12:37) and he was greeted with cries of 'Hosanna!' as he entered Jerusalem, now the cry is, 'Crucify him!'

The Irish rebel Henry Joy McCracken said that the insurrection of the United Irishmen failed because 'the rich always betray the poor'. Jesus was betrayed by religion, the Roman empire and the poor. Mark gives us here a stark choice between different kinds of revolution. The revolution of Jesus is the only one which can make a real difference.

† 'He was oppressed, and he was afflicted, yet he did not open his mouth; like a lamb that is led to the slaughter, and like a sheep that before its shearers is silent, so he did not open his mouth' (Isaiah 53:7).

For further thought

• Can you see that choices still need to be made in our world today between the message of Jesus and that of Barabbas?

Readings in Mark (3) – Noel Irwin

November

Wednesday 7 November
Aha, aha! Mocked and jeered

Read Psalm 70

> Be pleased, O God, to deliver me. O Lord, make haste to help me!
>
> (verse 1)

I know this psalm as a plea for deliverance because the words of verse 1 are those I use every time I am in an aeroplane which is about to take off. So far so good! This whole psalm is duplicated with just a couple of small variations in Psalm 40:13–17. The dominant view seems to be that this psalm was the original one and whoever edited Psalm 40 included Psalm 70 within it.

This was a psalm which was important for Dietrich Bonhoeffer, the German pastor, when he was imprisoned by the Nazis for his part in the plot to kill Adolf Hitler. Bonhoeffer said this was a psalm which played through his mind and helped him to endure his time in prison. For Bonhoeffer any psalm which is about an oppressed individual asserting their innocence and then cursing someone afterwards should leave us feeling a little uneasy. He argues that psalms like 70 must be seen as a prayer of Christ. Only Jesus Christ was perfect, innocent and suffered unjustly. Thus Christ became the 'enemy' in Psalm 70 (and other psalms) for us. As the Body of Christ we can say Psalm 70 only with that in mind.

This interpretation is not a great one for Christian/Jewish relations. It perhaps makes the psalms less nasty for our modern sensibilities. But the important thing for Bonhoeffer was that this interpretation allowed him to both express his anger but also forgive his enemies. Because Christ became the enemy, we no longer have enemies. That is a powerful message indeed.

† Let us pray for our enemies.

For further thought
- Can you write a psalm or a prayer which expresses your anger and frustration, but which is also forgiving?

The Empire strikes back

Read Mark 15:33–41

Now when the centurion, who stood facing him, saw that in this way he breathed his last, he said, 'Truly this man was God's Son!'

(verse 39)

The first reaction by anyone to Jesus' death is from one of those who executed him on behalf of the Roman Empire. Traditionally this is seen as a 'confession' by the centurion (famously uttered by John Wayne in *The Greatest Story Ever Told* with his inimitable American accent) with the view that Jesus can only be understood properly through the cross. But is this the first conversion post-crucifixion? Apart from God speaking during the baptism and transfiguration of Jesus, the only characters who ascribe sonship to Jesus in Mark's Gospel are opponents of Jesus or demons. The whole of Mark's story is built around how those in power understand exactly who Jesus is and want to destroy him, while those who follow him around do not quite get it about him – but some of them, a small group of women, are faithful to him even to and through death.

So, you could argue that the crucifixion has changed everything and we should not be surprised one of the oppressors has had their life changed by the encounter with Jesus on the cross. Or, the difference is that when one of the opponents of Jesus had called him 'Son of God' up to now, Jesus was able to contradict them if necessary. Here that cannot happen and for us as readers we have to make the response in lieu of Jesus. So what seems an answer from the Roman centurion could actually be a question for us as the readers of the Gospel, just as the centre of Mark's Gospel is framed as questions in 8:21, 29.

† Pray for those who are facing judicial execution.

For further thought
• Jesus' preferred title in Mark is not 'Son of God' but 'Son of Man' or, better, 'Human one'. Why?

Readings in Mark (3) – Noel Irwin

November

Friday 9 November
The Jewish authorities strike back?

Read Mark 15:42–47

He then rolled a stone against the door of the tomb.

(verse 46b)

I love the ambiguity of Mark's accounts of both crucifixion and resurrection. For me they seem to be so much more appropriate for the times we are living in. So we have asked questions about the centurion; surely everything is more straightforward with Joseph of Arimathea? Well … yes and no. It is really the same question as yesterday: is this another example of a conversion caused by the cross or another of the groups who most strongly opposed Jesus seeing him off the stage?

Did Joseph want to provide some dignity to Jesus by burying him? It is interesting that Mark is the only Gospel to mention that Joseph buries Jesus on the eve of the Sabbath. Remember in the Gospel there is a lot of conflict with the religious authorities over the Sabbath. Is the concern here actually to make sure the body of Jesus does not defile the Sabbath? If this passage is all about giving Jesus a decent burial, then why does Joseph not do all the decent things required for a body at this time? Why is it left to the women to go to the tomb to tend properly to the body of Jesus? Perhaps ritual purity has had the last word over the one who defied it with his teaching and actions.

My sense with these stories, apart from marvelling at the cleverness and subtlety of the language, is that they are mostly about the enemies of Jesus having the very last word. As the political and religious establishment control the world, they are now seen to be in control of our story.

† Pray for those who mourn, that they will be comforted.

For further thought

- One of the issues in the UK today is funeral poverty. Read more about it on the website of the UK's ecumenical social justice charity, Church Action on Poverty.

Back to the future

Read Mark 16:1–8

'But go, tell his disciples and Peter that he is going ahead of you to Galilee; there you will see him, just as he told you.'

(verse 7)

The stone is rolled up against the tomb. The Jesus Movement is ended. The rulers of the world have won. Case closed. Another one bites the dust. But the reality is that actually the world has been turned upside down. These women, those who are entrusted with the message of the resurrection (and in terms of the gender roles of the time, why would you make something like that up?), are living out the message of the kingdom of God, where the 'last become first and the first last'.

The authorities have not had the final word. Jesus is not where Joseph had put him – he is risen (16:6)! In fact the story which seemed to be done begins again as they are to go 'back' to Galilee, where Jesus first called the disciples, to find the 'future' of their discipleship.

This is where I love Mark. In verse 7 the women are told to speak, but as Mark's account finishes in verse 8 they are terrified and silent! Surely that is not the effect the resurrection is supposed to have on you. You can understand why so many have wanted to find a better and neater end to the Gospel. We may come to accounts of the resurrection thinking it gives all the answers and ties it up neatly. Not in Mark. There is one ambiguous witness and all we are given is hope with questions. The only way we can ever find answers to our questions is through being disciples and following this Jesus to Galilee and then to the ends of the earth.

† As God entrusted the women who followed Jesus with the message of resurrection, may the Church today do the same.

For further thought
• Are hopeful questions enough, or do you want and need more certainty? Why?

Readings in Mark (3) – Noel Irwin

November

Held in God's hand
1 Remembrance

Notes by **Malcolm Carroll**

See p. 220 for Malcolm's biography. Malcolm has used the NIVUK for these notes.

Sunday 11 November (Remembrance Sunday)
We will remember

Read Luke 22:14–20

And he took bread, gave thanks and broke it, and gave it to them, saying, 'This is my body given for you; do this in remembrance of me.'

(verse 19)

It wasn't unconsciousness but some place equally lost to us. Her memory slipped away, first the short-term, then the ability to remember and recognise any of her living family. Yet there were still gems, including one hidden for 60 years or more. I guess it was a story she told to herself, how, disobeying her parents, she'd gone to the train station in London with her older brother Len, and waved him off as he went to war: 'They never knew we got to say goodbye.' Great-uncle Len was killed in action in 1918, towards the end of the First World War.

Why weary ourselves with remembering? Especially, why remember bad things? Firstly, so that we don't repeat the same mistakes – World War III is waiting for forgetfulness. Also, to acknowledge that we today participate in a reality that could have been far less pleasant. On this Sunday, I for one will remember them.

Every Sunday, Jesus invites us to remember him. It's a step change in remembrance, a full participation in what he has done. This week, we'll immerse ourselves in the Bible's distinctive take on remembering. Today we immerse ourselves in him.

† At the going down of the sun, and in the morning, we will remember them. Now and forevermore, God remembers us.

Commanded to remember

Read Exodus 12:21–28

'Obey these instructions as a lasting ordinance for you and your descendants. When you enter the land that the Lord will give you as he promised, observe this ceremony.'

(verses 24–25)

One of the problems I have with the Commandments is that I don't like being commanded to do anything; even if I do some good as commanded, I've probably done that good for a number of bad reasons. The other problem I have is keeping those Commandments. Jesus would transform the Commandments from a list of Don't's to the two great Do's – to love God; to love others. And here we have a commandment which is liberating, not only liberating, but saving.

Here we have the command to remember. 'Remember' is one of the most common words in the Old Testament. Why? Because it's a salvation word. You can't command faith, as faith is relational, but here we are commanded to remember, to remember God's decisive saving intervention in human history. Those decisive acts are told as story, then celebrated in festival and song, and in the unforgettable symbol of bread broken, blood shared out.

Remembrance and faith join hands. Remember that God has acted to save, that work was done while we were still far away from him, his enemies even, remember that fact – and faith, faith is to accept that accomplished work and enjoy the gift of a new relationship with God. Remembering who we are, in Bible terms, is part of becoming who we truly are in Jesus.

† Set me free, Lord, from worrying about my image, or my performance or how others perceive me. Help me to remember that I am a child of God. Amen

For further thought

- On a good day, properly to remember God's saving acts is to be saved. On a bad day, hey, it works just the same.

Held in God's hand – Malcolm Carroll

November

Tuesday 13 November
What we should remember

Read Isaiah 46:8–11

'Remember the former things, those of long ago; I am God, and there is no other; I am God, and there is none like me.'

(verse 9)

I'm sure there are mitigating circumstances, nevertheless my wife has had to endure me calling her by the wrong name several times, including 'Jackie' (that's her mother-in-law) and – I regret to say it was in a moment of passion – 'Rodney', yep, Rodney the pet rabbit. Human memory can be fickle.

Only a few of us have photographic recollection of events. For the rest of us, our remembering is a complex process of revisiting, replaying and reinterpreting events. Much of this is to do with our identity, as we (re-)construct that by drawing on the past.

But some things we can remember and fix in our minds. Remember when we did maths and learned the two times table? Well it remains exactly as it was, and two times two goes on equalling four. So there are some things that we remember the same way, especially when they are specific, shared by a community and brought out regularly.

God wants us to fix something in our minds: him. In a world of deities by the dozen, here's the one God and his decisive intervention. There are three great monotheistic faiths and all share this one God. He is the one, not the plethora of negotiable and accommodating go-to gods. He is distinctive not only for being the One, but for acting decisively within human history. He wants us to fix something about his nature, something about his saving actions, in our minds.

† What would God want us to remember him by? (Hint: think back to Sunday's reading.) Fix your mind on that.

For further thought

• Can you plan ahead today and secure a moment when you can pause and remember God?

What God will remember

> **Read Psalm 103:1–14**
>
> *He will not always accuse, nor will he harbour his anger for ever ...*
> *for he knows how we are formed, he remembers that we are dust.*
>
> *(verses 9, 14)*

Jenny was a church leader who gave me a gift to help cope with fractious deacons' meetings and church meetings: to use Pooh characters, those loveable animals from the children's stories. Ah, that person's being a bit of an Eeyore; that's a bit of a Rabbit attitude; all enthusiasm but little thought? Here comes Tigger. It was just so much like one of those stories when Jenny arrived at the door. On this day she had only to remember two things: an envelope to post in the postbox at the end of the street, and another envelope with a small sum of money meant for me. When she arrived at the door with one envelope, giggling uncontrollably, it was clear what had gone wrong.

What if God forgot, from time to time? Instead of speaking the word that brings order out of chaos he's humming one of his favourite tunes (Mozart, I reckon). Or answers the prayers of one generation with a blessing that was meant for another – er, thanks for the flocks of sheep and camels, Lord, but we have a traffic situation in Islington. Peter rushes in to see him to point out the large crowd outside the pearly gates, but God has forgotten who is for upstairs and who for down.

Various passages remind us that God remembers. God remembers us, he knows us, knows that we are dust. He chooses to remember. He also chooses to forget. In his grace, with the love of a father, through the self-giving of Jesus, he chooses not to remember our transgressions.

† Lord, you know me. You also know those who suffer oppression, those in need of compassion. I know some of them too – grant me your strength. Amen

For further thought
• Try not to liken your church leaders to Pooh characters. Oh, go on then.

Held in God's hand – Malcolm Carroll

November

Remember that you are dust

Read Ecclesiastes 12:1–7

… and the dust returns to the ground it came from, and the spirit returns to God who gave it.

(verse 7)

Those of us lucky enough to live in rich enough countries with long enough life expectancy can expect to become acquainted with diseases like Alzheimer's. For instance, 44 million people were thought to have Alzheimer's back in 2015; over 130 million sufferers are expected by 2050.

I remember Ivy. As her short-term memory went she became a danger to herself – she'd forget she had put saucepans on to boil, for instance. She'd remember that there were once real coal fires, which was why she'd stuff paper into the pretend coals of the electric one, and, sometimes, spit into the fire. She had been a postmistress and, although no longer able to talk with anyone, would stop and total up a list of numbers put in front of her. On weekdays, her son took her to day care; evenings and weekends he cared for her at home. She no longer recognised him, she seemed cheerful in her own thoughts wherever she was, but he felt the need to treat her as she had always been – family; and to interact with her as a person, acknowledging her personhood.

At some point, for all and for each of us, it will slip away. Dissolution may come fast or slow but comes to us all. In this passage, it comes big time, the end of all things.

Remember those things of first importance while you can! But who, at the end, will be left to remember anything at all? Our remembering God.

† Pray for those whose memories no longer supply them with dignity; our prayer and care show how much we value them.

For further thought

• Who, at the end, will remember? The thief crucified with Jesus asked Jesus to remember him. And it was so.

Friday 16 November
Remembering who you are

Read Deuteronomy 26:1–9

'Then we cried out to the Lord, the God of our ancestors, and the Lord heard our voice and saw our misery, toil and oppression. So the Lord brought us out of Egypt ...'

(verses 7–8a)

They are small, live in burrows and found only in one part of London. They have a distinctive characteristic: that they use, reuse and recycle rubbish, making use of what would otherwise go to waste. They are, of course, the Wombles – the British book series, BBC TV show and even pop group from the 1970s. I remember a slogan, 'Remember you're a Womble!' (I think I remember it. With the usual apologies to womblephiles worldwide if I've misremembered; human memory is fickle.)

'Remembering' sounds like a reaching back, a word that takes us to the past. It's the other way around. To remember is to bring the past into the present. It is about now and it is formative as to how we go forward. Being human, we have the capacity to remember, and also to forget, for proper remembering can be about healing and moving on.

God's people remember the past to bring the salvation story into the present, to give momentum to that healing and that moving on.

Where was I? Oh yes, remember you're a Womble – if you remember that, then you remember your identity, your sense of purpose, where you belong. (And you remember that you are half a metre tall and made of badly reconstituted upholstery material.) Memory helps constitute our identity. The cultural memory of the people of God is not about flicking through the records of yesterday, it is a memory which helps drive our identity, purpose and sense of belonging today.

† What the world considers broken or worthless, God remakes and values. Lord, help me, help my church, to be compulsive menders, to go out of our way to value those whom society deems worthless. Amen

For further thought

• When God's people remember, they are remade.

Held in God's hand – Malcolm Carroll

November

Cut from one rock

Read Isaiah 51:1-3

'Listen to me, you who pursue righteousness and who seek the Lord: look to the rock from which you were cut and to the quarry from which you were hewn.'

(verse 1)

I don't recall now what had gone wrong with the engine, but it was irreparable. I had to wait in the Shropshire village of High Ercall, at the Cleveland Arms pub (I do recall that), for a breakdown van to arrive. The van and its driver were local, and what I especially recall is his chat about High Ercall and the war. He pointed out places that had been damaged, pointed out high ground where artillery had been based. It was remarkable stuff, it was a first-person account ('and they were shelling us from over there'), it was clear whose side he was on, and it was all about the English Civil War. He was remembering the rock from which he was hewn – the Royalists – and seemed quite ready to continue the English Civil War, 370 years on. I just kept my (Round)head down.

The Christian memory is not mere recall but the grace of participation. We remember past acts, and recreate them in the present; the past act of God in Christ recreates us in every present moment. We are now full participants in all that those acts accomplished.

Properly to 'remember' is to shift the focus from ourselves to what God has done. So it is not about the quality of our memory, just like it isn't about the amount of our faith – nothing to do with salvation derives from us, it only comes from what God has already accomplished. We are cut from that one rock; the Christian way is derived wholly from, and grounded securely in, the saving acts of God.

† How to tell the future: the prophets were those with the best memories, who best remembered the covenant and all that God had done. Take a moment to give thanks for them.

For further thought

- The Christian memory is a shared memory, it shapes us, enriches us, challenges us. Other than the Bible, where else do we encounter that shared memory?

Held in God's hand
2 Letting go

Notes by **Vron Smith**

 Vron Smith has worked as a laywoman in the Church for over 20 years. Her ministry has included work with young people in a parish and as a chaplain in school, university and hospice settings. She currently lives and works in a residential spirituality centre in Wales which is run by the Jesuits. Much of the time is spent accompanying others on silent retreats and delivering training in Ignatian spirituality and spiritual accompaniment both in the UK and further afield. Vron has used the NRSVA for these notes.

Sunday 18 November
Let go for a goal

Read Philippians 3:12–16

This one thing I do: forgetting what lies behind and straining forward to what lies ahead, I press on towards the goal for the prize of the heavenly call of God in Christ Jesus.

(part of verses 13–14)

Imagine being in the Olympic 100 metre final, set on the starting blocks, muscles tense, your whole being centred on one thing only. Imagine that in the space of one breath of about ten seconds, all that you have lived and trained for, the years of hard work, the perseverance, the injuries, the frustrations, the sacrifices, will gain you a glorious prize, or not.

I hugely admire those athletes and their depth of commitment and desire. Even more because so totally focused are they on their desire to win that all that lies behind them is forgotten in that moment of straining towards the goal.

I wonder what goal would draw out in me or you that same single-mindedness, that same recognition that in the moment, this is my focus, my goal, what I give my all for? Knowing Christ and the power of his resurrection is St Paul's response. He recognises too that this response takes striving and takes a lifetime of training. This week we explore the deeps of this invitation to let go and to look towards the glorious prize that is God.

† In your mind gather your life so far, breathing in slowly as you do so. Then breathe out, letting it go, noticing to whom or what you surrender it.

Monday 19 November
Let go and live the more

Read Matthew 6:25–34

Is not life more than food, and the body more than clothing? Look at the birds of the air; they neither sow nor reap nor gather into barns, and yet your heavenly Father feeds them. Are you not of more value than they?

(verses 25b–26)

In a recent film a man sentenced to death was asked now and again why he didn't seem worried about dying. His response was to ask if worrying would make any difference to the outcome. Recent scientific evidence suggests that the outcome of anxiety is the shortening of a person's life expectancy rather than adding to the quality of life. So the man was right.

Yet it's natural to be worried about having food to eat or clothing or any of the other basic needs we require in order to grow and flourish, as the Charter of Human Rights identified. But we don't stop there. We worry about the unknown, what is around the next corner, the bits of life that might hit us side-on and that we cannot yet control.

In this passage what catches my attention is the word 'more'. 'Is not life more …', 'the body more …', 'Are you not of more value …' There is something about the 'more' that draws us to look more largely at our purpose, our reason for being, rather than being grasped by the instinct that life is to eat, to drink and to be clothed and having that be what fills our waking hours. The invitation here is to see the 'more' that is the kingdom of God – both the 'more' I am created to be and do and the 'more' that God is and does in my life. To let go of the less and live the 'more'.

† Lord, give me a desire for you today that frees me to live more for you and others. Amen

For further thought

• Find one thing during each hour of today that you consider a gift to you from God.

Held in God's hand – Vron Smith

November

Tuesday 20 November
Let go and give all

Read Ecclesiastes 3:1–8

For everything there is a season, and a time for every matter under heaven:
a time to be born, and a time to die;
a time to plant, and a time to pluck up what is planted.

(verses 1–2)

Time is a very human concept, a way of measuring life and its passing events, and we often view it as a precious commodity. Physicists are fascinated by time – they've discovered that time is personal to you and me and that past, present and future are there all at once. Imagine that our every moment may somehow be contained in one whole!

I'm not sure what today's author, Ecclesiastes, would have made of that thought. He looked at a human's life span in terms of trying to discover the meaning of the time we have been given. He struggled to make sense of everything coming and going and how death cancelled any possible profit we may gain in our day-to-day activities.

Time demands we make choices. We act, feel and think and in their very doing they cause us to let go of other actions, choices, feelings and thoughts. Why are you reading this now? It means that you aren't doing the laundry or washing your face or the myriad of other acts that make up our time. I guess you're reading this because you have chosen to give this time for God. Yet, in this moment, why not give God the time for washing your face or the time for doing the laundry or the time for playing football or the time for dancing to your favourite music? Because my sense is that if we gave God all our time, it wouldn't be without profit. It would be a time for a rich return.

† Lord, I offer you today all my time and all the actions and choices that each moment will hold. May you make of them a rich return. Amen

For further thought
• What it is time for in your life? Maybe write your own version beginning with 'A time for ...'

Let go the old and desire the new

Read Isaiah 65:17–25

For I am about to create new heavens and a new earth;
the former things shall not be remembered or come to mind.
But be glad and rejoice for ever in what I am creating.

(verses 17–18)

Imagine yourself sitting next to God who is hunched over the old heavens and earth, looking at them from every angle, considering how they are now. The rough, frayed edges and well-worn cracks hold memories of distress, weeping, hunger, short life and uprooted-ness. In God's mind's eye is the dream of new heavens and a new earth, and they will be so spectacular that no one will remember what came before. Imagine seeing God's hands, the hands of a creator, poised in that 'about to' moment, perhaps trembling slightly in anticipation of what will unfold, what those hands will invent and transform and reshape. God's face wears an expression of concentration, brows pushed together, eyes seeing what the past can become, lost in this moment where design is about to be matter. Right now, God is about to weave a world in whose very fabric are joy, delight, dwelling, fruit, harvest, harmony and long life.

What is it like for you to be present with God at this in-between moment? Imagine God turns to you and says, 'Find joy forever in what I am creating.' What response does that stir in you?

When you experience something of God's desiring, I wonder what it does to your sense of what you desire for this world?

† For your prayer, simply speak with your Creator about how you feel about sharing in God's creating of this new world.

For further thought

• What might God be creating in your life? What of the old can be forgotten and what of the new celebrated?

Let go and be mine

Read Jeremiah 31:31–34

I will put my law within them, and I will write it on their hearts; and I will be their God, and they shall be my people. No longer shall they teach one another, or say to each other, 'Know the Lord,' for they shall all know me.

(part of verses 33–34)

There's a game we used to play where you had to work co-operatively with each other in order to win. You made deals with other people, shared resources and trusted that they would do what they said. But each player also had their own hidden objective; players had to compete to win and inevitably someone would betray another player and break a deal. Days after the game, the one who had been cheated on would be grumbling about it and holding a grudge. They couldn't let it go. And that was only a game!

We have probably all experienced being let down by someone, being hurt, not knowing if we can trust them again. God too knows what it's like. Today we hear God telling the houses of Israel and Judah, 'In times past, I made a heartfelt promise with you and I trusted you, yet you kept on breaking it.' Fortunately for them, God comes up with another plan. God doesn't hold grudges, refuses to have anything to do with them, doesn't write up their wrongdoing to refer back to when they do the same thing again, and again and again. When it comes to their failure to love, God gets memory loss and instead writes words on their hearts that claim them as God's own. You can almost hear God saying, 'What was it I had to remember about you? Ah yes, I wrote it on your heart. You're mine.'

God does the same for us. Can we do the same for others?

† Lord, let me see the words you have written on the hearts of my brothers and sisters, that I may learn to love and forgive as you do. Amen

For further thought
• As you meet people today, think about what God might have written on their heart.

Let go and be held

> **Read Psalm 95**
>
> *In his hand are the depths of the earth;*
> *the heights of the mountains are his also.*
> *The sea is his, for he made it,*
> *and the dry land, which his hands have formed.*
> *O come, let us worship and bow down …*
>
> *(verses 4–6a)*

Recently I visited the Canadian Rockies mountain range. It was the response to a serious health scare that left me floundering. Where was God amid the months of fear, stress and uncertainty? When I had recovered, I sure needed a holiday. I remember one particular day, standing on the stony shore of a breathtaking turquoise, ice-melted lake which was towered over and around by mountains capped with thick snow. The vastness and wildness of this incredible landscape left me awestruck and in no doubt that somewhere there had to be a God, much as I had struggled with believing it before. More so, that if God could shape this rugged, beautiful place and hold it in being, then who was I to think that my life was too much for God's holding and handling? I was given the invitation to let go and find my place with God in the world again.

The psalmist proclaims an invitation to his people to worship their Creator and Lord, to bow down before their Maker, who claims all as his own. He also makes a plea – don't harden your hearts, don't put God to the test as in times past. God *is* looking after his people and providing for them, even when it's tough going. Sometimes we only learn slowly that if the depths of the earth can fit in God's hand, then there has to be space for us too.

† Lord, I want to know more deeply that you hold me and all my life in your hands. Unmake in me anything that gets in the way. Amen

For further thought

• Imagine God's hands, in which all the familiar world around you, including you, is being held. What's that like?

Held in God's hand – Vron Smith

November

330

Saturday 24 November
Let go and rise

Read Luke 23:44–46

Then Jesus, crying with a loud voice, said, 'Father, into your hands I commend my spirit.' Having said this, he breathed his last.

(verse 46)

The end of a life is such a mystery and being present to it always stops me in my tracks. With one breath they are there and then they are gone. According to World Health Organization statistics, over 55 million people die every year in the world, about two people every second. But even though we know death is unavoidable, even though one day it will happen to you and me, we find the thought difficult to live with. Death leaves us feeling out of control and we don't like that. We don't know the when or the how. No one can come with us. No one comes back to tell us what it's like. It's the ultimate letting go into the unknown. No wonder science and medicine seek the key to immortality!

Jesus knows how it is for us. He didn't experience what dying would be like until he hung nailed to a wooden cross. He will have taken each breath painfully, knowing one would be his last, but not which one. The only certainty he had was that if there was to be anyone to whom he would abandon himself at the last, then it would be his Father, the one whom he loved and was loved by. As a human being Jesus didn't know for sure, as we now do, that there is resurrection, that death is not the end. It's a mind-blowing hope to hold to when we finally let go of all else.

† Lord, I pray for those who today will die alone or unexpectedly. May they welcome your presence with them and go gently into your hands. Amen

For further thought

• Imagine that today you were going to die. What simple things would you be grateful for having experienced? What would be hard to let go?

Held in God's hand – Vron Smith

Held in God's hand
3 A future and a hope

Notes by **Kate Hughes**

See p. 7 for Kate's biography. Kate has used the NRSVA for these notes.

Sunday 25 November
Working for peace and reconciliation

Read Isaiah 40:1–5

The uneven ground shall become level, and the rough places a plain. Then the glory of the Lord shall be revealed.

(part of verses 4–5)

Living in Coventry is a great privilege. It calls itself 'The city of peace and reconciliation' and it takes that title very seriously. Coventry was bombed twice in World War II. Compared with somewhere like Dresden, the casualties of fewer than 1,000 people were not high. But the city centre was flattened, factories in the suburbs were destroyed and thousands of people lost their homes. The city was small enough for almost everyone to know someone who had died.

The Anglican cathedral was also destroyed. But next day the Provost (Dean) of the cathedral made a cross of two burnt roof beams, put it on what remained of the main altar and commissioned a stonemason to carve the words 'Father forgive' on the stone. This was the beginning of a ministry of reconciliation for both the cathedral and the city of Coventry. The cathedral reaches out to places of conflict and peacemakers throughout the world through its Community of the Cross of Nails; the city is actively linked with other cities which have suffered in war, such as Dresden, Stalingrad, Warsaw and Sarajevo.

The uneven ground, the desolation, left by war can be transformed, revealing the glory of the Lord.

† Lord, make me a channel of your peace in the world. Amen

Monday 26 November
The salvation of our God

Read Isaiah 52:7–10

… all the ends of the earth shall see the salvation of our God.

(part of verse 10)

This passage is full of expectancy. The watchmen are on the walls, looking out for someone coming. The people are getting ready to welcome the messenger, but, even more, to welcome the coming Lord. Everyone is looking out from the city, at the road stretching away into the distance. 'Is that a speck in the distance? Could it be the messenger? Is the Lord really coming back to Zion?'

It is right that we should remember those who have died in conflict, both military and civilian. But as the second week of readings on this theme has shown us, there comes a point when we have to let go of memories of injustice, suffering, enmity and violence. We have to learn forgiveness, because we follow a God who in the midst of terrible suffering said, 'Father, forgive them; for they do not know what they are doing' (Luke 23:34).

To sum up the theologian Paul Tillich from his 1963 sermon, 'The Eternal Now': forgetting in spite of remembering is forgiveness. We may remember being hurt by someone, but in order to forgive them we have to forget what they did to us and give them our trust again. To refuse to forgive cuts us off from God because we are turned in on ourselves and our hatred and our constant remembering. When we can forgive, we can move on and the Lord re-enters our life, as Isaiah foresaw him coming joyfully back to Jerusalem. Our capacity to forgive reflects the greatness of God's salvation – we cannot do it without his grace.

† Lord, help me to forgive, so that there is space in my heart for you to come into. Amen

For further thought
• Whom do you find it hard to forgive? Talk to the Lord about your feelings and the steps you can take together to forgive.

Held in God's hand – Kate Hughes

Moving on

Read Jeremiah 29:4–14

For surely I know the plans I have for you, says the Lord, plans for your welfare and not for harm, to give you a future with hope.

(verse 11)

Jeremiah is writing to the Jews who have been taken into exile by the Babylonians. This was a devastating event, following the destruction of Jerusalem. It was tempting to sink into bitterness and despair, to question God's purposes, to sit down and weep beside the rivers of Babylon (see Psalm 137). With the help of Jeremiah and other prophets, the Jews came to see that God was using the Babylonians and the exile to confront them with the ways in which they had been failing in their role as his chosen people. They would not be co-operating with God's purpose for them if they just sat around in Babylon feeling sorry for themselves. They needed to see their exile as an opportunity for a fresh start, a chance to examine themselves and recognise where they had gone wrong. So Jeremiah tells them to settle down in Babylon, contribute to the well-being of the city, increase their numbers and prepare themselves for the distant return to their own land.

We may not be experiencing the actual devastation, destruction and grief of war, but even times of personal conflict and difficulty can seem like an exile from our former life. They can easily overwhelm us, but we can learn, like the Jews in exile in Babylon, to use the experience as a time of growth, a time of self-knowledge and repentance. We can trust God to use the experience for our welfare, to lead us through it and take us out into a better future. With him we can emerge into a time of hope – hope that we can continue to have the courage to go forward with God, to let him change us into the person he has created us to be.

† O God, grant me the courage to trust you in the dark times so that you can lead me into a new future and a new hope. Amen

For further thought
• Can you think of contemporary experiences of exile in our world today? How do you think God feels about those?

Held in God's hand – Kate Hughes

November

Wednesday 28 November
Clothed with joy

Read Psalm 30

You have turned my mourning into dancing; you have taken off my sackcloth and clothed me with joy.

(verse 11)

Christians are people of both Good Friday and Easter Day. Following in the footsteps of our Lord, we experience both dying and resurrection. It may be our own physical suffering, grief at the death of a friend or family member, a relationship gone wrong, a failure that destroys our good opinion of ourselves or a recurring sin that messes up our relationship with God. Things such as these can seem like the darkness and loneliness of death. God often seems to hide himself and leave us to flounder on our own.

But as another psalm says of God, 'Even the darkness is not dark to you; the night is as bright as the day, for darkness is as light to you' (Psalm 139:12). Blinded by our pain or sin, we may not be able to see God; we may experience him as distant or even entirely absent. But that doesn't mean that he isn't there, only that our human emotions blind us to his presence. He is with us every step of the way, guiding us, fighting on our side, compassionate when we suffer but tough when we are less than our best selves.

And our experiences of darkness and death are like travelling in a train through a long, dark tunnel. While we are going through it there is only blackness around us. But then we reach the end of the tunnel and burst out into daylight once more. Then we feel like dancing, we feel made new, strengthened in ourselves and in our relationship with God, clothed with joy and renewed in hope.

† O God, help me to trust you to be there with me in the darkness, so that we may rejoice together when light returns.

For further thought

- Does the picture of times of darkness as travelling through a tunnel and eventually emerging into daylight resonate with your own experience?

Held in God's hand – Kate Hughes

November

Thursday 29 November
Stand firm and hold fast

Read 2 Thessalonians 2:13–17

So then, brothers and sisters, stand firm and hold fast to the traditions that you were taught by us, either by word of mouth or by our letter.

(verse 15)

Our faith in God can be severely tested in times of devastation, destruction and conflict. People can do terrible things to each other, and it is often the innocent civilians, rather than the fighters, who suffer most. We can lose everything that is precious to us: our homes, our family, our work. If we experience times of conflict that are not actual war but are personal, emotional or spiritual, they may be triggered by losing a loved one or being made redundant. Where is God in all this? How can he be called a loving God when he allows terrible things to happen to us? Why doesn't he use his power to intervene and change things?

But Paul writes to the Christians in Thessalonica and tells them to 'stand firm and hold fast'. If we had a relationship with God before the darkness descended, if we had been taught and believed certain truths about him and had experienced them in our lives, there is no reason why we should lose them or abandon them. As we saw in yesterday's notes, God is with us in the darkness just as much as in the light and our faith may actually grow in the time of testing. We can build on the faith we had before; we can get to know God in new and different ways. But what we must not do is allow the temptation to reject God to overwhelm us. We must 'stand firm and hold fast', and then we can emerge into the light with our faith in God strengthened and deepened.

† Lord, help me in everything that life throws at me, to stand firm and hold fast to you. Amen

For further thought
• What in your life helps you to 'stand firm and hold fast' when the going gets tough?

Friday 30 November
A new heaven and a new earth

Read Revelation 21:1–4

[God] will wipe every tear from their eyes.

(part of verse 4)

Former Archbishop Rowan Williams, in his book *Meeting God in Mark*, describes the coming of the kingdom of God as 'regime change'. The bad ruler of the world, who can be described as Satan or the Devil, or the human impulse to disobey God, and who has caused so much harm to God's creation and imprisoned and tortured so many people, has been taken out and destroyed. In his place, sitting on his throne, is God. This change of ruler took place on a wooden cross, on a hill called Calvary.

The new regime is totally different from the old. The new ruler is our loving creator, a merciful and just lawgiver, someone who wipes away tears and lives among his people instead of being shut away in a fortress-like palace. One of the enemies destroyed when the regime changed was death, so that 'mourning and crying and pain will be no more' (verse 4). The old regime has truly gone; the new regime is what matters from now on.

Anyone can be a citizen of this new regime. Those who are Christians have been given the new citizenship when they were baptised, and the Church into which they were welcomed is meant to represent the new order. It replaces the regime represented by the old Jerusalem, and should always celebrate the change, just as a bride dresses up in all her finery on her wedding day.

† Lord, help me always to rejoice that I live under a new regime, the regime of your kingdom in which I can truly have a future and a hope. Amen

For further thought
• To what extent do you and your church, both nationally and locally, live as citizens of a new regime?

Held in God's hand – Kate Hughes

Nothing can separate us

Read Romans 8:35–39

For I am convinced that neither death, nor life, nor angels, nor rulers, nor things present, nor things to come, nor powers, nor height, nor depth, nor anything else in all creation, will be able to separate us from the love of God in Christ Jesus our Lord.

(verses 38–39)

This is the reading I am going to have at my funeral! It is one of the most important things that Christians can share with other people: God never gives up on us or allows anything to come between him and us, whatever is happening in our lives. He is always there, loving, teaching, rescuing, guiding – often, when we fail, showing us tough love, but always helping us to become our best selves, the people he has created us to be. We have free will, so we can refuse God's love, go it alone, turn our backs on him. But nothing we can do, nothing that is done to us, will stop him loving us. And that love is made clear to us in the life, death and resurrection of Jesus. As St Paul says in his second letter to the Christians in Corinth, 'in him every one of God's promises is a "Yes"' (2 Corinthians 1:20).

So however much we may have suffered in the past, however deep our grief, however real our sadness, however much we despair about what human beings can do to each other, especially in times of war and persecution, we are never without a future and a hope, because we are never without God. And when we stand in church and say 'We believe and trust in Jesus Christ', we are affirming that what Jesus shows of God in his words and actions is a true revelation of how much God loves us.

† Lord God, I rejoice that nothing can ever separate me from your love; whatever happens to me, you give me a future and a hope, alleluia! Amen

For further thought
• In the light of God's love for you, what do you see as your hope for the future?

Advent with the Gospel of John
1 The Word of God

Notes by **Sham P. Thomas**

 Sham P. Thomas is an ordained priest serving The Mar Thoma Syrian Church, Bangalore, India. He was the James S. Stewart scholar at the University of Edinburgh and professor of communication at the United Theological College, Bangalore. He continues to lead conferences and retreats. Sham has used the NRSVA for these notes.

Sunday 2 December
In the beginning, God

Read Genesis 1:1–5

In the beginning when God created the heavens and the earth, the earth was a formless void and darkness covered the face of the deep, while a wind from God swept over the face of the waters.

(verses 1–2)

Well begun is half done! Not all good beginnings may culminate in good endings. Nevertheless, tremendous care and attention are the ingredients for a successful journey, as attested by the proverbial saying, 'even a journey of a thousand miles must begin with the first step!'

This week's reading draws our attention to God as the 'prime mover', be it in creation, incarnation or eternal life. The first scene of the Bible is the preface for the whole biblical testimony that everything begins with God. Advent is a season in which we reflect on the decisive intervention of the triune God in coming down to earth as a human being.

God is creative. God, his Word and his Spirit act in conjunction to bring forth the cosmos out of the chaos. As everything that the triune God created was found to be good, the Bible invites us to affirm the goodness of creation – including our own self. This poses a great challenge and redefines the world's norm of segregating people into beautiful and less beautiful. It is also an invitation to delight in God's other creations like the sun, moon or stars, while at the same time to fear and worship only God, their creator, who is not only the beginning but also the end, the alpha and omega!

† Lord God, thank you for creating everything good. May we also continue that legacy by making this world beautiful through our lives. Amen

Monday 3 December
Mending the gap

Read John 1:1–18

And the Word became flesh and lived among us, and we have seen his glory, the glory as of a father's only son, full of grace and truth.

(verse 14)

In some countries an announcement that echoes at a railway platform, when a train approaches, is in the form of the warning, 'mind the gap'! It is to caution us of the danger of falling between the train and the platform. The danger increases as the gap widens! The world witnesses the widening of gaps at various levels, be it between the generations, urban and rural, global North and South, man and woman, rich and poor, or in recent years between the information rich and information poor. All this may be epitomised in the danger that arises from the gap between a holy God and sinful humanity.

Incarnation is God's initiative for 'mending' or bridging the gap: the gap between the creator and creation. This initiative stems from the fact that God is not a 'spectator', a passive onlooker or an indifferent viewer of what is happening with creation. Instead, God is a 'spect-*actor*' who acts and intervenes in order to shape and direct the creation to its desirable conclusion. The incarnation is thus an act of love on God's part to ground, guard and guide our human lives.

God bridged the gap as the creative Word became flesh and lived among humans – speaking human language, becoming accessible, available and touchable. God pitching his tent among humans is the supreme manifestation of his identification with humanity in order to reveal himself and his will. It is also a heavenly gift which ensures that those who receive the incarnate Son will become the 'children' of God. It is ironical that such a priceless gift can be dismissed as worthless.

† Incarnate Word, may we receive your revelation and be born anew so that we may receive you when you come again. Amen

For further thought
- How do we understand God's identification with humans as a challenging model in our mission contexts?

Tuesday 4 December
Word unbound

Read Isaiah 55:6–11

So shall my word be that goes out from my mouth; it shall not return to me empty,
but it shall accomplish that which I propose, and succeed in the thing for which I sent it.

(verse 11)

In a pre-literary world, when reading and writing were almost wholly absent or not popular, 'giving one's word' was considered a solemn act, demanding full compliance. 'I have given my word and I cannot change it' was the common refrain. People chose to suffer great loss rather than go back on their word. Taking an 'oath' had become more binding as it was taken in the name of the Ultimate. When the medium changed to literacy, the word was written or printed in the form of signed documents or affidavits. 'Give it in writing' was the new refrain as if the spoken word was not sufficient in itself. The loss of the value of the spoken word has brought in another refrain: 'mere words are not enough'!

Irrespective of the mode of communication, words are important and valuable. The Word is a means of creation, blessing and curse. The prophet Isaiah eloquently affirms the efficacy of God's Word as unfailing and purposeful. It is indeed greatly reassuring to remind ourselves that God's Word will continue to work in history, serving its purpose. It cannot be thwarted or defeated. God's messengers can be imprisoned, but God's Word cannot be bound.

The prophet brands the wicked and the unrighteous as those who use thoughts and words to move away from God and God's words. It is in line with the biblical branding of Satan as the 'father' of all lies who uses empty words to pervert the will of God.

As God's Word is alive, active, effective and powerful, so human words should be. Our words need to be honest, meaningful and purposive. For the children of God, the call is to redeem words from abuse and meaninglessness and to make them redemptive and full of truth.

† God of all truth, make us speakers of truth and let us remain your children. May our words be honest, creative, meaningful and relevant for your purposes. Amen

For further thought

• Are our words honest, creative, meaningful and relevant for God's purpose?

Advent with the Gospel of John – Sham P. Thomas

December

Wednesday 5 December
His master's voice

Read John 1:19–28

Then they said to him, 'Who are you? Let us have an answer for those who sent us. What do you say about yourself?' He said, 'I am the voice of one crying out in the wilderness, "Make straight the way of the Lord"', as the prophet Isaiah said.

(verses 22–23)

Most of us like to be photographed and we take care to preserve photographs. One of the advantages of the digital age is the way it makes it possible for anyone with a digital camera to take a 'selfie', or the self-portrait photograph! It is a wonderful opportunity to focus on ourselves, both literally and figuratively, at our own will. However, if care is not taken, it may become yet another way of narcissistically defining ourselves as being at the centre of everything.

Defining oneself in relation to the Messiah is the call of Advent and that of John the Baptist. John remains a challenging model in declaring what he is not and what he is. John was given an opportunity to declare himself as the Messiah, a prospect that would have made him a 'star', gaining attention, attraction and adoration. He declined that opportunity because of his conviction about who mattered the most.

He defined himself in relation to the Messiah. Rather than making any claims about himself, however genuine they might have been, he marked himself as a fleeting voice that witnessed to the Eternal Word. He identified himself as a servant of the Messiah, paving his way and pointing to his identity. He was not looking for a popularity campaign or any fan club for himself; instead his objective was to make followers for the Messiah. John emptied himself in order to honour the self-emptied Son of God. Now, that is what we are inspired to call an antidote to the self-obsessed and selfie-obsessed world we find ourselves in!

† Eternal God, in ourselves we are but fleeting voices. Help us to recognise that and make our lives valuable by pointing to you. Help us to define ourselves in relation to you, as you are the One who has come and will come again. Amen

For further thought

• How far do the commercials we watch persuade us to be someone else?

Thursday 6 December
Folly of the mighty

Read Psalm 2

Why do the nations conspire, and the peoples plot in vain? The kings of the earth set themselves, and the rulers take counsel together, against the Lord and his anointed, saying, 'Let us burst their bonds asunder, and cast their cords from us.'

(verses 1–3)

One of the ironies of the world we live in lies in its lopsided loyalties. The irony even becomes comical when we realise that God and his vision for the world are hardly acknowledged by the majority of humanity, who lavish their praises on ephemeral things or persons, despite the fact that God alone deserves the highest acclaim. The psalm for today depicts this rebellion against God.

In their vanity, many in the world collude against the Almighty God by arrogantly assuming confidence in their own might. They make concerted efforts to derail God and the will of God and may even appear at times to have had their way. However, that is not to be so. The conspiracy will have its own consequences.

In the whole of the Bible, it is only in this psalm that God is portrayed as laughing and scoffing. It is God's uncharacteristic laughter of derision at the folly of the mighty. God laughs in utter disdain of the arrogance of the rebel powers, but it must be said that this divine laughter is an empowering one for the few who are willing and available to pledge their loyalty to the Almighty. God, in a show of strength, anoints his Son and bestows on him authority to crush the rebels. There is also a clear warning to fall in line and to move from folly to wisdom by grateful and loving submission before him. God cannot be threatened!

† Almighty God, may we not be foolish and naïve enough to believe that our loyalty to you will be lauded by one and all. Even then, make us wise enough to remain loyal to you. Amen

For further thought
• How do we understand, expose and resist the systemic rebellion against God in today's world?

Advent with the Gospel of John – Sham P. Thomas

Passion of God

Read Exodus 3:1–15

Then the Lord said, 'I have observed the misery of my people who are in Egypt; I have heard their cry on account of their taskmasters. Indeed, I know their sufferings, and I have come down to deliver them from the Egyptians ...'

(verses 7–8a)

As the 'prime mover', God is neither an idol nor idle. God is alert and dynamic and defies prediction and stereotyping in puncturing human routes and routines. 'Theophany', or 'revelation of God', is one such act as narrated in today's text.

There is a mundane character about God's revelation. It occurs in the midst of everyday life and perhaps in the least expected ways and manner. It may happen in a barren land like 'Horeb' as in Moses' case or in a manger in Bethlehem. One may be baffled by such commonplace appearances of God, shorn of the extraordinary paraphernalia associated with divine appearance in popular imagination and individual exaggerations. It is at the same time a warning against attempting to place any kind of limits on the ways of God as exemplified by God's given name, 'I AM WHAT I AM'.

God intervenes as God is moved by pain in seeing, hearing and feeling the sigh of agony and misery of the wronged ones. The cry of a nameless and speechless group of slaves was accepted as an invitation to intervene in a distinct act of solidarity. It was also an act of judgement on the victimisers and dissociation from them. God is not neutral or passive in the face of injustice.

God intervenes to initiate an interaction and solicit partnership. It is a search for those who will share God's pain and set out, even if initially unwillingly as in the case of Moses, on the long road to freedom for the enslaved. All who join in this project will have the privilege of becoming partakers of a transforming mission. The Advent season reaffirms this call.

† Liberator God, when you reveal your passion and purpose, may we receive your revelation and become partakers in them for your glory and for the freedom of your people. Amen

For further thought

• How do we understand and emulate 'God's preferential option for the marginalised' in the context we find ourselves in?

Receive or reject him

Read John 8:42–59

Jesus said to them, 'If God were your Father, you would love me, for I came from God and now I am here. I did not come on my own, but he sent me.'

(verse 42)

One of the recurring themes in the Bible is the consistent rejection of God's offer of life and life eternal. We see it in the life of Jesus from his birth to his death. What is perhaps more paradoxical is that the Son of God himself was rejected in the name of God.

Jesus did not camouflage his identity and what he has to offer. He candidly presented himself as the revealed Word of God, constantly conveying the will of God which leads lives to its fullness. He even extended the offer of a life without death itself. While humans make all kinds of effort to preserve life and its posterity, the rejection of this priceless offer of fullness/eternal life defies logic or any rationale.

Today's reading emphasises two possible reasons for rejecting this 'lifeline'. Firstly, some of the Jewish audience of Jesus' day claimed a glorified spiritual ancestry and proudly dwelled in it without recognising the need for legitimising credentials. They had Abraham as a mascot, without having any significant hallmark traits of Abraham in their lives. More ironically, they were acting in a way opposite to the way of Abraham. Secondly, they were expecting Jesus to speak, work and live in a way conforming to them. Their acceptance of God was conditionally subject to his adherence to their ways. If God does not follow their norms then God will be done away with. In such a scenario Jesus chose to pray for their forgiveness when they shamelessly displayed such arrogance and ignorance at the cross of Calvary!

† Forgiving God, help us to accept you on your terms so that we may be found acceptable in your sight. Amen

For further thought
• How should we prevent 'holy wars' (wars in the name of God)?

Advent with the Gospel of John – Sham P. Thomas

Advent with the Gospel of John
2 I am ...

Notes by **Jennifer Smith**

 Jennifer Smith is a Methodist minister serving diverse congregations in urban west London. An American citizen, before ordination she lectured in history and politics with a focus on the development of *liberty* of conscience. As part of her present work she has travelled in Nigeria and Sierra Leone to teach with the Methodist Churches there, and she has a particular focus in Christian leadership development and women's ministry. Jennifer has used the NRSVA for these notes.

Sunday 9 December
I am ...

Read Exodus 16:1–9

Then the Lord said to Moses, 'I am going to rain bread from heaven for you, and each day the people shall go out and gather enough for that day. In that way I will test them, whether they will follow my instruction or not.'

(verse 4)

This week's readings play with the question of who God is, in relation to what God does and how God loves. But as in today's reading, any spiritualised version of these questions gets trumped by the real needs of God's people: what am I going to eat today? Where am I going to sleep? Will I be safe?

Jesus, the embodiment of Yahweh, answers these real-world questions by going back to who God is: I am the Lord who took you from slavery, I will rain bread upon you, I am light, I am resurrection, I intend abundant life. Our God is no spiritualised abstraction, but God in flesh, need and practical compassion.

My parents observed with humour that after a few weeks in Sunday School I started saying grace before meals. Eyes shut, I mumbled unintelligible syllables from my high chair before the loud and hopeful benediction: 'juice and cookies!' Manna did rain from heaven in the form of apple juice and cinnamon crackers. While my conversation with God since has rarely had as straightforward a return, the sense of prayer as hope expressed and answered is durable. It echoes in our readings this week, as we consider who God is.

† Where has the wilderness been, in your life with God? Pray for an immediate need or anxiety that you have today.

Monday 10 December
Doing the work of God

Read John 6:25–35

Jesus said to them, 'I am the bread of life. Whoever comes to me will never be hungry, and whoever believes in me will never be thirsty.'

(verse 35)

When someone tells me they do not believe in God, if we have time I ask them to tell me about the God they do not believe in. Often I find that I don't believe in that God either, especially if they describe a God who tries to buy belief with signs and wonders, and then does a poor job of it so as not to make the sale.

The problem with this image of God is that when the blessings dry up, so does the evidence of God's love. And then the very situations where Jesus is closest to hand – places of grief, illness, violence – seem to be most abandoned by God, as opposed to being the most precious. Who would want to believe in that God? Rejection of that God is surely a sign of health!

Ironically, in our reading today Jesus had just done exactly the kind of sign the people asked for, multiplying bread and fish to feed the five thousand (John 6:1–14). And yet he specifically told the people, 'Do not work for the food that perishes' (verse 27). Jesus' whole point was that the sign was not separate from his person: 'I am the bread of life' (verse 35).

Believing in God is not about having one's rationality bought off with magic tricks or ecstatic experiences, but simply about recognising that God is alongside us in the world as the 'Son of Man'. Our work is simply to notice God's presence and that God loves us – this is another word for faith.

† Jesus, Son of Man, give me eyes to see you, ears to hear you in the heart of each moment. Nearer than the breath that eases in me now, may I know your love. Amen

For further thought

• Where does God seem most absent in the world today? Is there a way to witness God's love there by practical action or service?

Constancy and security

Read Isaiah 60:19–20

Your sun shall no more go down, or your moon withdraw itself; for the Lord will be your everlasting light, and your days of mourning shall be ended.

(verse 20)

I get in the post and through my email inbox a fair amount of educational, financial and health advertising aimed at 'successful' people. Much of it is good advice, but much seems geared towards fearful preparation for a day that recedes ever further into the future: pass your exams to get to university, get the degree to get on the job ladder, get the first mortgage and get into the property market, build your bone mass before it's too late, save for your retirement, your children's education, their first home etc.

Added to this, I am aware of stress and anxiety among 'successful' teenagers and young adults as an epidemic, of the possibility of living entirely in preparation for that receding day when something called 'real life' will finally begin. In the meantime, the rising of the sun and its setting in the turn of days are marked out with hurdles, each one higher, a treadmill of anxious toil. I would call this a life of mourning, if I were to proceed through life not noticing the glory of God today, but fearfully looking over my shoulder as if I could outrun my mortality.

Of course it matters to do well in exams, of course prudent financial planning and self-care are good things. Yes, to work hard and well is a great blessing. And yet, today's verses remind us that we live in a constancy of God's blessing, because of who God is. Then I can work, study or save not in fear, but as a gesture of freedom and delight in that small part of God's gifts for which I have stewardship.

† Lord, may I know your steadfast love, mercy and loving kindness to carry me all my days. Amen

For further thought

• Write yourself a private letter of encouragement, giving reassurance for any fears or hopes for the near future – seal and date it to be opened in six months' time.

Wednesday 12 December
Walking in the dark, towards the light

Read John 8:12

Again Jesus spoke to them, saying, 'I am the light of the world. Whoever follows me will never walk in darkness but will have the light of life.'

(verse 12)

The first time my British husband met my extended family, we arrived late on a November evening in northern Vermont, in the USA. We parked at the start of a barely distinguishable track after a long drive on dirt roads. I had explained that we would walk the last half mile up to the cabin where food, light, warmth and 25 relatives awaited.

Thick snow was falling and muffled sound, the night was flat dark and very cold. We loaded provisions onto a sled which I tied around my husband's waist, keeping his hands free for his umbrella. Umbrellas are unusual to the point of non-existence in Vermont, in the snow on a mountain, but he had his.

I pointed him up the hill: 'Walk up that way and when you see a light, go towards it.' Off he set, into the dark. I loaded up my sled and followed a few minutes later.

Walking in the dark is a hazardous business. That night we knew where we were heading, how to get there, and that at the end there would be light, warmth and welcome. Often we may be on paths in life where we do not know what lies ahead, or know with certainty that there are sharp edges and events we will not avoid. Jesus' promise is that following him, our steps will find light in the most foreign and unwelcoming places. Even in the dark, we can remember his light and close our eyes to trust, stepping forward. Umbrella optional.

† Light of the world, lighten my darkness and shine on my path. Amen

For further thought

• Is there someone you know in an uncertain time? Send a card or care package of small things to encourage them.

Thursday 13 December
Rest in peace, rise in glory

Read John 11:17–27

Jesus said to her, 'I am the resurrection and the life. Those who believe in me, even though they die, will live, and everyone who lives and believes in me will never die. Do you believe this?'

(verses 25–26)

We often hear words from today's reading at the beginning of funeral services. They are the first words said as a traditional funeral procession enters the church. As a minister I have said them many times, equally for friends and strangers. I hope that these words will accompany my body when I have died and that people will also gather to say them for me.

But we do not usually read the full verse including Jesus' question to Martha: 'Do you believe this?' Note that Jesus does not imply that the resurrection of her brother is dependent on her believing what he has said. Her belief does not create or earn Lazarus' call from the tomb. And presumably Lazarus went on to die later, after how much longer a life we do not know. We are not meant to live forever on this earth and few of us would want to, as much as we love life.

Because of who God is, we rest from our labour on earth and die. And because of who God is in Jesus, we rise from that rest and meet God and each other in eternal life. We are already part of the resurrection which Jesus embodies.

But none of that obscures the kind of pain that would make a woman run out away from her kitchen and the duties of grief along the road to Jerusalem. Rather than trying to argue her out of her pain, Jesus answers Martha's grief for her brother by reminding her who he is, who God is, alongside her in death as in life.

† Holy God, draw near to those who come to the end of life today, and those who grieve. Amen

For further thought

- Consider making a note of any special hymns, music or readings you would hope for at your own funeral, and why.

What it is to build with rejected stones

Read Psalm 118:15–24

The stone that the builders rejected has become the chief cornerstone.
This is the Lord's doing; it is marvellous in our eyes.
This is the day that the Lord has made; let us rejoice and be glad in it.

(verses 22–24)

All the readings this week ask us to consider in one way or another who God is, and how God works or loves. In today's reading the psalmist gives examples of God's working to say something about what kind of God this is. What emerges is a deeply paradoxical picture. What kind of master builder uses stones that the others have rejected? If a builder has not used a stone, it will be for good reason: a chief cornerstone needs to bear much weight and stress from all sides. How will a rejected stone make for a building that is safe? Will I want to live in that house? And yet the call is to rejoice, because this is the day the Lord has made.

Two possibilities present themselves to me. The first possibility is that in God's economy, the things that make a stone unacceptable won't matter, and a misshapen stone will be as safe as houses. If I read the verse to be about God's celebration and reuse of things the world throws away, I have important lessons about the value of persons and things that our world does not choose. The second possibility is more mysterious, and more compelling: what if the safety of the arch matters less than the inclusion of the stone? God entered into the world God had made as a limited, human, fragile person. And died. The arch fell. What kind of God does this? Ours.

† O Lord, let me rejoice today in life, and breath, my ageing body and your love. Amen

For further thought
• Consider who or what is the rejected stone in your community. What would it mean to make them or it the centre?

Saturday 15 December
Hearing the voice of home

Read John 10:1–10

I am the gate for the sheep … I came that they may have life, and have it abundantly.

(part of verses 7, 10)

Jesus highly rates the intelligence of the sheep he speaks about in this passage. He has confidence that they will recognise the voice of their own shepherd, and when he calls they will come. Obviously they will not follow a stranger, why would they? But until they hear the voice of their own shepherd, they will not have good pasture: he leads them through the gate so that they will have food, space, ease and freedom. He leads them into their home pasture.

Many of us live far from the place we think of as home, or indeed have no specific place that feels like home any more. Who then is this God who says he will call to us, and we will recognise his voice?

Once in a while I meet someone in the course of my day who says or does something that seems to tug at my subconscious, to be a sign of God's love and presence if only fleetingly as if in a dream upon waking. Sometimes I am moving quickly enough in a busy day that I miss it until later or completely. But I am convinced that the familiar voice of home, the voice of the shepherd saying 'I am the gate', echoes in our day-to-day lives. If only we can learn to slow down enough to hear it: any clever sheep can, why not us? Follow it, when you do.

† Holy God, my gate, my way, my light and life, call me so that I may hear. Amen

For further thought

• Where could you listen more for the voice of Jesus in your life at the moment? What is God saying to you this Advent season?

Advent with the Gospel of John
3 The good shepherd, the way, the true vine

Notes by **Lesley G. Anderson**

 Lesley G. Anderson is a Methodist Minister of the Methodist Church in the Caribbean and Americas (MCCA). He is pastor of Thomas Memorial Wesleyan Methodist Church in Harlem, New York City, USA. He studied in the UK and the USA and enjoys the arts, music, reading, writing and Scrabble. Lesley has used the NRSVA for these notes.

Sunday 16 December
Jesus, the true shepherd

Read Ezekiel 34:1–16

'I will seek the lost, and I will bring back the strayed, and I will bind up the injured, and I will strengthen the weak, but the fat and the strong I will destroy. I will feed them with justice.'

(verse 16)

One night I was driving alone to church in bad weather. I took a wrong turn and found myself in unfamiliar surroundings. I was like a lost sheep, desperately in need of help. When I did receive it, I arrived safely to my destination. Surely, to be lost can be a very challenging, frightening and overwhelming experience.

The people in this passage were like lost sheep without a shepherd. They were in a state of helplessness. They were left as prey to be slaughtered by their enemies. When we have been led astray by false shepherds we too will experience a sense of separation from God, being lost to self and wounded by sin. As a result, our peace and joy will be shattered. It was while we were in this state of spiritual darkness that God in the fullness of time and history sent his only Son Jesus, the true shepherd, to seek and save the lost.

Advent is a reminder that none of us as God's children are irretrievably lost. When we go astray like lost sheep, Jesus will search for us until he finds us to restore us back to himself at the throne of his pardoning grace.

† Lord, my true shepherd, pour your healing balm into my broken life. Restore me to yourself and keep me confident of your love. Amen

Sufficient presence

Read Psalm 23

Even though I walk through the darkest valley,
I fear no evil; for you are with me;
your rod and your staff – they comfort me.

(verse 4)

I learned Psalm 23 as a child. It is certainly one of the most beloved to me. It provides me with a vision of a God who is able to meet all my needs. In times of sorrow, it gives me encouragement and courage; it enables me to see beyond my doubts to a God who walks with me in the darkest moments of my life. He is the comforting shepherd, who loves and cares for you and me.

This psalm draws us to an ever-present God, who as shepherd embraces every sheep in his thoughts, as well as in every changing scene of life. Whether we are going through the darkest valley or the valley of the shadow of death, God is with us. His presence with us is real, recognisably continuous, and evidently sufficient in the face of death!

Death is one human mystery which causes fear in many. This psalm points us to the Lord, who by offering his life in death on Calvary's cross is able to take away all our fears and shepherd us through the valley of death to the valley of everlasting life. His presence with us is symbolised by his 'rod and staff', which physically is one item. A 'rod', a club, is at one end to protect the sheep and at the other end is a 'staff', a hook, which gives comfort to the shepherd.

I will die my own death without fear, 'for you are with me'. I am assured that the incarnate God, who came to save you and me, will never leave nor forsake us!

† O Lord our God, we thank you for your presence with us in all circumstances of our life. Amen

For further thought

• What are your thoughts about Psalm 23? Reflect on ways in which you can provide tangible help to persons who are grieving during this Advent season.

Tuesday 18 December
The great 'I am'

Read John 10:11–18

'I am the good shepherd. The good shepherd lays down his life for the sheep.'

(verse 11)

Jesus made seven 'I am' declarations about himself in the Gospel of John. In chronological order he declares:

'I am the bread of life.' (John 6:35)

'I am the light of the world.' (John 8:12)

'I am the gate.' (John 10:7)

'I am the good shepherd.' (John 10:11)

'I am the resurrection and the life.' (John 11:25)

'I am the way, and the truth, and the life.' (John 14:6)

'I am the true vine.' (John 15:1)

Advent is a marvellous time to remember the life and work of modern-day shepherds like Ida Walker of Trinidad, who lovingly and faithfully cared for the suffering poor, the sick and shut-ins.

Jesus, the true shepherd, however, is distinct from all others. He calls on us, his sheep, to follow him. Like Ida, we can follow him because he knows the way and where to take us. We can follow him because he will protect us from all danger. He makes it possible for us to put our trust and confidence in him, for he is able to provide for all our needs. He knows all about our challenges, difficulties, struggles, concerns and pains. Most importantly, he knows us by name (John 10:27; Isaiah 43:1) and calls on each one of us to place our life in his hands.

The good shepherd 'lays down his life for the sheep'. He broke his body and poured out his blood in love on the cross for each of us. He paid the ultimate price for our sins. He has forgiven us and has opened for us the 'gate' that leads to eternal life!

† O blessed Lord, the shepherd of my life, make me mindful to love, care for and feed your sheep, with the 'bread of life'. Amen

For further thought

• How can you participate with Jesus, the Good Shepherd, in transforming your society for the good of all?

Advent with the Gospel of John – Lesley G. Anderson

Trust amidst trial

Read John 14:1–7

'Do not let your hearts be troubled. Believe in God, believe also in me.'

(verse 1)

Many of us are carrying heavy burdens. Some of us are stressed out. Others of us are overwhelmed with a variety of problems, sicknesses, difficulties and challenges, and that awful feeling of loneliness and abandonment. We face gloom and despair, darkness and discouragement, sadness and sorrow and many hearts are troubled.

In the midst of our brokenness, distress and pain of heart, we are reminded that Advent is a time of joyful expectation of the coming of the Lord Jesus, the Saviour of the world. We are reminded too of what he said to his worried and anxious disciples: 'Do not let your hearts be troubled. Believe in God, believe also in me.' Jesus is assuring us that his Father's love for us is exemplified in his person. His care for us will never cease. He will meet all our needs. He will show us mercy.

Jesus is God's gift for our salvation. Salvation for us meant crucifixion for Jesus, who suffered pain, agony and ultimately death. He knew his disciples would be troubled by his death. He knew that by the power of the living God, he would rise from the dead on the third day, and open the door to the kingdom of heaven.

Believing and trusting in Jesus' words, we know that beyond this earthly life, Jesus has provided for us a heavenly life, where the Church remains triumphant, life is full and complete, and where there are no pain, trials, or sorrow. Jesus speaks again: 'Do not let your hearts be troubled. Believe in God, believe also in me.'

† O loving Father, we thank you for Jesus, for his life, death and resurrection. Believing in him, we rejoice in his gift of salvation. Amen

For further thought

• What does it mean to believe in God? To what extent are you prepared to place your entire trust in God? What anticipated challenges do you think you will encounter?

Advent with the Gospel of John – Lesley G. Anderson

God's expectations

Read Isaiah 5:1–7

For the vineyard of the Lord of hosts is the house of Israel,
and the people of Judah are his pleasant planting;
he expected justice, but saw bloodshed;
righteousness, but heard a cry!

(verse 7)

The Song of the Vineyard begins as a love song. This love-song imagery is fascinating. God is the vine-grower and groom. His bride, the Israelites, is of 'the house of Israel and the people of Judah', whom he loves. He calls her his vineyard. He cares for the vines and contributes to their growth by providing a watchtower to safeguard their productivity. He has high expectations for the vines and wants them to be fruitful. God did all he could for the Israelites. He liberated them from slavery in Egypt. They survived the crossing of the Red Sea, the ravages of the wilderness, and finally arrived into the Promised Land. God, having poured out his mercy and grace on them, expected them to thank him profusely and to spend their lives in service for others. God expected, from them, us and others, good grapes of love, mercy and kindness, but instead received sour grapes of abuse, selfishness and wickedness.

Some persons live lives that are reasonably peaceful and prosperous. Underlying these positives in their societies are the damaging effects of injustice, violence and corruption. The absence of justice is replaced by (bloodshed) bleeding of the suffering poor to death and righteousness by the (cry) anguished screams of the oppressed. God wants us to be merciful and kind to others as he has been to us.

God's option is for the poor and oppressed. God's love for all persons regardless of age, gender, religion, nationality or denomination is revealed in the coming of his Son, Jesus, to conquer evil and save us from sin and death.

† O Lord our God, teach us to know the difference between good and evil, and to practise mercy and righteousness all the days of our lives. Amen

For further thought

• Apply Isaiah 5:1–7 to the church. What challenges are we facing today? How prepared are we to meet them?

Advent with the Gospel of John – Lesley G. Anderson

December

Friday 21 December
Jesus, the true vine

Read John 15:1–11

'I have said these things to you so that my joy may be in you, and that your joy may be complete.'

(verse 11)

Jesus, and no other, is the true vine. He fulfills in his person the gifts of the fruit of the Spirit: 'love, joy, peace, patience, kindness, generosity, faithfulness, gentleness, and self-control' (Galatians 5:22–23). God, his Father, is the gardener, who protects and cares about the fruit.

We rejoice as beneficiaries of the fruits of the Spirit and live to use them meaningfully for the good of others. This relationship with Jesus is vital if we Christians are not to become withered branches. When we begin to live lives of unfruitfulness, Jesus has only one purpose in mind: to assist us to bear fruit to the honour, praise and glory of his Father, who loves us. We need the fullness of the Spirit if we are not to experience emptiness or lack of power. Jesus climaxed his remarks by telling us: 'I have said these things to you so that my joy may be in you, and that your joy may be complete' (verse 11). This is our victory!

During this year's Christmas season let us celebrate the true vine, Jesus. He is the reason for the season. God gave us his greatest gift, his Son Jesus, the Saviour of the world. He came to save us from sin and to give us the essential gift of salvation (eternal life). Let us rejoice in accepting this gift from God, for Jesus makes it possible for us to increase our gift of joy in living dynamically as children of God. Our true joy begins with our connection to Jesus, so we sing: 'Joy to the world, the Lord has come.'

† O Lord, the true vine, keep us connected to you that we may bear fruits that are pleasing to you. Amen.

For further thought

• What image helps you remember that Jesus wishes that you might have his joy, and that your joy might be complete?

Saturday 22 December
Above and below

Read John 3:1–21
'What is born of the flesh is flesh, and what is born of the Spirit is spirit. Do not be astonished that I said to you, "You must be born from above."'

(verses 6–7)

During this Christmas season, we are made aware that Jesus, the Light of the world, came to shine his marvellous light into our lives to remove from us the darkness of sin and death. Nicodemus, the centrepiece of today's scripture passage, exemplifies a person of power and success, who lived a strict religious life and adhered to high ethical standards. He heard about Jesus, but had no personal experience of him, so he took the initiative to meet him by night. He wanted privacy and Jesus' undivided attention.

Taking his religious life seriously, Nicodemus was in earnest search for the truth which would provide him with a spiritual experience of peace of mind and heart. Like many persons today, he had no knowledge that Jesus is the sole Messiah sent by God to bring hope and salvation into the world. He had no experience of the joy of knowing and accepting him for who he is. He saw Jesus only as a great teacher of the things of God. In this encounter, Jesus informed Nicodemus about the 'New Birth' which is possible through God alone, and not by means of the flesh (natural birth/'his mother's womb'). This view Nicodemus found perplexing and difficult to understand.

What is it Jesus wants Nicodemus and us to understand? That God's Word is a word of grace, forgiveness and salvation, and that like Nicodemus we must be born of the Spirit 'from above'.

Amazingly, once Christ Jesus, the 'difference maker', steps into our lives we become new beings/new creations (2 Corinthians 5:17). Now, let us worship and adore him!

† O God, I thank you for the gift of your only Son Jesus, and for his gift of a new life, born of the Spirit. Amen

For further thought

• How relevant is Jesus, the 'difference maker', in your life? What does it or will it mean to experience a changed life for the better?

Advent with the Gospel of John – Lesley G. Anderson

Treasured in our hearts

Notes by **Aileen Quinn**

Aileen Quinn is a copywriter and lay member of the Church of England. Her blog, *The (mal)Contented Mother: Ranting and reassurance for parents who aren't perfect*, satirises the oppressive advice culture that overwhelms new parents and has been featured on websites such as Mumsnet and *The New York Times*. Aileen is passionate about creative writing in all forms and in November 2016 her first play, *Rebrand*, which she co-authored with her father James Quinn, was staged in Manchester. Aileen lives in South Manchester with her son, Isaac. Aileen has used the NRSVA for these notes.

Sunday 23 December
God is with us, but what does that mean?

Read Matthew 1:18–23

God is with us.

(part of verse 23)

In this week's readings, the story of Jesus' birth is interspersed with visions of salvation – God's light writ large in the world. A predominant theme is one of divine presence. A God who is closer than we may have thought, a God who is *here* with us.

This language of God's presence has always at once rung true for me and felt quite problematic. It is sometimes hard to look at the world and imagine the close and quiet presence of God as its backdrop. Yet I *do* believe that, though perhaps *believe* is the wrong word; it is something less cerebral than a belief. The presence of God is, after all, something that cannot be fully captured by human language, or it wouldn't be divine.

In today's reading we hear two names for the son that will be born of Mary: Emmanuel, meaning 'God is with us' and Jesus, meaning 'God saves'. The themes of presence and salvation seem to intertwine in this week's readings, as if there cannot be one without the other. For me, there is something sublimely redemptive in the humility that comes with accepting that God is here, and that I don't fully know what that means.

† In the bustle of the days to come, may we sense your quiet closeness, and may we know that you, God, are with us. Amen

Monday 24 December
Naughty or nice?

Read Titus 3:4–7

He saved us, not because of any works of righteousness that we had done, but according to his mercy.

(verse 5)

I once attended a midnight mass service where the sermon focused on the similarities and differences between Jesus Christ and Santa Claus. Spoiler alert: one of them isn't real! One of the other differences was that Jesus doesn't keep a list of who is naughty or nice. Salvation is not conditional on us behaving ourselves.

This is a concept I struggle with because as people of God it is my understanding that we are required to, in the words attributed to St Francis of Assisi, 'always preach the gospel; use words if necessary'. If salvation is not lived out in our actions, if it hasn't touched us deeply enough to imbue a core of compassion and kindness, then what's the point of it?

Today's reading is an extract of Paul's letter to Titus, and this small passage proclaiming God's merciful grace comes in the midst of instructional teaching that very much centres on behaviour, namely that of the new Christian community in Crete.

Many of Paul's instructions don't sit easily with me, yet whatever moral standards we may hold ourselves to in contemporary society, these four verses appearing where they do serve to interrupt any idea that this striving to be blameless is somehow the point of being Christian. Far from excusing us from doing 'works of righteousness', this promise of salvation through God's very 'appearance' among us releases us to do such works with an open heart rather than seeing them as a requirement that must be fulfilled to earn a place on the 'nice' list. What a relief.

† In all our doing, striving and trying to be good enough, may we remember that your loving presence is never offered conditionally. Remembering this, may we serve you in a spirit of freedom. Amen

For further thought

• Where in your life are you striving to be good enough? How would it change if you stopped striving?

Treasured in our hearts – Aileen Quinn

Tuesday 25 December
An ordinary arrival

Read Luke 2:1–7

And she gave birth to her firstborn son and wrapped him in bands of cloth, and laid him in a manger, because there was no place for them in the inn.

(verse 7)

We have all been to school nativity plays in which the innkeepers, one by one, turn Mary and Joseph away until at last they are offered a lowly stable in which to spend the night. This image of Christ born homeless has some power and a certain sense of drama, but is likely to be inaccurate.

The Greek *kataluma*, translated here as 'inn', can also mean 'guestroom' and it is much more likely that hospitality was offered to the young couple in a house that was already full of guests. Humble households would have a 'lower room' where animals where brought in at night, and this is where they would have housed the overflow of guests. Not such a desperate scene; in fact it's one that at the time would have been utterly unremarkable.

In our sterilised modern world, the thought of giving birth close to domestic animals, or wrapping a newborn in bands of cloth, seems alien; it alludes to poverty. Yet in the year of Jesus' birth there were no romper suits, no maternity wards, and this setting would have been distinctly normal.

We like to impose poverty on the nativity story, we want to begin building the narrative of 'Jesus the outsider' from day one. But I find that the idea of his being born in an ordinary house, greeted by ordinary people, has a more powerful impact. Here he is: God with us.

Not into a palace nor abandoned in a stable, but into a modest, normal home comes the light of the world.

† Jesus, on this day we remember your incarnation, help us to welcome you into our own homes, remembering that you are present in even the most ordinary moments. Amen

For further thought

• How will you welcome Jesus into your own ordinary home today?

Wednesday 26 December
Quiet strength

Read Luke 2:8–20

But Mary treasured all these words and pondered them in her heart.

(verse 19)

I like Mary; there is a quiet strength about her, and by that I don't mean she is 'meek and mild'. For me, I imagine that Mary must have been a remarkable young woman in possession of steely determination and enormous faith. Her quietness is not a sign of meek submission, but of a trust in God that eludes most humans.

Luke 2:19 might be my favourite verse of the Bible; it's so rich and poetic and I feel it communicates something of Mary's wisdom but also that there is more than one way to hear and react to the 'good news'.

In contrast to the overjoyed (some might even say overexcited) shepherds, Mary is far more subdued. No doubt this is partly to do with the fact that she is a young girl who has just given birth, but I'd like to think there's more to it.

For me, 'the good news' is a knotty, complex thing – salvation is something at work within us, not something we see writ large on the world stage. Perhaps Mary knows this; she doesn't leap for joy because she acknowledges that she doesn't yet know what it means that her little child is 'a saviour'. Or what it means to be saved. We know, of course, that it certainly doesn't mean to be saved from suffering or pain, not in this life at any rate. But I like Mary's approach, it sits more easily with me. I am a ponderer rather than a proclaimer, and Mary's dignified silence helps me feel that that's OK.

† May we ponder the mysteries of incarnation in our hearts in the hope that we are shown a closer glimpse of your salvation. Amen

For further thought

• Where today could you be less demonstrative and more meditative?

Treasured in our hearts – Aileen Quinn

Thursday 27 December
Longer light

Read Psalm 97

Light dawns for the righteous, and joy for the upright in heart.

(verse 11)

For me, the days between Christmas and New Year are ideally a time of hibernation: curling up indoors, away from the cold and maybe even getting a chance to sleep off the excesses of December. Cocooned in my own cosy world I often fail to notice that the days are getting longer again; yet in the northern hemisphere the light has begun to return.

Today's reading makes reference to light dawning in the context of God's glorious reign over the earth. It speaks of a vision of divine might quite in contrast to the little baby we have been hearing about during this season. Of course, these ancient words were written long before the birth of Jesus, yet their talk of righteousness invokes hope too and raises similar questions to those we have been exploring already this week.

Just before we read of the light dawning for the righteous, the psalmist tells us that God 'guards the lives of his faithful; he rescues them from the hand of the wicked' (verse 10). Yet, whatever worldly dominion is proclaimed here, we all know that righteousness is not always rewarded on earth, just as wickedness goes too often unpunished.

Again, then, the question arises as to what it means to be rescued, guarded by the Almighty. Many of the psalms read, to me, like mantras of hope for the oppressed – words of promise, salvation and the coming of new life. Much like the light lengthening in late December it can be hard to notice God's own presence with us. We cannot judge it by the world's standard, or confuse the seen with the unseen.

† God, before you the mountains melt like wax. May we know the power of your love and connect with it in ever more real ways. Amen

For further thought

• We are the light of the world – how can we offer this light to others today?

Friday 28 December
Revelations of love

Read Luke 2:21–40

'This child is destined for the falling and the rising of many in Israel, and to be a sign that will be opposed so that the inner thoughts of many will be revealed – and a sword will pierce your own soul too.'

(part of verses 34–35)

When my son was born I was utterly unprepared for the tumult of emotions that arose in me. Hollywood movies had duped me into believing that, however tough your labour was, once the baby arrived there'd be an 'instant rush of love' that made it all worth it. Painfully, when the time came I didn't feel that great outpouring.

I cared for my son better than I cared for myself in the early days, when I spent most of the time fighting an inner churning of guilt and anxiety; I would see others enjoy my baby and wonder why I couldn't do the same. Thanks to inner strength, an amazing family and the National Health Service combined I was eventually able to wake up from this long, bad dream to love with my baby.

I wonder how Mary felt that day in the Temple; had her quiet resolve been shaken by sleepless nights? Could she take in the enormity of what Simeon and Anna had to say about her son? This tiny being who cried in her arms in the wee hours?

There are times when the present is so demanding that we lose all awareness of anything larger than ourselves or those we must care for. Yet my experience is that, though we may not always feel it, a connection remains. Just as my love for my son grows more and more, so too can the revelation of God's love; it doesn't come all at once, but grows with us, revealing itself in new ways when we least expect it.

† Dear God, sometimes life is so constricting we can barely breathe. Help us find the space to meet you and experience deeply the fullness of your love. Amen

For further thought

• Is there somewhere in your life that you are expecting too much from yourself? Can you ease that internal struggle today somehow?

Treasured in our hearts – Aileen Quinn

December

365

Let God be God

Read Ezekiel 36:22–32

… you shall be my people, and I will be your God.

(part of verse 28)

As with many parts of the Old Testament, in today's reading God is adamant that the abundance and good fortune he will bestow on Israel are not for the nation's own sake but to 'sanctify [his] great name'. These divine acts are exemplification of the Lord's great power for all the world to see, not a gift for his chosen few.

For me, it would be easy to focus on the beautiful promise of a 'new spirit' and renewed hearts of flesh in verse 26 but I can't ignore the words surrounding it, which disrupt my cosy vision of a warm, fuzzy, benevolent God. In fact, for me disruption and discomfort are two of the most important aspects of reading the Bible.

In the Christian tradition there is an emphasis on the unconditional, abounding nature of God's love, something I have been keen to dwell on in this Christmas week, yet I hope I have also made clear that God's salvation is different from comfort, and *very* different from achievement.

The few words from verse 28 that I have chosen to highlight today are key. God reminds us of the order of things. Too often we make ourselves, others and, of course, things into Gods. Not perhaps in the crude idolatrous way Ezekiel is raging against here, but we do forget that our job is simply to be God's people. Stop thinking we know best, stop trying to control everything, stop believing that everything will be OK if we just get this or do that … Just stop. Be a person doing your imperfect best. Let God be God.

† You shall be our God, and we will be your people. Amen

For further thought
• If you can, spend some time today reflecting on verse 28.

Sunday 30 December
A dwelling-place

Read Psalm 90:1–2, 12–17

Lord, you have been our dwelling-place in all generations.

(verse 1)

What a prayer this psalm is. I find it quite perfectly complete, and endearingly human. There is praise, a fair bit of moaning and the most beautiful supplication for God's favour. 'Satisfy us in the morning with your steadfast love' (verse 14); aren't these words we could all do with uttering every night?

My favourite thought, though, comes in the very first line. 'You have been our dwelling-place in all generations.' That word 'all' is key for me. This psalm in part documents the suffering of the Israelites, it speaks of God's face turned away from them, and yet it begins by affirming his constant presence. More than this, that God is the place where each generation has lived. He has encompassed their worlds at all points.

When thinking about God's presence, this language of a 'dwelling-place' provides a rich source for reflection. God as a place, as a home. Not some being who can come and go, but the space in which our lives exist, in which all things occur. I like that a lot.

I am not afraid to admit that I don't really know what God is. Not a person; perhaps a being, an entity, a source from which to draw, the very presence of love. All of these ring true for me and yet none do. Perhaps because God is not a thing we can pin down in human language, though it helps to try.

Yet this inescapable presence, this dwelling-place, is something I know. It is strange as a writer to know something I can't express but there it is; there is God.

† You are our dwelling-place in times of feast and famine, pain and joy, birth and death; may we know this more and more. Amen

For further thought
• Where or in what would you like to dwell? What would the abode God built for you look like?

Treasured in our hearts – Aileen Quinn

Monday 31 December
Arise, shine!

Read Isaiah 60:1–9

Arise, shine; for your light has come, and the glory of the Lord has risen upon you.

(verse 1)

What better way to beckon in the New Year than with this emphatic calling to abundance? Isaiah calls upon God's people to arise and meet these divine promises with heads held high.

I don't know how your year has been. Perhaps you're sad to see 2018 go, or maybe you can't wait to see the back of it? The latter is how I felt about 2016 for many reasons, both personal and global, and though I am well aware that the turn of the calendar from 31 December to 1 January contains no magic qualities and no more real potentiality than any other time of year, there is something powerful, I suppose, in the collective focus on a new start. Whatever you think of New Year's resolutions, how often do groups of friends sit and discuss ways they'd like to improve their lives and the steps they're willing to take to do so? It's a rare and precious thing.

This year, as a focus for my own resolutions – which are always more powerful in their setting than their acting out – I'd like to ask myself how I will rise to meet Isaiah's call to shine. How will I let that light that Christmas time always bestows seep out into the darkness of January? How will I carry it throughout the year? What would nurture it in me?

Whether you celebrate or get an early night, I wish you the happiest of New Years and an increasing awareness of God's delightful, disruptive and deeply loving presence in your life.

† How shall we arise, O Lord? How shall we shine your light? Let us be beacons in the world's darkness. Let us shine like the stars. Amen

For further thought
• Is there a resolution you could make that would nurture the light within you?

IBRA International Fund: would you help us?

Will you work with us and help us to enable Christians from different parts of the world to grow in knowledge and appreciation of the Word of God by making a donation of £5, £10, or even £50? 100 per cent of your donation will be used to support people overseas.

How your donations make a difference:

- **£5.00** prints 6 translated copies of *Fresh From the Word* in Ghana
- **£10.00** buys 8 copies in Nigeria
- **£25.00** sends 5 copies to South Africa
- **£50.00** prints 60 copies in India

Our partners are based in 16 countries, but the benefit flows over borders to at least 32 countries all over the world. Partners work tirelessly to organise the translation, printing and distribution of IBRA Bible study notes and lists into many different languages from Ewe, Yoruba and Twi to Portuguese, Samoan and Telugu!

Did you know that we print and sell 8,000 copies of *Fresh From the Word* here in the UK, but our overseas partners produce another 42,000 copies in English and then translate the book you are reading to produce a total of 136,000 copies in 11 local languages? With the reading list also being translated and distributed, IBRA is still reaching 1,081,113 Christians around the world.

Faithfully following the same principles developed in 1882, we still guarantee that 100 per cent of your donations to the International Fund go to support our international brothers and sisters in Christ.

If you would like to make a donation, please use the envelope inserted in this book. Send a cheque to IBRA, 5–6 Imperial Court, 12 Sovereign Road, Birmingham, B30 3FH or go online to shop.christianeducation.org.uk and click the 'Donate' button at the top of the page.

Making a difference

Donations to the IBRA International Fund have supported the All India Sunday School Association (AISSA), our partner in Nagpur, India, for over 35 years. Recently Revd Dr Ipe Joseph shared the following story:

'For some people *Fresh From the Word* is like a life companion. We have a lady in Chennai who is an ardent user. In October 2015 she wanted to go to Australia for six months to be with her daughter. She called me urgently and asked if *Fresh From the Word 2016* was ready. I had just one copy which the printing press sent as the first copy. I decided to send her my copy by courier. That was the time when the Chennai floods started. She called me a few hours before her departure and said, "Thank God, and thank you! Just now the courier brought me *Fresh From the Word*. He was wading in flood water. Only the cover of the book is wet!"'

The AISSA print *Fresh From the Word* in English. Each year they distribute over 4,000 copies for free. As part of their wider work they plan and carry out intensive training programmes for Christian educators and those teaching in Sunday schools.

Your donation can help the AISSA reach even more people. Just £10 can fund the printing of 12 copies of *Fresh From the Word* in India.

Where people are following IBRA daily readings:

Global community

Our partners enable IBRA readings to be enjoyed all over the world; from Spain to Samoa, New Zealand to Cameroon. Each day when you read your copy of *Fresh From the Word* you are joining a global community of nearly a million people who are also reading the same passages. Here is how our readings impact people across the globe:

Nigeria

IBRA Nigeria has translated and distributed materials for over 30 years, and say the following about IBRA daily readings:

66 The readers are happy, they like the way every topic is explained. In view of this various people from different states joined IBRA ...The readers of IBRA materials have a better understanding of the Bible, making them more happy to join IBRA group to preach the gospel to others. 99

India

B. Matthew, age 20 from India, was a first-time reader in 2017:

66 It's my first time to use IBRA devotional book, *Fresh From the Word*. It helps open my mind to see the deeper meaning of the word of God and helps me to see the word from different perspectives. 99

Fiji

Seru L. Verebsluvu of the Methodist Bookstore in Fiji, where the lack of reading materials in local dialect is a major challenge, says:

66 They are very informative and useful, especially in a country where we do not have much resources in our churches. [IBRA] help and support the mission of the church through the provision of Christian literature and other resources at a cost they can afford. 99

Vamavasi, age 42, a reader of the Fijian edition, adds:

66 It gives me hope every morning. 99

UK

Sue, from the UK, has read IBRA notes for twenty-two years:

66 I have had many days where it feels as though the notes have been written just for me. I like the short reading for each day as this can easily be fit into a daily routine and be kept up with. I also really like reading the views of the writers from overseas for an international view. 99

Thank you!

IBRA partners and distributors

A worldwide service of Christian Education at work in five continents

HEADQUARTERS
IBRA
5–6 Imperial Court
12 Sovereign Road
Birmingham
B30 3FH
United Kingdom

www.ibraglobal.org
ibra@christianeducation.org.uk

SAMOA – TOKELAU
Congregational Christian Church in Tokelau
c/o EFKT
Atafu
Tokelau Island

hepuutu@gmail.com

AMERICAN SAMOA
Congregational Christian Church in American Samoa
PO Box 1537
Pago Pago
AS96799

cccasgs@efkas.org

WESTERN SAMOA
Congregational Christian Church in Western Samoa
CCCS
PO Box 468
Tamaligi
Apia

isalevao@cccs.org.ws / lina@cccs.org.ws

FIJI
Methodist Bookstore
11 Stewart Street
PO Box 354
Suva

mbookstorefiji@yahoo.com

GHANA
Asempa Publishers
Christian Council of Ghana
PO Box GP 919
Accra

gm@asempapublishers.com

NIGERIA
IBRA Nigeria
David Hinderer House
Cathedral Church of St David
Kudeti
PMB 5298 Dugbe
Ibadan
Oyo State

SOUTH AFRICA
Faith For Daily Living Foundation
PO Box 3737
Durban 4000

ffdl@saol.com

IBRA South Africa
The Rectory
Christchurch
c/o Constantia Main and Parish Roads
Constantia 7806
Western Cape
South Africa

Terry@cchconst.org.za

DEMOCRATIC REPUBLIC OF THE CONGO
Baptist Community of the Congo River
8 Avenue Kalemie
Kinshasa Gombe
B.P. 205 & 397
Kinshasa 1

ecc_cbfc@yahoo.fr

CAMEROON
Redemptive Baptist Church
PO Box 65
Limbe
Fako Division
South West Region

evande777@yahoo.com

INDIA
All India Sunday School Association
NCCI Campus
Civil Lines
Nagpur
440001
Maharashtra

sundayschoolindia@yahoo.co.in

Fellowship of Professional Workers
Samanvay
Deepthi Chambers, Opp. Nin.
Tarnaka
Vijayapuri
Hyderabad 500 017
Andhra Pradesh

fellowship2w@gmail.com

The Christian Literature Society
No. 68, Evening Bazaar Road
Park Town
Chennai 600 003
Post Box No. 501

clschennai@hotmail.com

REPUBLIC OF KIRIBATI
KPC Bookstore
PO Box 80
Bairiki, Antebuka
Tarawa
Republic of Kiribati

Fresh From the Word 2019
Order and donation form

IBRA
International Bible Reading Association

ISBN 978-0-85721-883-4	Quantity	Price	Total
AA180101 Fresh From the Word 2019		£9.95	
10% discount if ordering 3 or more copies			
UK P&P			
Up to 2 copies		£2.50	
3–8 copies		£5.00	
9–11 copies		£7.50	
12 or more copies		Free	
Western Europe P&P			
1–3 copies		£5.00 per copy	
If ordering 3 or more copies please contact us for revised postage			
Rest of the world P&P			
1–3 copies		£6.00 per copy	
If ordering 3 or more copies please contact us for revised postage			
Donation Yes, I would like to make a donation to IBRA's International Fund to help support our global community of readers.			
		£5.00	
		£10.00	
		£25.00	
		£50.00	
		Other	
TOTAL FOR BOOKS, P&P AND DONATION			

Ebook versions are available. Please see our website: shop.christianeducation.org.uk. A Kindle version can be purchased via Amazon.

Gift Aid declaration *giftaid it*

If you wish to Gift Aid your donation please tick the box below.

I am a UK taxpayer and would like IBRA to reclaim the Gift Aid on my donation, increasing my donation by 25p for every £1 I give.

☐ I want IBRA to claim tax back on this gift and any future gifts until I notify you otherwise. I am a UK taxpayer and understand that if I pay less Income Tax and/or Capital Gains Tax than the amount of Gift Aid claimed on all my donations in that tax year it is my responsibility to pay any difference.

Signature: _____ Date: _____

Thank you so much for your generous donation; it will make a real difference and change lives around the world.

Please fill in your address and payment details on the reverse of this page and send back to IBRA.

Please fill in your order on the reverse

Title: _____ First name: _____ Last name: _____

Address: _____

_____

_____

Postcode: _____ Tel: _____

Email: _____

Your order will be dispatched when all books are available. Payments in pounds sterling, please. We do not accept American Express or Maestro International.

☐ **I have made a donation**

☐ **I have Gift Aided my donation**

☐ **I would like to know more about leaving a legacy to IBRA**

☐ **I would like to become an IBRA rep**

☐ **I enclose a cheque (made payable to IBRA)**

☐ **Please charge my MASTERCARD/VISA**

Cardholder name: _____

Card number: ☐☐☐☐ ☐☐☐☐ ☐☐☐☐ ☐☐☐☐

Start date: ☐☐ ☐☐ **Expiry date:** ☐☐ ☐☐

Security number (last three digits on back): ☐☐☐

Signature: _____

Please return this form to:

IBRA
5–6 Imperial Court
12 Sovereign Road
Birmingham
B30 3FH

You can also order through your local IBRA rep or from:

• website: shop.christianeducation.org.uk
• email: ibra.sales@christianeducation.org.uk
• call: 0121 458 3313

◆IBRA
International Bible Reading Association

Registered Charity number: 1086990